WORLD HISTORY BY ERA

The Middle Ages

VOLUME 3

W9-AHA-769

Withdrawn

Other titles in the
World History by Era series:

WORLD HISTORY BY ERA

The Middle Ages

VOLUME 3

Jeff Hay, *Book Editor*

Daniel Leone, *President*
Bonnie Szumski, *Publisher*
Scott Barbour, *Managing Editor*

Greenhaven Press, Inc., San Diego, California

Every effort has been made to trace the owners of copy-righted material. The articles in this volume may have been edited for content, length, and/or reading level. The titles have been changed to enhance the editorial purpose.

Library of Congress Cataloging-in-Publication Data

The Middle Ages / Jeff Hay, book editor.
    p. cm. — (World history by era; vol. 3)
    Includes bibliographical references and index.
    ISBN 0-7377-0721-6 (lib. bdg. : alk. paper) —
ISBN 0-7377-0720-8 (pbk. : alk. paper)
    1. Civilization, Medieval. 2. Middle Ages—History.
3. Europe—History—476–1492. 4. Civilization, Islamic.
5. Asia—Civilization. I. Hay, Jeff. II. Series.

D117.A2 M53 2002
909.07—dc21   00-069922
                                                        CIP

Cover inset photo credits (from left):
Corel Professional Photos; Photodisc; Corel Professional
Photos; Corel Professional Photos; Planet Art; Digital Stock;
Photodisc
Main cover photo credit: Giradon/Bridgeman Art Library
International
Dover Publications, 182
Library of Congress, 207, 238
North Wind Picture Archives, 40, 159
Prints Old and Rare, 19

Copyright © 2002 by Greenhaven Press, Inc.
10911 Technology Place, San Diego, CA 92127

Printed in the USA

CONTENTS

powers of the Middle Ages and its capital, Constantinople, was a cultural and trade center that attracted settlers from many regions.

Chapter 3: The Emergence of Islam

Chapter 4: Trade Expands Across the Old World: 600–1400

Chapter 5: Science and Technology Develop in Asia: 800–1300

Chapter 7: Medieval Europe Reaches Out: The Crusades

into the local culture and enjoyed a high standard of living.

6. The Crusades Enriched Europe Economically and Culturally

The Crusades exposed Europe to the more advanced cultures of the Byzantine Empire and Islamic world, and provided Europeans greater access to Asian trade.

Chapter 8: Challenges and Transitions in the Fourteenth and Fifteenth Centuries

1. The Black Death Strikes the Old World

An epidemic of plague killed huge populations as it spread from Central Asia to China, India, the Middle East, and Europe. The military campaigns of the Mongol Empire and the expansion of trade facilitated the rapid spread of the plague.

2. The Plague in Italy

A contemporary writer describes some of the unusual effects of the Black Death in Florence, Italy, in 1348.

3. Famine and Church Corruption in Europe

In the 1300s, Europeans suffered from chronic famine, which made them susceptible to disease. Moreover, they lacked religious leadership as the Roman Catholic Church became both weak and greedy.

4. England's Henry V Triumphs During the Hundred Years' War

England enjoyed a moment of glory during its interminable war with France when King Henry V won an unexpected victory at the Battle of Agincourt in 1415.

FOREWORD

The late 1980s were a time of dramatic events worldwide. Tragedies such as the explosions of the space shuttle *Challenger* and the Chernobyl nuclear power plant shocked the world out of its complacent belief that humankind had mastered nature and firmly controlled its technological creations. In U.S. politics, scandal rocked the White House when several high-ranking officials in the Ronald Reagan administration were convicted of selling arms to Iran and aiding the Nicaraguan Contra rebels. In global politics, U.S. president Ronald Reagan and Soviet president Mikhail Gorbachev signed a landmark treaty banning intermediate-range nuclear forces, marking the beginning of an era of arms control. In several parts of the world—including Beijing, China, the West Bank and Gaza Strip, and several nations of Eastern Europe—people rose up to resist oppressive governments, with varying degrees of success. In American culture, crack cocaine and inner-city poverty contributed to the development of a new and controversial music genre: gangsta rap.

Many of these events were unrelated to one another except for the fact that they occurred at about the same time. Others were linked to global developments. Greenhaven Press's World History by Era series provides students with a unique tool for examining global history in a way that allows them to appreciate the seemingly random occurrences as well as the general trends of human progress. This series divides world history—from the time of ancient Greece and Rome to the end of the second millennium—into ten discrete periods. Each volume then presents a collection of both primary and secondary documents that describe the major events of the period in chronological order. This structure provides students with a snapshot of events occurring simultaneously in all parts of the world. The reader can then see the connections between events in far-flung corners of the world. For example, the Palestinian uprising (*Intifada*) of December 1987 was near in time—if not in character and location—to similar

protests in Beijing, China; Berlin, Germany; Prague, Czechoslo-
vakia; and Bucharest, Romania. While these events were different in many ways, they all involved ordinary citizens striving
for self-autonomy and democracy against governments that
were attempting to impose strict controls on their civil liberties.
By making the connections between these events, students can
see that they comprised a global movement for democracy and
human rights that profoundly impacted social and political systems worldwide.

Each volume in this series offers features to enhance students'
understanding of the era of world history under discussion. An
introductory essay provides an overview of the period, sup-
plying essential context for the readings that follow. An anno-
tated table of contents highlights the main point of each selection. A more in-depth introduction precedes each document,
placing it in its particular historical context and offering bio-
graphical information about the author. A thorough chronology
and index allow students to quickly reference specific events
and dates. Finally, a bibliography opens up additional avenues
of research. These features help to make the World History by
Era series an extremely valuable tool for students researching
the rise and fall of civilizations, social and political revolutions,
cultural movements, scientific and technological advancements,
and other events that mark the unfolding of human history
throughout the world.

Charlemagne. Muhammad. Genghis Khan. Marco Polo. All of these historical figures lived in the period of world history known as the Middle Ages, spanning approximately A.D. 450 to 1450. By the beginning of the Middle Ages most of the world's major cultural traditions and religions had been established. Vast empires had risen and fallen in China, India, and the Mediterranean. Little new, it seemed, remained in the establishment of major civilizations.

Nonetheless, the Middle Ages was an era of consolidation and expansion. A network of trade and cultural contact knit reborn empires across the Old World of Asia, Europe, and Africa. The Byzantine Empire of the Middle East and southeastern Europe kept alive the traditions of the Roman Empire. A new religion and civilization, Islam, appeared out of the Arabian deserts. And through it all, settled civilizations were constantly threatened by warlike nomads from Central Asia.

A GLOBAL DARK AGE

The Middle Ages began in an unsettled world. Stable and influential empires lay dismembered across the Old World. China was frequently subjected to invasions by Central Asian nomads. Chinese historians refer to the period as the era of Six Dynasties, lasting from 220 to 589, a time of relative decline after the glories of the Han era.

Other groups of Central Asian nomads, the Huns, had helped to destroy the Roman Empire in western Europe and the Gupta Empire in India. Both empires had provided political unity under which trade, culture, and religion flourished. The Hun invasions of the fifth century, however, helped to splinter both empires into numerous smaller states preoccupied with survival. India, for its part, lay disunified for over one thousand years, a center of trade and culture but also of political fragmentation.

THE EASTERN ROMAN EMPIRE SURVIVES

The Byzantine Empire, however, survived the Hun invasions and other challenges of the fifth, sixth, and seventh centuries. It remained one of the dominant civilizations of the Middle Ages. The empire, based in Constantinople, was the eastern portion of the former Roman Empire. The Byzantines had largely converted to Christianity and their emperor saw himself as the head of all Christians, including the Christian Church based in Rome in the dismembered western empire.

Among the greatest of the early Byzantine emperors was Justinian, who ruled from 527 to 565. He helped turn Constantinople into one of the most impressive cities on earth, sponsoring the construction of such masterpieces as the Church of Hagia Sophia. Moreover, he helped keep alive much of the classical culture of Greece and Rome by, for instance, assembling a collection of Roman law known as the Body of Civil Law. This collection decisively influenced legal systems in the revived Europe of the Renaissance era.

Justinian also tried to reestablish his authority over western Europe and, in so doing, reassemble the Roman Empire. Beginning in 533 he sent a number of armies to Italy, Spain, and North Africa in an attempt to bring the Germanic peoples who now controlled those areas under his control. The Byzantine forces enjoyed a few successes but were soon forced to withdraw. Not only had the Mediterranean region begun to suffer an outbreak of plague, but Justinian faced enemies closer to home such as the Sassanid Empire of Persia. After Justinian's death the Byzantine Empire was largely ignored by western Europe.

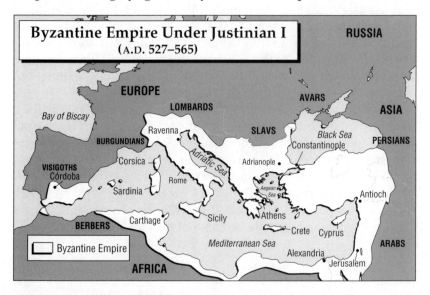

The Germanic tribes of Europe—notably the Goths, Vandals, Lombards, Franks, Angles, and Saxons—toppled the Western Roman Empire in 476. But the kingdoms they established in Spain, France, Italy, Germany, and Britain could not maintain the sophisticated civilization the Romans had built. The Germans were largely illiterate and ignorant of trade, manufacturing, and the politics of managing large kingdoms. In addition, they remained extremely warlike, often fighting one another for land and other spoils. Success on the battlefield, in fact, was the only way in which a Germanic warrior could acquire status and leadership for himself and his kinfolk.

The Germans had mostly converted to Christianity by the sixth century, but the church had little real influence over their lives. Until the Germans established stronger ties with the Roman Catholic Church, and with the Greek and Roman past, western Europe remained in a state of chronic warfare. The church emerged as the dominant political and cultural institution of Europe in the first centuries of the Middle Ages. Monasteries became Europe's closest equivalent to trade and cultural centers. The bishops of Rome, the popes, maintained that they, not the Byzantine emperors, were the leaders of European Christianity.

CHINA'S GOLDEN AGE

China was reunified in 571. Under the Tang and Song dynasties, which governed China until 1279, China once again became a vigorous civilization. Indeed, for much of the Middle Ages, China was arguably the richest, most vibrant, and most creative civilization in the world.

The Middle Ages was an era of great cultural accomplishment in China. Architects built numerous Buddhist temples, which sculptors filled with statues of the Buddha in various materials. Craftsmen created intricate works in silk, porcelain, and lacquer that were highly valued throughout Asia, Africa, and Europe. Philosophers and scholars revived the Confucian system of administration by which candidates for the highest offices in the state had to pass examinations in philosophy, history, and poetry.

Although the Chinese had invented paper centuries earlier, not until the eighth and ninth centuries was paper put to a variety of new uses ranging from currency to clothing. Among the greatest of the Chinese uses of paper, however, was block printing and, subsequently, the paper book. The earliest known printed book is a Buddhist document published in 868. Block printing helped to popularize a literary culture in China by creating an audience for historical writing, ethical texts, and poetry.

The Middle Ages was indeed a golden age of Chinese poetry.

Li Po, who lived at Chang'an, the Tang capital, in the eighth century, remains a popular poet in China. According to legend, an unpretentious man, he supposedly drowned when he walked into a river in a drunken revery, staring at the moon. Many of his poems reminded the Chinese of the beauties of the countryside; others are concerned with dreams and visions. Another Tang poet, Du Fu, wrote verse that contained ethical lessons and reflected the revived Confucianism of the period.

The philosopher Zhu Xi, who created neo-Confucianism, also lived during China's golden age. He sought to reinvigorate Confucianism by combining it with Buddhist influences. Zhu Xi maintained the traditional Confucian respect for order and family, but he was also interested in more obscure philosophical issues such as the nature of reality. Among his most important writings was *Family Rituals*, which provided instructions for important ceremonies such as weddings, births, and funerals. Neo-Confucianism proved to be an important influence on society and politics not only in China but also in Korea, Japan, and Vietnam, where Chinese culture had a major influence.

China also made great contributions in science and technology. Technicians developed the ability to create high-quality metal by burning coke rather than coal in blast furnaces. According to state records, iron production increased tenfold between the ninth and eleventh centuries. The iron was mostly used for household tools and weapons, although it was also used to strengthen bridges or buildings. As they had adopted neo-Confucianism, China's neighbors were quick to adopt this new technology. Central Asian nomads learned, in fact, to use Chinese weapons against China.

In other fields, philosophers and alchemists invented medicines, potions they believed might prolong life, and devices they thought could help them predict the future. Among these devices was the magnetic compass, which soon found practical uses on Chinese ships, then the best in the world. In the twelfth century, Chinese thinkers invented the first mechanical clock, although it was too large and cumbersome to be of much use. Another technological advance was the invention of gunpowder; the first gunpowder weapons on earth were used by Chinese armies against Central Asian nomads.

THE POPE AND CHARLEMAGNE CHALLENGE THE BYZANTINE EMPIRE

While China established itself as the dominant civilization in East Asia, the Byzantine Empire continued to dominate the eastern Mediterranean and parts of the Middle East. Constantinople not only served as the imperial capital, housing treasures from its Greek, Roman, and Christian past, but also attracted merchants and mercenaries from as far away as Sweden, Russia, and sub-Saharan Africa. Between 600 and 1000, the Byzantines survived threats from the Persians, the Slavs, and the Muslims as well as internal conflicts. The emperor still saw himself as the head of Christendom; as far as he was concerned, the pope in Rome was just one of many bishops in the church hierarchy.

The pope, however, helped to bring about a reemergence of empire in western Europe in the eighth and ninth centuries. Known as the Holy Roman Empire, it was an attempt to combine the influence of western Christianity with the political power of the strongest of the Germanic tribes, the Franks.

In the eighth century the Franks established dominion over much of France, Germany, and Italy under kings belonging to the Carolingian family, notably Charlemagne, or Charles the Great. Unlike other Germans, the Franks proclaimed allegiance to Roman Catholic Christianity as opposed to the Eastern Orthodox Christianity practiced in the Byzantine Empire.

Taking advantage of a temporarily empty Byzantine throne, Pope Leo III crowned Charlemagne Holy Roman Emperor on Christmas Day, 800. Charlemagne's empire was short-lived, but it inspired a brief cultural revival, the Carolingian Renaissance,

Charlemagne, shown here during his coronation ceremony, established social stability throughout Europe and ignited a cultural revival during his reign.

as well as trade ties with the Byzantine Empire and the Islamic world. Moreover, the Holy Roman Empire established Frankish feudalism as the basis of western Europe's social and political order. Feudal arrangements helped tie Europe together in an intricate network of military and family relationships and began to provide Europe with a social stability it had not known since the Roman Empire.

EUROPEAN CRUSADERS TRY TO CONQUER THE HOLY LAND

This stability helped rapidly expand European society after 1000. Population swelled, cities grew in importance, and large kingdoms began to form in England, France, and Germany. As a reflection of Europe's revival, both the pope and the aristocracy tried to expand their authority by conquering the Middle East. This attempt, the Crusades, was one of the most dramatic events of the Middle Ages.

The origins of the Crusades lay in the invasion of the Arabic Middle East by groups of Turks from Central Asia. With their victory over the Byzantines at Manzikert in 1071, a group of Turks known as the Seljuks took possession of the city of Jerusalem, holy to Muslims, Christians, and Jews and an important destination for religious pilgrims since long before the birth of Jesus Christ.

In 1095 the Byzantine emperor Alexius, claiming that he needed military help against the Turks, wrote a letter to Pope Urban II. Alexius, clinging to the Byzantine belief that he was the head of all Christendom, believed that Urban, like any good church official in the east, would do as he requested in the letter and organize a small force to send to Constantinople.

Urban, however, had other ideas. He was the heir to a great reform movement that was trying to establish Roman Catholic control over both the warring nobles of Europe and the Christians of both east and west. Alexius's letter gave him the opportunity he needed to assemble a huge Christian army. Claiming, falsely, that the Turks were abusing Christians and preventing Christian pilgrims from visiting Jerusalem, Urban called upon all European knights to give up fighing one another. Instead, he demanded that they unite, march to the Holy Land, and take control of Jerusalem. Any crusader, as these warriors came to be called, would be forgiven all his sins and entitled to any spoils of war won on the way. Urban's "call to crusade" in 1095 set off nearly two hundred years of crusading fever in western Europe. Wave after wave of crusaders set off for Byzantium and the Holy Land.

Not all who left, however, were knights. The First Crusade, also known as the Peasants' Crusade, was more a mass movement than a proper military campaign. Led by Peter the Hermit, the Peasants' Crusade reached Constantinople in 1096. Alexius, expecting a small group of soldiers, was surprised to see thirty-five thousand peasants camped outside the city walls. He urged them to wait for the pope's army, but they pressed on into Turkish territory. Most were massacred in a valley not far from Constantinople, although Peter the Hermit escaped. Decades later the Children's Crusade suffered perhaps an even worse, though still mysterious, fate at Muslim hands in Spain and North Africa.

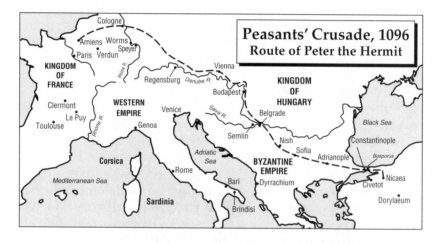

The First Crusade arrived in Constantinople in 1096, taking three more years to reach Jerusalem. Crusaders conquered the city in 1099, massacring nearly all its inhabitants and claiming to have won "a splendid victory for God." The First Crusade was the only one to achieve notable success, as the crusaders established a string of European-style kingdoms, the Crusader States, to add to the possession of Jerusalem.

The success of the First Crusade had much to do with disunity among the Muslims of the area, as Arabs and Turks had little reason to like one another. During the twelfth century, however, Arabs and Turks put aside their differences and formed alliances against their common enemy, winning territory back from the crusaders, especially under the Egyptian warlord Saladin.

Back in Europe, such Muslim successes inspired calls for more Crusades. Few achieved their goals. The Fourth Crusade of 1202–1204, in fact, was directed at Constantinople more than any Muslim territory, and it dealt a nearly fatal blow to the Byzantine Empire, which found itself caught in the middle of the madness between the Roman Catholic world and the Muslim Middle East. The final Crusader State, Acre, was lost in 1291.

THE MAYAN CIVILIZATION

Across the Atlantic Ocean from Europe, and unknown to the Franks, Byzantines, and Chinese, another major empire rose to dominate much of southern Mexico and Central America. Although the Mayan civilization had been in existence for centuries, it reached its greatest extent in the so-called Late Classic period, approximately 600 to 800. During that era the Mayans constructed a number of urban centers, the most important being Tikal in Guatemala. The Mayans had a sophisticated economy based on agriculture, fishing, crafts, and trade with the tribes and cities of Central Mexico. In addition, they created a culture based on astronomy and time-keeping. Their astronomical charts were accurate enough to predict solar eclipses years in advance, and their mathematical system included the concept of zero. The Mayans also had writing, which they used for both political and ritual purposes. Although this rich and advanced civilization fell into decline after 800, and many of its cities were abandoned for reasons that are still unknown, it left a lasting mark on early America.

The revived empires in China and western Europe, as well as the thriving Byzantine Empire, faced a new rival in the emergence of Islamic civilization. Islam, indeed, was to play a decisive role in the Middle Ages. Not only did the Islamic religion spread rapidly across the Middle East, Asia, Africa, and even parts of Europe, Islamic conquerors from Arabia established an empire that was in every way the rival of China or Byzantium.

THE PROPHET MUHAMMAD AND ISLAM

The religion of Islam emerged out of the Arabian deserts in the early seventh century. A merchant from the trade center of Mecca, Muhammad, declared in 610 that he had been called on to be a prophet of God, or "Allah" in Arabic. Over a period of two decades Muhammad and his followers continued to receive divine recitations from both Allah and the archangel Gabriel. These recitations were later assembled into the Koran, the holy book of Islam.

Muhammad's supporters were few at first. In 622 they were forced to flee from Mecca to the nearby city of Medina, an event known in Islamic history as the hegira, or exile. The first true Islamic community was formed in Medina. From there, Muhammad sent a conquering army to various points including Mecca, his home. Muhammad cleansed the city of its earlier religions and idols and established Mecca as the holiest city of Islam. Islam, the Prophet and his followers argued, was the perfection and completion of all religions, including its two predecessors, Judaism and Christianity, and should properly replace them. All

Arabia in Muhammad's Time

Aral Sea

Black Sea

Caspian Sea

Constantinople

B Y Z A N T I N E
E M P I R E

Nineveh

Nishapur

P E R S I A N
E M P I R E

Sergiopolis

Ctesiphon

Mediterranean
Sea

Kufa

Hora

Jerusalem

Mu'ta

Jarba

Alexandria

Eilat

Adrhuh

Dumat al-Jandal

Tabuk

Magna

Fadak

Khaybar

Medina

Badr

A R A B I A

MECCA

Taif

Red Sea

Najran

Marib

San'a

A B Y S S I N I A

- - - - - - - - - Border between Persian and
Byzantine Empires and Arabia

Persian Empire

Byzantine Empire

devout Muslims are asked to make a pilgrimage to Mecca, the "haj," in commemoration of the Prophet's return to the city.

After Muhammad's death in 634, Arab Islamic armies led by caliphs, or "successors to the prophet," continued to spread the religion. Often following the trade routes used by Arabian caravan merchants, and in search of plunder as well as religious expansion, these armies quickly conquered an empire stretching from Spain in the west to Persia in the east.

The Islamic Arabian Empire was originally based in the city of Damascus in modern-day Syria. The caliphs moved their capital to Damascus from Mecca largely because of the city's proximity to both Jerusalem and the Byzantine Empire. Jerusalem, like Mecca and Medina, was holy to Muslims because they believe that Muhammad ascended to heaven from the city. The Byzantine Empire offered the Arabs a strong rival as well as access to wealth and trade goods.

In the eighth century, the Islamic Empire reached its greatest geographical extent. Indeed, Muslim leaders very nearly added western Europe to their conquests. One of the most decisive battles of the Middle Ages was fought in 734 at Poitiers in France. There the Arabs, fresh from the conquest of Spain, met a Christian army led by the Frankish warlord Charles Martel, Charlemagne's grandfather. Charles Martel's forces proved victorious, and the Muslim advance into western Europe was halted.

BAGHDAD: A GREAT CULTURAL CENTER

In 750, Arab leaders moved to a new capital, Baghdad. The great attraction of the city was its proximity to Persia, which was undergoing conversion to Islam. Persia was a wealthy and ancient civilization, and it had much to offer the desert Arabs in the way of culture and riches.

Baghdad grew to be one of the three great cities of the Middle Ages, a rival to Constantinople and Chang'an. The city was the center of a wide network of trade and finance connecting the capital with such important urban centers as Cairo in Egypt and Cordoba in Spain, as well as with foreign centers in India, China, and Europe.

Baghdad was also an important cultural center. There, Arab thinkers drew heavily on the traditions of Greece, Rome, Persia, and India in creating a hybrid culture centered on Islam. Writers and storytellers at the courts of such Abbasid caliphs as Harun al-Rashid, who governed in the early ninth century, developed a new literature combining Islamic teachings with folktales from Islamic areas. Their legacy includes such memorable works as *The Rubaiyat of Omar Khayyam* and *The Thousand and One Nights,* which includes stories about Aladdin and Sinbad the Sailor.

Islamic accomplishments in science and technology were also significant. As in literature, work in these areas demonstrated the Arabs' skill in combining ideas and techniques from different countries. Baghdad scientists invented optics, developed weapons using gunpowder (which they referred to as "Chinese snow"), and invented advanced techniques for measuring the movements of the stars and planets. They also began to widely use Indian mathematics, producing textbooks on arithmetic and algebra that were still in use in the Middle East and Europe centuries later. India is the source of the mathematical system still in use today; what are referred to as "Arabic" numbers, ten symbols (0–9) that can be assembled in any combination, were in fact originally developed by Hindu mathematicians in India. The system was introduced into Europe by Arab scholars, and Europeans quickly found these "Arabic" numbers a huge improvement on Roman numerals.

Arab doctors were the most accomplished in the world. Again combining knowledge from a number of times and places, they worked on the assumption that human health was not a matter of religion or magic but rather a true science. Arab physicians understood that the blood was circulated by the heart (five centuries before Europeans knew), that disease could be carried by dirt or stagnant water, and that mental health was closely related to physical health. Among the greatest of the Arab physicians was Ibn Sina, or Avicenna, as Europeans referred to him. His text, the *Canon of Medicine*, written in the first decades of the eleventh century, was the fundamental medical textbook in the Middle East and Europe until the seventeenth century. The reputation of Arab medicine, in fact, was so high that European Christians who traveled to the Middle East during the Crusades preferred Arab doctors to their own.

ISLAM SPREADS TO ASIA AND AFRICA

A truly global Islamic culture developed between 800 to 1200. Merchants, conquerors, and political exiles expanded the religion throughout Asia and Africa. India, a rich cultural center, was a natural target for Muslim expansion. Beginning in the ninth century traders, religious mystics, and conquerors made their way to India, where they found many converts. Military conquest turned India into an important Islamic center in 1206 when a Turkish Muslim government known as the Delhi Sultanate established control over much of the country.

Muslims also followed old overseas trade routes beyond India to the spice-producing areas of Southeast Asia. They found many willing converts among Southeast Asian kings seeking trade and military advantages. Islam, indeed, was still spreading in Southeast Asia when Europeans arrived there in the 1500s.

In East Africa the first Muslims were political exiles from Arabia. But such cities as Malindi and Mogadishu eventually became part of a vast network of trade controlled by Muslims. East Africa grew to be the center of a sophisticated trading civilization, an ethnic hybrid of Africans, Arabs, and Indians who mostly practiced the religion of Muhammad. By the tenth century, overland trade routes connected East Africa, as well as Mecca and Cairo, to the gold-producing regions around the Niger River in West Africa.

Little known to the outside world, West Africa had become a center of large empires and big cities by the tenth century. The region slowly became attached to the Islamic world, as African kings, merchants, and scholars converted to the new religion. The greatest of the West African empires was Mali, which thrived from approximately 1250 to 1380 and produced much of the gold circulated in Europe and the Middle East. Mali received attention in the outside world partly because of Arabian visitors like Ibn Battuta, but also because one of its kings, Mansa Musa, made the required Muslim pilgrimage to Mecca. Along the way, Mansa Musa impressed Islamic leaders with his wealth, sophistication, and devotion to Islam. And on his return to West Africa, he brought with him Islamic scholars who helped to turn cities such as Timbuktu into centers of Islamic scholarship.

A Vast Network of Trade Connects the Old World

Muslims were adventurous merchants, but the Middle Ages after 600 was a period of expanding trade overall. An international trade network, anchored at one end by Tang and Song China and at the other end by Islam, inspired a vigorous circulation of money and goods. Trade routes crossed both land and sea. The overland Silk Road, actually a network of roads through the deserts and mountains of Central Asia, connected China with the Middle East and Europe. Its eastern end was at Chang'an, and the Silk Road led not only merchants but also scholars, entertainers, and even religious pilgrims and exiles to the Chinese capital.

Overseas trade routes took advantage of the seasonal monsoon winds of the Indian Ocean. They connected the ports of East Africa, Arabia, Persia, India, Southeast Asia, and China. Many of the sailors were Arabs, who until the Song dynasty had the best boats as well as the most advanced seafaring knowledge. As a result of this Indian Ocean trade, Chinese porcelain was used to decorate Islamic mosques in Africa and Arabia, African and Indian slaves could be found in China, and the most highly desired products of the region, spices, were circulated worldwide. In some areas spices were so valuable they were used as currency.

The dominance of China and Islam in the Old World after 1000 was interrupted by yet another challenge from Central Asian nomads. Groups of these nomads, who were known as Turks because of the languages they spoke, invaded the Islamic Middle East. Although they converted to Islam and settled permanently, they also fought viciously against the Arabs. It was Turkish conquerors, in fact, who sacked Arab Baghdad in 1055 and defeated a strong Byzantine force at Manzikert in 1071. Moreover, Turkish Muslims repeatedly attacked India from a base in Afghanistan. By 1206 they were able to establish a new empire, the Delhi Sultanate, which controlled large parts of northern India.

THE MONGOL CONQUEROR GENGHIS KHAN

The most powerful of the Central Asian nomads, however, were the Mongols, who wandered the dry, empty areas north and west of China. Various Mongol tribes made sporadic raids into China in the late twelfth century, but in 1206 these tribes decided to combine their forces. They chose as their leader Temujin, who took the title of Genghis Khan, or "Great Lord." Under Genghis Kahn, a brilliant warrior and inspirational leader, the Mongols established the largest land empire in world history. By 1279 Mongol armies had conquered China, taken control of much of the Islamic Middle East, and even entered central Europe. Their empire, at its greatest extent, stretched from Poland to Korea.

Although Genghis Khan was able to take advantage of disunity and weakness in some areas, particularly China and the Middle East, the success of his conquests can be attributed to the military superiority and brutal tactics of the Mongol horsemen. They could travel long distances very quickly with few provisions. Their attacks featured repeated hit-and-run tactics until the enemy was weak enough to be destroyed. The Mongols even used psychological warfare, quickly learning that their reputations as savage, merciless conquerors terrorized enemies even before they attacked.

The great prize, as far as the Mongols were concerned, was China. Genghis Khan initially attacked China in full force in 1211, but the conquest of China, and with it the end of the Song dynasty, was completed by Kublai Khan, Genghis Khan's grandson. Kublai Khan settled in as the emperor of a new Chinese dynasty, the Yuan dynasty, and governed from the city of Kanbalu, near Beijing. Kublai Khan's brief reign (1264–1294) was perhaps the high point of the Mongol Empire, an era of a "Mongol Peace," which made travel and trade across the Old World relatively easy. Moreover, Kublai Khan tried in many ways to adapt the Mongols to Chinese ways.

MARCO POLO VISITS THE GREAT KHAN

One of the many visitors to Kublai Khan's court was the Italian merchant and adventurer Marco Polo, whose published account of his journey across Asia proved very popular in the Europe of the Late Middle Ages. Marco Polo served for a number of years as an official in the government of the Yuan dynasty. He reported that Kublai, the Great Khan, governed with elaborate ritual and ceremony. He also noted that Chinese cities, such as Hangshou, the second Song dynasty capital, were more impressive by far than European cities, full of unique trade goods, impressive architecture and technology, and a vast array of peoples. Marco Polo's descriptions of Kublai Khan's China were to have a great impact on the European explorers of the 1400s and 1500s.

Marco Polo traveled from a revitalized Europe. After 1000, agricultural innovations and the opening of new lands had provided a stable food supply, which led to longer life spans, healthier children, and a growing population. Strong kingdoms had begun to emerge in Germany, France, and England, while the city-states of Italy, such as Marco Polo's Venice, grew prosperous with trade and manufacturing. Cultural life had once again begun to flourish with the establishment of universities and sponsorship of philosophy and the arts.

A REVIVED EUROPE

Another reflection of the revived Europe of Marco Polo's day was the reentry of western Europe into the mainstream of Mediterranean and Middle Eastern civilization during the Crusades. Europeans learned of the cultural advances of the Muslim world, particularly in such areas as medicine, mathematics, and navigation. They had new access to the trade goods of Asia and Africa available in the markets and bazaars of Egypt and Syria. The constant seagoing traffic across the Mediterranean helped make Venetian and other Italian sailors familiar figures everywhere, and cultural contacts were renewed between the Muslims and Jews of Spain and those of the Middle East. Finally, many argue that European nobles learned how to behave in a more civilized fashion thanks to contact with their more gentlemanly Arab and Byzantine counterparts. The courtly culture of knights, jousts, and romance that so many associate with the European

Middle Ages first appeared in the twelfth century and is perhaps a direct consequence of the Crusades.

THE BLACK DEATH

The Middle Ages ended with a series of crises and transitions in the 1300s and 1400s. Among the greatest of the crises was an epidemic of disease that emerged in Central Asia, spread by Mongol horsemen and international trade caravans, and devastated civilizations from China to Europe. The disease was plague in both its bubonic and pneumonic forms. Between 1325 and 1355 it killed, records claim, at least one-third of the populations of China, India, Central Asia, the Middle East, and Europe. Known by European chroniclers as the Black Death, the outbreak of plague may have been an unforeseen consequence of the population growth and expansion in trade that much of the world had seen since 1000. Crowded cities facilitated the spread of the disease, and trade caravans often carried the rats whose fleas acted as hosts for the plague bacteria.

No one at the time understood how the plague was spread. People blamed it on foreigners or people who followed religions different from their own. Others claimed it was the wrath of God. Those of a more scientific bent blamed it on bad air and sought escape from the air of the towns and cities by fleeing to the countryside. This was a sensible response to the epidemic as there was less crowding and better sanitation, and therefore fewer rats, in the country.

The devastations of the plague may have contributed to political and cultural upheaval. The Mongol Yuan dynasty in China, unable to maintain authority in an increasingly chaotic land, was finally overthrown in 1368. The new emperor was a peasant warlord known as Hongwu. He established a new dynasty, the Ming, or "brilliant dynasty."

In Europe, the plague also had important social, economic, and political effects. The death of so many people resulted in a labor shortage. Those who survived were able to buy land cheaply or demand better terms from their landlords and employers. The many peasant revolts of the late 1300s are a direct consequence of feudal serfs demanding greater freedom. Moreover, the labor shortage forced employers to develop innovative methods of production. Western Europe experienced a surge in entrepreneurial activity as a rising merchant class found new ways to organize work. Their new wealth helped to weaken the landowning aristocracy, itself suffering from the effects of the Black Death. Merchants established alliances with some of the more powerful nobles, while weaker nobles languished on estates that had lost much of their value.

The Hundred Years' War between England and France worsened conditions in the countryside. Both armies lived off the land, and the general lawlessness made it easy for bandits to steal what remained. The costs of the war, moreover, required the kings of England and France to raise taxes. Both had begun to move to mercenary armies rather than armies made up of loyal vassals, thinking mercenaries more reliable. In turn, many nobles began to harbor resentment toward their kings. By the end of the fourteenth century, both Crowns were disputed by new claimants to royal power.

A CRISIS IN THE CATHOLIC CHURCH

Europeans also suffered from a lack of religious authority in the fourteenth century. Church leaders had not only lost some of their credibility due to the failures of the Crusades, but it seemed to many that the church had become no more than a political pawn. In 1307, at the behest of the French king, the papacy was moved from its traditional seat in Rome to Avignon in southern France, where it remained until 1379. During this era, known as the Babylonian Captivity, religious leaders seemed to enjoy a life of corruption and luxury. Even after the papacy was returned to Rome, religious and political leaders dithered over what sort of authority the church should have. At one point in the early 1400s, there were actually three popes, each one representing a particular political faction.

Not until the Council of Constance in 1414 and 1415 did leaders settle on an Italian papacy. But the damage had been done. Some Europeans began to look outside the church for religious authority, and it grew clear that kings, not popes, wielded the greater power in European affairs.

THE END OF THE BYZANTINE EMPIRE

Political change also shook the Middle East. In the early 1300s a new power emerged: the Turkish Ottoman Empire. Named after their first sultan, Osman, the Ottomans originally possessed no more than a small kingdom bordering the Byzantine Empire. Military success against the Byzantines, who were greatly weakened by the Crusades, attracted other Turkish warlords to the Ottomans. They rapidly established domination over most of Turkey and Syria, their success impeded only by the brief empire established by Tamerlane, the last of the Central Asian conquerors.

The goal of the Ottoman warriors, by the early fifteenth century, was the conquest of Constantinople. The warlike traditions of the Ottomans, as well as their fierce devotion to Islam, made them natural enemies of the Byzantines. Constantinople, however, was a difficult city to conquer. It was situated on a peninsula jutting out into the Bosphorus, a narrow waterway connecting the Black and Mediterranean seas. The land approach to Constantinople was defended by a series of thick walls. Indeed, many conquerors from the Persians to the Slavs to the Crusaders had attempted to conquer the city with no lasting success.

By 1453, Ottoman conquests had reduced the once large and powerful Byzantine Empire to the city of Constantinople itself. That year the Sultan, Mehmed II, prepared his final assault on the Christian capital. Mehmed enlisted the help of many mercenaries, including weapons experts from western Europe who were able to effectively deploy heavy cannon against the city walls. Gunpowder weapons such as cannon were very new in the Middle East and Europe, and the Byzantine emperor, Constantine, had no answer for them.

Constantinople's defenses were finally breached by both land and sea on May 29, 1453, as the city's Christian inhabitants both prayed for deliverance and prepared to fight. Constantine's forces, which included many mercenaries from among the sympathetic Christians of western Europe, proved no match for the Ottomans. Constantine himself died in the fighting, and as the Turks established control over the city, they massacred and plundered freely.

Over the next years, Mehmed the Conqueror, as he was now known, made Constantinople the capital of the Ottoman Empire. The ancient Church of Hagia Sophia became a mosque, and the imperial treasures, which represented over one thousand years of Roman and Byzantine glory, fell into Muslim hands. The Byzantine Empire was at an end, and with it, the Middle Ages.

A Dark Age: 477–600

CHAPTER 1

THE GERMANIC KINGDOMS OF WESTERN EUROPE

H.G. KOENIGSBERGER

The Roman Empire in western Europe finally disappeared when the last western emperor, Romulus Augustulus, was deposed in 476. His soldiers, most of whom belonged to Germanic tribes, ousted him in favor of their general, Odoacer. Although a Roman emperor continued to govern the eastern empire from Constantinople, western Europe was now under the control of various Germanic kings.

In the following selection, H.G. Koenigsberger describes how the tribes these kings led—the Ostrogoths, Vandals, and others—the transition from a seminomadic existence to the settled life of rulers. The Germanic peoples, whom Koenigsberger refers to as barbarians in contrast to the more urbanized and sophisticated Romans, could never produce a culture as impressive as that of the Romans. Koenigsberger argues that until Germanic traditions were combined with those of the Roman past and the Christian Church, a process that took several centuries, western Europe experienced a cultural decline, a true dark age.

H.G. Koenigsberger was professor of history at King's College, London.

The different barbarian peoples who overthrew the political authority of the western Empire were all faced with a similar problem: how to adapt the customs and traditions of a tribal society that had only just broken camp and trekked—

warriors, old men, women, children and animals—over hundreds of miles to a new life among strangers, strangers who lived in a structured, urban, literary and self-consciously civilized society. Except possibly in Britain and in the northernmost parts of Gaul the barbarians were always a small minority. In some areas such as the Po valley and the high plateau of central Spain they settled fairly densely, elsewhere much more sparsely. Provided they could survive outside attack—and the Vandals in Africa, the Ostrogoths in Italy and the Suevians in north-western Spain did not—there was still this paradox: the more successfully the Germanic tribes adapted to their new environment, the more they lost their original identity and the more they were absorbed into the Roman society they had conquered. This was a slow process, lasting at least two centuries and producing in the end quite new societies, different from both the late-Roman and the German-tribal societies from which they had originated.

Because our sources for this period, mainly the sixth and seventh centuries, are few and difficult to interpret, this process of the formation of new societies is still rather obscure in detail; and yet it is one of the most important developments in the whole of European history. This becomes clear when the history of western Europe is compared with the history of those parts of the Roman Empire which were conquered by the Arabs in the seventh century. Here too a new society emerged as the result of the conquest of a Hellenized and Romanized society by a relatively primitive people. What emerged was, and has remained into our own times, a very different society from that which developed in the west. The reasons for this difference lie deeply embedded in the very old, pre-Hellenistic and pre-Roman traditions of Egypt and the middle east but also, and vitally, in the different religious histories of the Germans and the Arabs. For those Germanic people who survived, all found that they had to adopt the religion of those they had conquered, Catholic Christianity. . . .

A CULTURAL DECLINE

There was no way in which the barbarians could have matched the richness, sophistication and variety of the artistic achievements of such an old civilization as that of the Roman Empire. Tribal societies, living on pasturage and primitive agriculture and without fixed settlements for more than two or three generations, could develop neither the resources nor the skill to produce a permanent architecture, not to speak of paintings, mosaics or statues. Their artistic achievements were concentrated on jewelry and on armour. This is what we would logically expect in such societies, and this expectation is confirmed by archaeological finds. Tens of thousands of graves have been discovered—more than 40,000 in France alone—showing men buried with their weapons and women with their brooches, armbands and hairpins. These were evidently their most precious possessions. The styles and decorations of these artifacts are certainly very different from Roman styles. Even so, they appear mostly to have been borrowed originally from central Asian and near Eastern models and then developed according to the Germans' own tastes.

When the Goths, the Franks and the Lombards set up their kingdoms in the provinces of the Roman Empire, they came to rule over a Roman provincial population that maintained its craft skills. In many areas, no doubt, these skills declined both in quality and, perhaps even more important, in the number of persons who still managed to learn them. Yet masons could still build Roman arches, sculptors could still carve in stone, ivory or wood, and painters could still paint icons and decorate the pages of books. This last skill seems to have had an expanding market as, with declining literacy, books became less utilitarian and consequently rarer and more precious.

The invasions, wars and devastations, and the decline of population in the terrible plagues of the sixth century meant that there were now fewer resources for building and the arts and also that much of what still was built or painted has not survived. The relatively small number of craftsmen, however, was open to outside influences, perhaps precisely because there were so few. Jews, Syrians and Greeks travelled in barbarian kingdoms, trading precious fabrics, carved ivories, books and other valuable objects. The prestige of Constantinople remained enormous. The emperor and the barbarian kings exchanged gifts. Thus we find Coptic, Syrian and, above all, Byzantine stylistic influences in the art and architecture of the sixth and seventh centuries, as far north and west as the Rhine and Guadalquivir.

At the same time Germanic tastes in artistic style and decoration began to affect western Roman provincial art in much the same way. In some cases it is clear that the royal courts favoured it. In the recently excavated tomb of the Frankish queen, Arnegunde, of the middle of the sixth century, there was preserved her rich clothing and jewelry, all in essentially Germanic style. This contrasts with the tomb of King Childeric of 482 in which was found, together with some Germanic jewelry, much more that was essentially Roman. Artists, builders and craftsmen, working in a still living Roman tradition, were subject to influence from the whole Mediterranean world, including those of the Germanic tribes who had settled there. Gradually they evolved strong regional variations on the basic Roman style. These variations can be observed as early as the sixth and seventh centuries, as for instance in the use of the horseshoe arch in Spain, well before the Muslim invasions. Their first full flowering, however, was not reached until the eighth and ninth centuries.

ROMAN AND GERMANIC TRADITIONS COMBINED

Not until our own time have there ever been such far-reaching changes in the structure of European society as there were in the 300 years between AD 400 and 700. A politically unified empire with an urban and literate culture was replaced by a number of separate kingdoms whose culture was provincial, rural and largely non-literate. And yet, the life style of the vast majority of ordinary people, the country-dwellers, had neither changed as much as we might have expected, nor had it greatly deteriorated. Literacy and the Latin language had not disappeared altogether but continued to be cultivated by churchmen. The Christian Church had survived triumphantly and had, moreover, achieved great successes in the conversion of the Germanic tribes.

The head of the Church in the west, the pope in Rome, continued to acknowledge the authority of the emperor in Constantinople. But in practice he was almost completely independent of the emperor. This independence of the papacy—in sharp contrast to the dependence of the Christian patriarchs on the emperor—was to have the most profound consequences for the development of the Christian Church and of Christian civilization in the west.

Among the reasons which historians have proposed for these changes, and especially for the fall of the Roman Empire in the west, those which stress the internal developments of the later Roman Empire, whether religious, moral, racial or social, have been found insufficient; for none of them explains satisfactorily why the eastern half of the Roman Empire survived. The decisive force was the invasion of the Germanic tribes. The fusion of the tribal Germanic and the settled Roman societies took several centuries to accomplish and, since it took place in different ways and at different speeds, it produced a rich variety of new political, social, ethnic and cultural structures and societies. Nevertheless, all these looked back to and often tried to recapture a common Christian and Roman heritage.

Neither trade nor travel and cultural exchange ceased on the Mediterranean and in the lands of the former Roman Empire, though there was a good deal less of both than there had been before the barbarian invasions.

THE BYZANTINE EMPIRE AND ITS ATTEMPT TO RECAPTURE ROME'S GLORY

HENRI PIRENNE

Beginning early in the fourth century, most Roman emperors ruled not from Rome itself but from Constantinople in the eastern, Greek-speaking part of the empire. Sometimes two emperors ruled: a weaker one from Rome itself and the stronger one from Constantinople. When the final western emperor was deposed in 476 and Germanic tribes took control of western Europe, the eastern empire remained intact. Known as the Byzantine Empire, it survived until Constantinople was conquered by the Ottoman Turks in 1453. The Byzantine Empire combined Greek and Roman traditions with adherence to Christianity. The emperor not only considered himself the head of the Christian Church, he continued to believe he held authority over the Germanic kings.

According to historian Henri Pirenne, the events of 476 meant little as most Christians, east or west, looked to the emperor in Constantinople as their true sovereign. Even the pope, who then was merely the bishop of Rome, acknowledged the supremacy of the emperor. However, Pirenne asserts, most Germanic Christians were heretics rather than orthodox Christians. In an effort to reassert his authority over the Germans, Byzantine emperor Justinian's armies conquered much of Italy and Spain in the sixth century.

Excerpted from *A History of Europe,* by Henri Pirenne, translated by Bernard Miall (New York: University Books, 1956).

Henri Pirenne was professor of history at the University of Ghent in Belgium.

I t is usual to date the latter period of the history of the Roman Empire, which is quite properly known as the Byzantine period, from the reign of Justinian. Yet it was Constantine . . . who made Byzantium the capital of the Imperial government of the East. Henceforth, while Rome was abandoned for Milan or Ravenna by the successors of Theodosius, Byzantium was always, until in 1453 it fell into the hands of the Turks, the residence of the Emperors, the city of the Tsars, the *Tarsagrad* of the Russians. Favoured from the first by its incomparable geographical situation, the privilege of sheltering the court, and with it the central government, soon had the result of making it the chief city of the East. We may even say that from the time of the Muslim conquests it was to become the one great city of the Christian world. While after the Muslim invasions all the urban centres of the West became depopulated and fell into ruin, Byzantium retained a population of several hundreds of thousands, whose alimentary needs placed under requisition all the territories bordering on the Black Sea, the Aegean, and the Adriatic. It was Byzantium that promoted the trade and the navigation of the Empire, and the attractive force which it exerted on the whole of the Empire was the surest guarantee of its unity. Thanks to this force, the Byzantine Empire presented, so to speak, an urban character, in a much greater degree than the old Roman Empire. For Rome had merely attracted to herself the exports of the provinces, but had given them nothing in return; she restricted herself to the rôle of consumer. Byzantium, on the contrary, both consumed and produced. The city was not only an Imperial residence; it was a trading centre of the first order, into which were poured the products of Europe and Asia, and it was also a very active industrial city.

By language it remained a Greek city, but a Greek city more than half Orientalized. Incomparably richer, more thriving, and more populous than Thrace or Greece proper, the provinces of Asia Minor exercised an irresistible ascendancy. Syria, the most active of the provinces, exerted a preponderant influence on the capital. Byzantine art is really a Hellenic art transformed through the medium of the art of Syria.

CHRISTIANITY AND POLITICS

But of Greek thought and Greek science only as much survived as Christianity had seen fit to spare; and this was little enough.

Justinian, as we know, closed the school of Athens, where a faint echo of the ancient philosophers might still be heard. But the dogmas and mysteries of religion provided an abundance of material for the passionate love of dialectic which had for so many centuries characterized Hellenic thought. No sooner did Christianity appear than the East began to teem with heresies: there were pitched battles in the great cities, Council attacked Council, and the three Patriarchs of Byzantium, Antioch and Alexandria engaged in conflict. Naturally, all these heresies had their repercussions in the capital, and in every conflict the Emperor had to take sides, for the old conception that made him the religious leader, as well as the head of the State, had been perpetuated in Constantinople. In the capital every theological debate became a governmental affair. The parties pulled what wires they could at court, each seeking to obtain the all-powerful support of the sovereign. Turn and turn about, orthodoxy or heresy, according to the choice he made between them, became the religion of the State.

With all this the Empire, though confined to the East, was, nevertheless, the Roman Empire. . . . To speak, as we do for convenience' sake, of the Empire of the West and the Empire of the East, is to employ an inaccurate description. In actual fact, although for administrative purposes it was divided into an eastern and a western portion, the Empire was nevertheless a single organism. If the ruler of one of these two halves disappeared, it passed, by this very fact, under the power of the other ruler. And this is precisely what happened at the time of the invasions. The Emperor of the West having disappeared, the Emperor of the East found himself henceforth the sole Emperor. And as we have seen, he did not cede any portion of the Empire; his right to the possession of the whole remained intact. Even after the conquest the memory of his supremacy lingered. The Germanic kings recognized that he exercised a sort of primacy over them; it was not clearly defined, but they betrayed their feeling by the respect which they paid to the Emperor. For the Pope, he remained the legitimate sovereign, and the pontifical chancellery continued to date its Bulls from the year of the Consulate—that is, from the accession of the Byzantine Emperor. Moreover, in the Church the tradition persisted that the Empire was both necessary and eternal. Did not Tertullian and St. Augustine proclaim its providential nature?

THE GERMANIC HERETICS

The Romans had yet another reason to regret the Empire. Their new masters, the Germanic kings, were not orthodox. Apart from the King of the Franks, who was converted to Catholicism at the beginning of the conquest of Gaul by Clovis, the others—Visigoths,

Byzantine emperor Justinian, pictured here with his ministers, controlled much of western Europe and helped to revive Greek and Roman culture.

Ostrogoths and Vandals—were Arians by profession. To the Arian heresy, which had been so formidable in the 4th century, and which had caused so much bloodshed in the East, the Germans obstinately adhered. In actual fact it was not very dangerous. The Arian Church was making no proselytes in the heart of the Roman population, and there is reason to believe that as the Barbarians became absorbed by the latter the number of its adherents was progressively decreasing. But enraged by its very impotence, and confident of the favour of the kings, it was aggressive and intolerant in its treatment of the Catholic clergy. And the quarrels of the priests embittered and exasperated the orthodox population. In Italy the conflict became so acute that the Pope, in his despair, having invoked the intervention of the Emperor, Theodoric flung him into prison, to the great scandal of the faithful.

All this was known in Byzantium; it was known also that the strength of the new kingdoms was not very alarming. In all of them the dynasty was destroying itself by intestine quarrels and domestic murder. In the Visigoth and Ostrogoth kingdoms the various competitors for the crown begged the Emperor to come to their assistance. In the Ostrogoth kingdom, after the death of Theodoric, Theodatus had his wife Amalasontha, the daughter of the late king, assassinated, in order that he might reign alone. What with religious persecution and political scandals, there were plenty of pretexts for intervention!

Justinian (527–565) did not fail to profit by them. He had restored peace in his States, reorganized the finances, and renovated the army and the fleet; he now employed them to reconstitute the Roman Empire. The first blow was struck at the Vandals. In the year 533, five hundred ships landed in Africa 15,000 men, led by Belisarius. The campaign was as brief as it was brilliant. Within a few months the Vandal kingdom was completely conquered, and its king sent to Byzantium to figure in the Emperor's triumph. The Visigoths, who had stood aside indifferently while their neighbours were being defeated, now suffered the same fate. The whole maritime region was occupied and subdued without difficulty; the Byzantines did not trouble to pursue the king, who had fled to the mountains. The Ostrogoth kingdom held out longer. Only after eighteen years of warfare was its fate decided by the bloody defeat of its last forces on the slopes of Vesuvius (553).

The Mediterranean had once more become a Roman, or should we say, was becoming a Byzantine lake. On every side the Byzantine dukes and exarchs were organizing the administration of the reconquered provinces. Rome was once again part of the Empire, and, as in the good old days, the Emperor's orders ran as far as the Pillars of Hercules.

It might well have seemed that the Byzantine civilization, after performing such brilliant services, would become the European civilization, and that Constantinople, where Justinian was building the basilica of St. Sophia in lieu of a triumphal arch, was destined to draw the entire West into its orbit.

AN ERA OF DISUNITY IN CHINA

J.A.G. ROBERTS

Like the Roman Empire far to the west, the ancient civilization of China had been unified under a strong, centralized government. Known as the Han dynasty, it ruled from 204 B.C. until A.D. 220. From geographical unity to thought and culture, Han China set the pattern for later dynasties. Also like Rome, however, Han China suffered a decline and fall. In the fifth and sixth centuries, China still lay disunified, the victim of both internal dissension and outside invasion.

In the following selection, historian J.A.G. Roberts describes the varied rulers who controlled different areas of China during this period of disunity. While the southern part of the country lay under Chinese rule, dynasties rose and fell, beset by rivalry and rebellion. Northern China, the country's traditional heartland, was invaded and controlled by outsiders. Chinese civilization began to revive in the fifth century when the inhabitants of two cities, Pingcheng and Louyang, recovered the administrative traditions of the Han era.

J.A.G. Roberts is professor of history at the University of Huddersfield in Great Britain.

From 316 to 589 China was divided politically between dynasties of the south which sought to revive the tradition of the Han, and dynasties of the north, generally established by non-Chinese peoples. To describe the political succession in the south, the term the Six Dynasties is used, referring to the dynasties which had their capital at Jiankang, or modern Nanjing.

In the north the fragmentation of authority was even more extreme and the period between 316 and 384 is known as that of the Sixteen Kingdoms. But from that time onwards a new power began to emerge, headed by a branch of the Xianbei known as the Toba, who had originally settled in northern Shanxi. In 386 the Toba adopted the dynastic name of the Northern Wei and from then on they became increasingly sinicised. In 493 the Toba emperor established his capital at Luoyang and inaugurated a period of peace and prosperity. In 534, however, the dynasty split and the north again experienced division under dynasties known collectively as the northern dynasties. From one of these emerged a general named Yang Jian, who not only gained control of the north, but also defeated the last of the southern dynasties. In 589 the Sui dynasty reunited China. . . .

After the collapse of the Western Jin dynasty in the north, for two centuries China was effectively divided into two. It is convenient to describe first the developments to the south of the Yangzi. The record began with the establishment in 317, by a survivor of the Western Jin, of a new dynasty known as the Eastern Jin, with its capital at Jiankang. To the capital came many refugees from the north, while at the same time the Chinese population was increasing rapidly, causing tension between old and new settlers and between the Chinese and non-Chinese populations. The dynasty maintained its claim to be the true heir to the Han and sought to reconquer the north, but it was hampered by intrigues at court and rivalry among generals. In 399 the dynasty was faced with a different sort of threat, a popular rising along the southern coast, perhaps triggered off by tension between new and old settlers. Its leaders claimed a connection with the Yellow Turbans of the last years of the Later Han period. The rising was suppressed by an army commander named Liu Yu, who in 420 usurped the throne and established what became known as the Liu-Song dynasty. Under Liu Yu and his successor a period of political stability ensued, but after the fall of the Liu Song in 479 three more undistinguished dynasties were to rise and fall in quick succession. Despite the failure of any of the southern dynasties to recover political authority, this period was one of population growth and the rise of what has been called a manorial system.

MANY INVASIONS FROM CENTRAL AND NORTHERN ASIA

Meanwhile, in the north, there occurred the long period of anarchy known as the time of the Sixteen Kingdoms. During this era, the settled population of north China was invaded and overrun by various tribal groupings coming from the west and the north.

Among these, three major ethnic conglomerations have been distinguished. To the west, in the area of modern Gansu, Shaanxi, Sichuan and Qinghai, were the Tibetan Di and Qiang, peoples who were essentially sheep herders rather than horse breeders and whose states were based on a military rather than on a tribal structure. In the north-west were the Xiongnu, traditionally divided into nineteen tribes, and the Jie, both ethnically described as Turkic. Finally, to the north were the Xianbei, whose ethnic origins were variously described as proto-Mongol or Tungus. These ethnic labels must be treated with caution. At most they only refer to the language and culture of the leading tribe within a group or confederation. Tribes with different ethnic characteristics could and did join together in confederations.

The first major incursion into north China in this period came from the Xiongnu and resulted in the capture of Luoyang and Chang'an and the destruction of the Western Jin dynasty. The leading figure in this train of events was Liu Yuan, descendant of Maodun, whose dynamic leadership of the Xiongnu in the early years of the Former Han dynasty, five hundred years previously, has already been noted. Liu Yuan came from a new mould of Xiongnu leadership, one who had acquired a Chinese education and whose concept of empire was not the nomadic empire of the past, but one which laid claim to settled territory and to the imperial throne of China. To support this claim Liu Yuan could point to the intermarriage between the Xiongnu and the Han dynasty, to the fact that his surname was the same as that of the Han, and that at his capital, Pingcheng, Chinese court ceremonial had been adopted and to it he had already attracted educated Chinese. Liu Yuan died in 310, the year before the capture of Luoyang, though his successors established the short-lived dynasty known as the Earlier Zhao (304–20). But Liu Yuan's vision of empire was not shared by other tribal leaders. A new tribal confederation formed under Shi Luo, who rejected the Chinese model in favour of a return to the Xiongnu nomadic state, but who also broke with tradition by usurping the rightful succession and declaring himself ruler of the Later Zhao dynasty.

The second main challenge came from the Tibetan peoples in the west. When the Later Zhao dynasty collapsed, the leader of a Tibetan tribal confederation declared himself emperor of the Earlier Qin dynasty. In 357 he was succeeded on the dynastic throne by a man named Fu Jian, who built up a formidable fighting force, consisting not only of cavalry, but also of infantry, recruited among the Chinese. With this force he was able to conquer much of North China. In 383 he turned his attention to the conquest of the south and to the destruction of the Eastern Jin.

This campaign was the most famous of the period. Fu Jian is supposed to have mustered one million men when he descended the Yangzi to capture Jiankang. But his forces were accustomed to open terrain and were unable to adapt to the conditions of the Yangzi valley. They were defeated by the Jin troops at a decisive battle, which led not only to the failure of the expedition, but also to the rapid disintegration of the Earlier Qin empire.

The third instance of the rise of a non-Chinese dynasty, to be called the Northern Wei, was that of the tribal federation known as the Toba. The original Toba state had been destroyed by Fu Jian, but in about 385 it was re-formed in the north of the present province of Shanxi. Its leadership group may have been of Turkic origin, although the federation incorporated Xiongnu and Xianbei tribes and, as the state prospered, an increasing number of Chinese were employed as officials. Towards the end of the fourth century the Toba state extended its control over much of the North China Plain. It then began a process of adaptation and change, including progressive sinicisation, which gave it a strength and permanency which exceeded that of all previous non-Chinese dynasties.

A NON-CHINESE DYNASTY

This process had several components. The first was that the Toba developed sufficient military power to ward off rivals, which was achieved initially by the gradual subversion of the tribal system and its replacement by a military administration. This enabled the Toba to extend their influence in two directions. To the north, the settled Toba attacked and defeated yet another confederation of nomadic tribes, known as the Ruanruan, sometimes identified with the Avars who were later to settle on the Danube. There followed a series of successful expeditions which extended Toba influence into Gansu and gave access to the commerce of Central Asia. By 440 the Toba empire was the most powerful state in East Asia, ruling the whole of north China.

Another factor was the increasing participation of Chinese in the government of the Toba state. From 440, Pingcheng was developed as a capital city. Although still a barbarous place in the eyes of Chinese visitors, it had a huge palace complex, residential wards and religious buildings. Such a city required the service of Chinese officials accustomed to urban life. From 476, when the Empress Dowager Feng, herself from an aristocratic Chinese family, gained paramount power, the advancement of Chinese to high office gathered pace. Between 472 and 499 a series of decrees was issued, known as the Taihe reforms, which were 'a conscious and deliberate attempt to bring the country closer to the . . . ideal of a Han-Chinese, Confucian, bureaucratic monarchy ruling an ordered aristocratic state'. The reforms included the development of a Confucianised bureaucracy and the promotion of Confucian morality, control of Toba religious and social customs, and the introduction of more sophisticated systems of taxation and forced labour. They were accompanied by a change in frontier policy, with a switch away from the aggressive policy of sending powerful forces on raids against the Ruanruan, to one of wall-building, static defence and appeasement. Policies such as these, aimed at sinicisation and undermining tribal customs, inevitably excited the hostility of traditionalist Toba aristocratic families. . . .

Early in 493 the young Emperor Xiao had said of Pingcheng 'This is a place from which to wage war, not one from which civilized rule can come'. Before the end of that year the emperor announced his decision that the Northern Wei capital would be transferred five hundred miles south, to the site of the historic city of Luoyang. The move was probably intended as a further blow to the declining influence of the Toba aristocratic leadership. Luoyang was chosen because of its cultural associations—it was at the very centre of Chinese civilisation—and because it was at the heart of the most populous and wealthy agricultural region of north China. The move itself took time, two years to move the court and the bureaucracy to Luoyang and a further seven years to build the new capital. But then the city grew rapidly, achieving a population in excess of 500,000 and becoming one of the great cities of the ancient world. The inner city measured about 9.5 square kilometres and was surrounded by massive walls, the remains of which measure 25–30 metres thick. The roads were set out on a grid system and the city was furnished with a sophisticated water supply. Beyond the inner city lay an outer city, which contained the residential wards and over five hundred magnificent Buddhist monasteries and nunneries. One such, the Jingming, was an imperial foundation and it served not only a religious function but it also contributed to the revenues of the state. Within its walls the most advanced water-powered grain-processing machinery of the day was in use. This technology may have been developed by captives or émigrés from the south, and its use may have been monopolised by the imperial house. Another part of the outer city was set aside for the large community of foreign traders. Beyond the city lay the imperial domain and an intensively farmed countryside which supplied the city's food requirements. In 534, when the dynasty collapsed, this great city was to be abandoned in three days.

THE END OF CENTRALIZED AUTHORITY IN INDIA

ROMILA THAPAR

Like Europe and China in the fourth and fifth centuries, India suffered invasions from Central Asian Huns. According to ancient Indian scholar Romila Thapar, the Hun invasions helped speed the decline of the Gupta dynasty, which governed much of India in that era. Gupta emperors such as Chandra Gupta II ruled over a strong and prosperous nation and actively supported the arts. Yet despite their strength and accomplishments, they were unable to defend the country from the Huns.

Although Hun control of India was short-lived and weak, according to the author, the Huns nevertheless prevented the emergence of a new centralized empire in India. Instead, India was characterized for centuries by large-scale population migrations and competition among local rulers.

Romila Thapar, the author of numerous books on ancient India, was a professor of history at the University of Delhi.

C handra Gupta II took the title of *Vikramaditya* or Sun of Prowess, yet his reign is remembered for things other than war: for his patronage of literature and the arts—Kalidasa, the Sanskrit poet, being a member of his court—and for the high standard of artistic and cultural life. Fa Hsien, the Chinese Buddhist pilgrim who visited India during the years from 405 to 411 collecting Buddhist manuscripts and texts and studying at Indian monasteries, described the country as a generally happy one.

THE HUNS INVADE INDIA

It was during the reign of Chandra Gupta II's son and successor Kumara Gupta (*c.* A.D. 415–54) that there came the first hints of a new invasion from the north-west, but they were to remain only a distant threat during the first half of the fifth century. A branch of the Huns from central Asia had occupied Bactria in the previous century and were threatening to cross the Hindu Kush mountains, as had so many invaders before them, and attack India. On the whole, Kumara Gupta's reign was peaceful and he succeeded in keeping the empire intact. However, the Hun threat on the Indian frontier continued for the next hundred years and the Guptas were hard put to it to keep them back. Yet they succeeded up to a point, for, when the Huns finally broke through, they had been weakened and India did not meet with the fate of the Roman Empire. It has been plausibly suggested that the resistance offered by the Chinese and Indians to the central Asian nomads was partially responsible for the fury with which they fell upon Europe.

But the successors of Kumara Gupta could not defend their kingdom as he had done, each repeated wave of the Hun invasions making the Guptas weaker. Skanda Gupta battled valiantly but he faced domestic problems as well, such as the breaking away of his feudatories, and there are indications of an economic crisis which would explain the debasing of the coinage. However, by *c.* 460 he had managed to rally the Gupta forces, but 467 is the last known date of Skanda Gupta. After his death, the central authority of the Guptas declined at an increasing pace. The succession of the various kings that followed is uncertain. A number of administrative seals have been discovered with the names of the same kings, but following a varied order of succession, which points to a confused close to the dynasty. A major blow came at the end of the fifth century when the Huns successfully broke through into northern India. Gupta power was slowly eroded over the next fifty years, after which the empire gave way to a number of smaller kingdoms.

The 'Indian' Huns, or *Hunas* as they are called by Indian writers, were not entirely independent, since they ruled as viceroys for a Hun overlord. The Hun dominion extended from Persia right across to Khotan, the main capital being Bamiyan in Afghanistan. The first Hun king of any importance was Toramana, who ruled northern India as far as Eran in central India. Toramana's son Mihirakula (A.D. 520) appears to have been more of the Hun as pictured by tradition. A Chinese pilgrim travelling in northern India at the time describes him as uncouth in manner and an iconoclast, especially in his hatred for Buddhism. Inscriptions from central India suggest that the Guptas were still making belated attempts to resist the Huns both by their own efforts and in collaboration with other local rulers. Mihirakula was finally driven out of the plains and into Kashmir where he died in about 542, after which the political impact of the Huns subsided. Gupta power would not in any case have lasted very much longer and the Huns had accelerated the process of decline.

DISUNITY AND CONFUSION

But this was not the sole effect of the Huns. Whatever potential there might have been for the creation of an imperial structure was now demolished, because political energy was directed towards keeping back the Huns. Defence on an all-India scale was unthought of: defence was conceived in local terms with occasional combinations of the smaller kingdoms, which sometimes led to consolidation accentuating the emergence of larger kingdoms under capable protectors, whose military powers rather than concern for their royal antecedents was a deciding factor. To add to the confusion and the atmosphere of insecurity there was a movement of populations and new ethnic combinations of peoples. Together with the Huns came a number of central Asian tribes and peoples, some of whom remained in northern India and others moved further to the south and the west. Among them were the Gurjaras, who rose to eminence a few centuries later. Many of the existing tribes in Rajasthan fled from their homeland when they were displaced by the new tribes who became the ancestors of some of the Rajput families, and again were to dominate the history of the north in later centuries. The tide of Hun invasions had receded by the end of the sixth century, when the Turks and the Persians attacked them in Bactria, but as elsewhere the Huns had acted as a catalyst in the affairs of north India.

From the decline of the Guptas until the rise of Harsha in the early seventh century the political scene is confused, and there are few records to illuminate it. The large-scale displacement of peoples continued for some time. This was a period when petty kingdoms vied with each other to succeed to the past glory of the Guptas.

Diverse and Rich Postclassical Empires: 600–1000

CHAPTER 2

THE BYZANTINE EMPIRE CONTAINED MANY DIFFERENT PEOPLES

CYRIL MANGO

The Byzantine Empire contained much of the earlier Eastern Roman Empire. This region, consisting of southeastern Europe, most of North Africa, and modern-day Turkey, Syria, Lebanon, and Israel, was often referred to as the Hellenistic world due to the influence of the Greek language and Greek customs. The capital of the empire was a Greek city once known as Byzantium, whose name was officially changed to Constantinople after the Roman emperor Constantine (and became modern-day Istanbul).

This rich civilization, which outlived Rome for a thousand years, comprised a wide variety of peoples and languages, as historian Cyril Mango shows in the following article. The region had been the location of such earlier civilizations as Egypt, Ancient Israel, and Armenia, and those regions and others maintained their own languages and many of their own customs, although virtually all except the Jews converted to Christianity. Moreover, Mango suggests, Constantinople's status as a trade and cultural center drew visitors and settlers from much of the rest of the world.

Cyril Mango is professor of Byzantine and modern Greek studies at Oxford University.

From *Byzantium: The Empire of New Rome*, by Cyril Mango (London: Weidenfeld & Nicolson). Copyright © by Cyril Mango, 1980. Used by permission of the author.

All empires have ruled over a diversity of peoples and in this respect the Byzantine Empire was no exception. Had its constituent population been reasonably well fused, had it been united in accepting the Empire's dominant civilization, it would hardly have been necessary to devote a chapter to this topic. It so happens, however, that even before the beginning of the Byzantine period—indeed, when the grand edifice of Rome started to show its first cracks towards the end of the second century AD—the various nations under Roman sway tended to move apart and assert their individuality. The rise of the Christian religion, far from healing this rift by the introduction of a universal allegiance, only accentuated it. We must, therefore, begin with the question: Who were the 'Byzantines'? In an attempt to answer it we shall undertake a rapid tour of the Empire, noting as we proceed the populations of the various provinces and the languages spoken by them. The time I have chosen is about 560 AD, shortly after the recovery by the Emperor Justinian of large parts of Italy and North Africa and several decades before the major ethnographic changes that were to accompany the disintegration of the Early Byzantine State.

It will have been sufficient for our imaginary traveller, provided he did not intend to stray far from the cities, to know only two languages, namely Greek and Latin. The boundaries of their respective diffusion were not in all places sharply drawn. It may be said, however, as a rough approximation that the linguistic frontier ran through the Balkan peninsula along an east-west line from Odessos (Varna) on the Black Sea to Dyrrachium (Dürres) on the Adriatic; while south of the Mediterranean it divided Libya from Tripolitania. With the exception of the Balkan lands, where there was a fair amount of mingling, the western half of the Empire was solidly Latin and the eastern half solidly Greek in the sense that those were the languages of administration and culture. Nearly all educated persons in the East could speak Greek, just as all educated persons in the West spoke Latin, but a great proportion of ordinary people spoke neither. . . .

BYZANTIUM'S MULTICULTURAL CAPITAL

Constantinople, like all great capitals, was a melting-pot of heterogeneous elements: all seventy-two tongues known to man were represented in it, according to a contemporary source. Provincials of all kinds had either settled there or would drift in and out on commercial or official business. The servile class included many barbarians. Another foreign element was provided by military units which in the sixth century consisted either of barbarians (Germans, Huns, and others) or some of the sturdier provincials like Isaurians, Illyrians and Thracians. It is said that seventy thousand soldiers were billeted on the householders of Constantinople in Justinian's reign. Syrian, Mesopotamian and Egyptian monks, who spoke little or no Greek, thronged to the capital to enjoy the protection of the Empress Theodora and impress the natives with their bizarre feats of asceticism. The ubiquitous Jew earned his living as a craftsman or a merchant. Constantinople had been founded as a centre of latinity in the east and still numbered among its residents many Illyrians, Italians and Africans whose native tongue was Latin as was that of the Emperor Justinian himself. Furthermore, several works of Latin literature were produced at Constantinople, like Priscian's famous Grammar, the Chronicle of Marcellinus and the panegyric of Justin II by the African Corippus. Necessary as Latin still was for the legal profession and certain branches of the administration, the balance was inexorably tilting in favour of Greek. By the end of the sixth century, as Pope Gregory the Great avers, it was no easy matter to find a competent translator from Latin into Greek in the imperial capital.

Facing Constantinople lies the huge land mass of Asia Minor which has been compared to a jetty attached to Asia and pointing towards Europe. Its most developed parts have always been the coastal edges, especially the gently shelving west face, favoured by a temperate climate and studded with famous cities. The Black Sea coastal strip is much narrower and discontinuous, while the southern shore has, with the exception of the Pamphylian plain, no low-lying edge at all. The coastal areas, save for the mountainous part of Cilicia (Isauria), where the Taurus range advances to the very edge of the sea, had been hellenized for a good thousand years and more before Justinian's reign. Along the Black Sea the limit of Greek speech corresponded to the present frontier between Turkey and the [former] Soviet Union. To the east of Trebizond and Rizaion (Rize) dwelt various Caucasian peoples, such as the Iberians (Georgians) as well as the Laz and the Abasgians (Abkhazians), the latter two barely touched by Christian missions. The Empire also possessed a Hellenized foothold on the southern shore of the Crimea, while the high tableland of the Crimean peninsula was inhabited by Goths.

THE BYZANTINE MIDDLE EAST

Quite different from the coastal areas of Asia Minor is the high inland plateau, where the climate is rough and much of the land unfit for agriculture. In antiquity as in the Middle Ages the plateau was sparsely populated and urban life was relatively undeveloped there. The more important cities were situated along the major highways, such as the so-called Royal Road that ran from Smyrna and Sardis, by way of Ancyra and Caesarea, to Melitene; the road connecting Constantinople to Ancyra by way of Dorylaeum; and the southern road that extended from Ephesus to Laodicea, Antioch in Pisidia, Iconium, Tyana and, through the Cilician Gates, to Tarsus and Antioch in Syria. The ethnic composition of the plateau had not undergone any notable change for some seven hundred years before Justinian's reign. It was a bewildering mosaic of native peoples as well as immigrant enclaves of long standing, such as the Celts of Galatia, the Jews who had been planted in Phrygia and elsewhere during the Hellenistic period and Persian groups of even more ancient origin. It appears that many of the indigenous languages were still spoken in the Early Byzantine period: Phrygian was probably still extant, since it appears in inscriptions as late as the third century AD, Celtic in Galatia, Cappadocian farther east. The unruly Isaurians, who had to be pacified by force of arms in about 500 AD and many of whom drifted all over the Empire as professional soldiers and itinerant masons, were a distinct people speaking their own dialect, often to the exclusion of Greek. Next to them, however, in the Cilician plain, Greek had solidly taken root, except, perhaps, among the tribes of the interior.

Lying to the east of Cappadocia and straddling a series of high mountain chains were a number of Armenian provinces that had been annexed to the Empire as late as 387 AD when the Armenian kingdom was partitioned between Persia and Rome. These were strategically very important, but practically untouched by Graeco-Roman civilization, and they continued to be ruled by native satraps until Justinian imposed on them a new form of military administration. In the fifth century the Armenians acquired their own alphabet and began building up a literature of translations from the Greek and the Syriac which strengthened their feelings of national identity. Indeed, the Armenians, who were to play a crucial role in later Byzantine history, proved very resistant to assimilation as did the other Caucasian peoples. . . .

It is unlikely that the use of Greek should have been more widespread in Palestine than it was in northern Syria, except for an artificial phenomenon, namely the development of the 'holy places'. Starting in the reign of Constantine the Great, practically every site of biblical fame became, as we would say today, a tourist attraction. From every corner of the Christian world people poured into Palestine: some as transient pilgrims, others on a longer-term basis. Monasteries of every nationality sprang up like mushrooms in the desert next to the Dead Sea. Palestine was thus a babel of tongues, but the native population—and we must remember that it included two distinct ethnic groups, namely the Jews and the Samaritans—spoke Aramaic as it had always done. . . .

Another element of the population of both Syria and Palestine consisted of Arabs who had spread as far north as Mesopotamia. Some of them, like the Nabataeans of Petra and the Palmyrenes, had become sedentary and lost their native language. Others roamed the deserts either as brigands or as vassals of the Empire whose duty it was to protect the settled areas and oversee the transhumance of the nomads. We should not, in any case, imagine that the Arab conquest of the seventh century introduced a foreign element into those provinces: the Arabs had been there all along, their numbers were increasing and, in Justinian's reign, they assumed more and more the role of keepers of the emperor's peace. When, for example, the Samaritans staged a bloody revolt in 529, it was an Arab chieftain, Abukarib, who put them down.

Closely linked with Syria by virtue of its situation was the island of Cyprus. Here Greek had been spoken since prehistoric times, but there was also a sizeable colony of Syrians as may be deduced from the prevalence of the Monophysite heresy. St Epiphanius, the most famous bishop of Salamis (d. 403), was a Palestinian and is said to have known five languages—Greek, Syriac, Hebrew, Egyptian and Latin. An exaggeration perhaps, but even so an indication of the multilingualism that characterized, as it still does, the more enterprising among the Levantines.

Separated from Palestine by an area of desert lay the rich and ancient land of Egypt. Here, too, the distribution of Greek was a direct legacy of the Hellenistic age. The capital, Alexandria, was a predominantly Greek city, but it was officially described as being *ad Aegyptum* [in Egypt], not *in Aegypto* [of Egypt], an intrusion into an alien country; and the farther one travelled from Alexandria, the less Greek was spoken. Apart from the capital, only two cities had been founded by the Greeks, Naukratis in the Delta and Ptolemais in the Thebaid; nor did Hellenization make much progress under Roman administration. Setting aside the Jewish colony, which in the first century AD is said to have numbered about one million, the bulk of the population, even though they were administered in Greek, continued to speak Egyptian (Coptic), and there are signs that in the Early Byzantine period Coptic was gaining ground so that, by the sixth century, even some official acts were published in the native tongue. Above all, Coptic was the language of Egyptian Christianity, while Greek was identified with the alien hierarchy that was imposed by the imperial government.

A TRAVELER TELLS OF THE WEALTH OF CONSTANTINOPLE

BENJAMIN OF TUDELA

For much of its history as the capital of the Byzantine empire, Constantinople was one of the greatest and most populous cities of the world. Trade goods and tribute flowed to the city from as far away as Sweden, China, and Africa, and scholars, monks, merchants, and mercenaries traveled there seeking enlightenment and wealth. The Byzantine emperor, for his part, saw himself as the heir to the emperors of Rome and the head of world Christianity, and he lived accordingly.

In the twelfth century, a Jewish merchant named Benjamin of Tudela visited the city and recorded his observations, excerpted in the following article. Benjamin confirmed that the city was a wealthy trade and religious center, and that the emperor lived luxuriously. However, Benjamin also noted that Constantinople's large Jewish community was forced to live apart from the city's Christians.

All sorts of merchants come here from the land of Babylon, from the land of Shinar, from Persia, Media, and all the sovereignty of the land of Egypt, from the land of Canaan, and the empire of Russia, from Hungaria, Patzinakia, Khazaria, and the land of Lombardy and Sepharad. It is a busy city, and merchants come to it from every country by sea or land, and there is none like it in the world except Bagdad, the great city of Islam. In Constantinople is the church of Santa Sophia, and the seat of

From *Itinerary*, by Benjamin of Tudela, translated by Marcus Nathan Adler (Oxford: Oxford University Press, 1907).

the Pope of the Greeks, since the Greeks do not obey the Pope of Rome. There are also churches according to the number of the days of the year. A quantity of wealth beyond telling is brought hither year by year as tribute from the two islands and the castles and villages which are there. And the like of this wealth is not to be found in any other church in the world. And in this church there are pillars of gold and silver, and lamps of silver and gold more than a man can count. Close to the walls of the palace is also a place of amusement belonging to the king, which is called the Hippodrome, and every year on the anniversary of the birth of Jesus the king gives a great entertainment there. And in that place men from all the races of the world come before the king and queen with jugglery and without jugglery, and they introduce lions, leopards, bears, and wild asses, and they engage them in combat with one another; and the same thing is done with birds. No entertainment like this is to be found in any other land.

A LAVISH PALACE

This King Emanuel built a great palace for the seat of his government upon the sea-coast, in addition to the palaces which his fathers built, and he called its name Blachernae. He overlaid its columns and walls with gold and silver, and engraved thereon representations of the battles before his day and of his own combats. He also set up a throne of gold and of precious stones, and a golden crown was suspended by a gold chain over the throne, so arranged that he might sit thereunder. It was inlaid with jewels of priceless value, and at night time no lights were required, for every one could see by the light which the stones gave forth. Countless other buildings are to be met with in the city. From every part of the empire of Greece tribute is brought here every year, and they fill strongholds with garments of silk, purple, and gold. Like unto these storehouses and this wealth, there is nothing in the whole world to be found. It is said that the tribute of the city amounts every year to 20,000 gold pieces, derived both from the rents of shops and markets, and from the tribute of merchants who enter by sea or land.

The Greek inhabitants are very rich in gold and precious stones, and they go clothed in garments of silk with gold embroidery, and they ride horses, and look like princes. Indeed, the land is very rich in all cloth stuffs, and in bread, meat, and wine.

Wealth like that of Constantinople is not to be found in the whole world. Here also are men learned in all the books of the Greeks, and they eat and drink every man under his vine and his fig-tree.

They hire from amongst all nations warriors called Loazim

(Barbarians) to fight with the Sultan Masud, King of the Togar-
mim (Seljuks), who are called Turks; for the natives are not warlike, but are as women who have no strength to fight.

No Jews live in the city, for they have been placed behind an
inlet of the sea. An arm of the sea of Marmora shuts them in on
the one side, and they are unable to go out except by way of the
sea, when they want to do business with the inhabitants. In the
Jewish quarter are about 2,000 Rabbanite Jews and about 500
Karaïtes, and a fence divides them. Amongst the scholars are several wise men, at their head being the chief rabbi R. Abtalion, R.
Obadiah, R. Aaron Bechor Shoro, R. Joseph Shir-Guru, and R. Eli-
akim, the warden. And amongst them there are artificers in silk
and many rich merchants. No Jew there is allowed to ride on
horseback. The one exception is R. Solomon Harmitsri, who is
the king's physician, and through whom the Jews enjoy considerable alleviation of their oppression. For their condition is very
low, and there is much hatred against them, which is fostered by
the tanners, who throw out their dirty water in the streets before
the doors of the Jewish houses and define the Jews' quarter (the
Ghetto). So the Greeks hate the Jews, good and bad alike, and
subject them to great oppression, and beat them in the streets,
and in every way treat them with rigour. Yet the Jews are rich
and good, kindly and charitable, and bear their lot with cheer-
fulness. The district inhabited by the Jews is called Pera.

A NEW EMPIRE IN WESTERN EUROPE: CHARLEMAGNE AND THE CAROLINGIANS

PIERRE RICHÉ

The Franks were one of the many Germanic tribes who controlled Europe after the fall of Rome in 476. They were, however, the first to convert to Roman Catholic Christianity, which predictably strengthened the relationship between the Franks and the pope. After leading an alliance against the invading Arab Muslims in the eighth century, a Frankish noble family known as the Carolingians gained even greater prestige in the eyes of the papacy.

In 768 the head of the Carolingians, Charlemagne, became king of the Franks. He established many alliances with other nobles, enjoyed great success on the battlefield, and helped sponsor literature and the study of philosophy. On Christmas Day 800, the pope crowned Charlemagne Holy Roman Emperor in an attempt to reassert the authority of the Western Roman Empire as well as the Roman Catholic Church.

As Pierre Riché points out in the following selection, however, Charlemagne's empire was something new. The Holy Roman Empire combined Roman and Christian traditions, to be sure, but also incorporated many Germanic customs. A noteworthy example of such customs was Charlemagne's insistence on sharing his authority with other nobles, provided they had sworn an oath of loyalty to him.

From *The Carolingians: A Family Who Forged Europe*, by Pierre Riché, translated by Michael Idomir Allen. Copyright © 1993 University of Pennsylvania Press. Reprinted with permission.

Pierre Riché is emeritus professor of medieval history at the University of Paris, Nanterre.

T he [Holy Roman Empire] was governed by a ruler who possessed absolute authority over politics, justice, legislation, and military affairs. This authority derived as much from the royal *bannum* [proclamations] of the Frankish kings as from the tradition of the Christian emperors of late antiquity, some of whose enactments were known to Frankish jurists. Charlemagne followed in the tradition of Constantine and Theodosius when he regulated such matters as religion, education, fair pricing, and coinage.

THE HOLY ROMAN EMPEROR SHARED HIS POWER

Nevertheless, the emperor was not a tyrant; his monarchy was not authoritarian after the fashion of Byzantium. Charlemagne maintained the traditional contact between Frankish kings and their subjects. Each year before the summer campaigns, he convened the *conventus generalis,* or "general assembly," where great matters of state were discussed in common. . . .

At the close of these assemblies, capitularies were drafted and issued as a series of ordinances in article form *(capitula).* To these well-known documents we owe much of our knowledge about life in the Carolingian realm, although we cannot be sure of their actual effectiveness in curbing abuse and prompting change. The general assembly was an extension of the closer circle of advisers that helped the king to govern and resided at the palace. Charlemagne lived amid friends to whom he entrusted various responsibilities. Some of these aides held offices in the royal household that survived throughout the Middle Ages: for example, the cellarmaster, cupbearer, and seneschal. . . .

In the case of misconduct, the king could dismiss a count, but this rarely happened. Charlemagne preferred to regulate his agents with the help of personal envoys, the *missi dominici.* Although they first appear in the mid-eighth century, the *missi* became most effective and visible as an institution after 800. Charles defined a series of separate inspection zones, the *missatica,* which generally comprised six to ten counties to be scrutinized by his *missi.* The emperor usually paired a layman and an ecclesiastic to travel for a set period of time and gave them instructions before their departure. Such guidance was even passed on by the *missi* to local counts, as in a document of 806:

> We admonish and command you to settle fully, equitably, and justly the claims for justice presented by

churches, widows, orphans, and all others, without fraud, undue cost, or excessive delay, whether these claims are laid before you or your subordinates. . . .

Above all guard that no one, in the hope of delaying or frustrating a judgment, deceives either you or some helper into saying: "Keep quiet until the *missi* have passed through, then we shall come to an arrangement among ourselves." Take care rather to settle the matter before we arrive. . . .

Read this letter often and keep it safe, so that it may serve as a witness to whether or not you have complied with its contents.

Not all subjects of the empire were subject to the administration of the counts. Under Charlemagne, the church benefited from the extension of grants of immunity, which had existed since the Merovingian period. These privileges entitled ecclesiastical rulers, especially abbots, to deal directly with the king and remain "immune" from the interference of local counts. An institution that possessed such immunity levied its own troops for the royal army, administered local justice, and collected fines and direct taxes, turning over a portion of the receipts to the king. To prevent individual abbots from becoming overwhelmed with worldly concerns and also to police their dealings, Charlemagne named a lay "advocate" to help them. The principal task of these advocates was to dispense justice within the immune territory.

Finally, Charlemagne also sought to ensure a personal bond between himself and his subjects by requiring an oath of fidelity from every free male in his realm. The leading agents of the emperor were also encouraged to become his vassals. Although the two procedures affected persons of different social stature, they were part of the same effort to ensure that personal ties linked individual subjects to the king: . . .

To our lord and most pious emperor, Charles, son of King Pippin and Queen Bertrada, I am a faithful servant, as a man lawfully ought to be to his lord, in the service of his kingdom and righteousness. This oath which I pledge, I shall keep, and I do intend to keep, to the best of my knowledge and understanding from this day forward, so help me God, who created heaven and earth and these relics of the saints. . . .

The formula prescribed by Charlemagne for the oath was closely modeled on the pledge of vassalage made by nobles. However, a vassal actually commending himself would have placed his hands between those of his lord, as had Tassilo in 757. To establish links between himself and the magnates, Charlemagne enjoined them to become his pledged supporters, or "faithful men." The chief interest of such personal ties lay in the promise of military support, since the king might call for immediate help from his vassals whereas his counts might delay in bringing contingents to the host. Moreover, the king could always count on the near presence of "faithful men" who would be ready to lend him their support, and this encouraged him to enlist all bishops, abbots, and counts as his vassals. In return, Charlemagne conferred a benefice on his vassal, generally in the form of land. In Aquitaine, Bavaria, and Italy, royal vassals often held immense domains in order to ensure an effective royal presence and authority. In turn, these royal vassals secured help from followers of their own to whom they parceled out land as a subbenefice, thereby creating a secondary level of vassal clients. This practice of vassalage, became increasingly widespread at the end of the eighth and the beginning of the ninth century. It was the product of royal initiative. In principle, the ties that arose were strictly personal and limited to the lifetime of the individuals involved. The death of either party broke the bond and returned to the lord, or his successor, whatever benefice had been conferred.

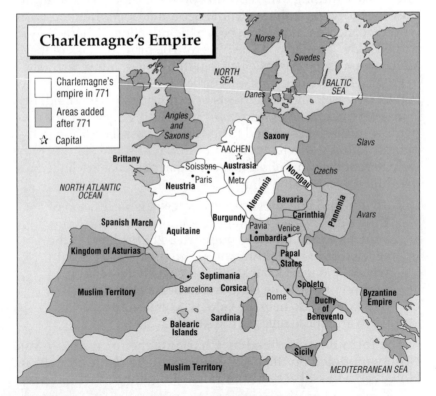

In the case of Charlemagne, royal authority was strong enough to ensure that this indeed happened, but under his successors, many vassals managed to keep for themselves and their progeny the lands conferred by the king. . . .

AN EMPIRE OF MANY PEOPLES

Carolingian Europe spread across more than one million square kilometers of territory. It comprised many different regions that had been marshaled around a common focus of authority in a relatively short span of time; each region retained its own history, laws, culture, and outlook. Francia was the center of the empire; it harbored many palaces, great abbeys, and domains of the royal fisc. The "land of the Franks" extended from the Atlantic Ocean to beyond the Rhine, bounded in the south by the Loire River and the plateau of Langres. Francia itself was subdivided into the former territory of Neustria (now more narrowly conceived as the lands between the Seine and the Loire), western Francia (between the Seine and the Meuse), middle Francia (between the Meuse and the Rhine and including Frankish Burgundy), and eastern Francia (beyond the Rhine and comprising Hesse, Thuringia, and Alemannia, thus encompassing former Austrasia). To the northeast lay the lands of the Saxons and Frisians, and to the southeast, the former duchy of Bavaria. Although Saxony was subjugated and Christianized by terror, it retained its ancient laws and social order. The nobles of Bavaria likewise managed to foster their own traditions despite the loss of political autonomy and the influence of Italy and the Franks. . . .

For the Franks, Italy always remained a land foreign in both tongue and mentality. A visit there required a lengthy and difficult voyage and posed health risks. Although Charlemagne sought to unify the entire peninsula under his own authority, he had to take account of the diverse character of its regions. The subject Lombard kingdom, the papal territories, and the duchies of Spoleto and Benevento all presented multiple landscapes and populations.

A traveler who voyaged across the Carolingian Empire would have been sorely tried by the variety of dialects and languages. While the Bretons and the Basques each possessed unique tongues, the peoples of Aquitaine and most of Francia spoke an array of highly vulgarized Latin dialects, known collectively as *lingua romana rustica,* or "Romance." In the Germanic linguistic areas, there survived some pockets where Rheto-Romance, or Ladin, was spoken, as in Bavaria around Salzburg, in West Tirol near Chur, and in Friuli. The Germanic language referred to in our sources as *lingua teudisca* (whence the word "Deutsch") also presented considerable dialectical variations. Saxons could not, for instance, understand Bavarians. The "Frankish" spoken at the Carolingian court was variable according to region, as is demonstrated by the few surviving written examples. Thus, it was necessary for the rulers and their functionaries to be bilingual or even trilingual. Hoping to impose order on his mother tongue, Charlemagne even began work on a written Germanic grammar, which has not survived.

FEUDALISM IN CAROLINGIAN EUROPE

SIDNEY PAINTER

One of the most significant legacies of the Carolingian age in Europe was the development of feudalism, the system of knights, vassals, and peasant serfs that provided the foundation of European societies for centuries. Although European feudalism emerged out of the context of the violent warrior nobles of the Germanic tribes who controlled Europe during its dark ages, it provided coherence to European life beginning with the reign of the Carolingian warlord Charles Martel, Charlemagne's grandfather.

According to Sidney Painter, the author of the following excerpt, feudalism evolved from the practice in which powerful nobles granted parcels of land, or fiefs, to the warriors who supported them. These fiefs were also known as benefices. A warrior who was granted a fief was considered a vassal of his lord. As such, he was expected to support the noble in war as well as swear an oath of loyalty, or fealty, to him. In addition, vassals were expected to pay homage to their lords in ways ranging from providing advice to lending money.

Painter argues that feudalism and feudal relationships helped keep Europe in an almost chronic state of war. Disputes over fiefs were frequent, success in war was the basis for granting or withholding fiefs, and warrior nobles generally chose to settle their differences on the battlefield.

Sidney Painter was professor of medieval history at Johns Hopkins University.

From "Feudalism and Civilization," by Sidney Painter, in *A History of the Crusades*, vol. 1, edited by Marshall W. Baldwin. Copyright © 1969. Reprinted by permission of The University of Wisconsin Press.

Feudalism was the most important of the few original creations of the period known to us as the Middle Ages. The product of an age of anarchy lying under the spectre of Imperial Rome, it became a fundamental element of the political institutions of Western Europe. Long after the disappearance of feudalism as a living political system, its traditions deeply affected the accepted political ideas of this region and inhibited the development of both absolutist government and nationalism. In it lay the foundations of the Anglo-American conception of government which has played so important a part in the modern world.

Feudalism Was Built Around the Landholdings of Warriors

Feudal institutions were restricted to a particular class of society—the warrior aristocracy. This class created for itself a set, or perhaps one should say several sets, of ethical ideas which were in accord with the requirements of the feudal environment. Their propagation was the work of writers and reciters who embodied them in an extensive literature intended to be heard rather than read. These ideas long outlasted the class that originated them and are still an important part of our social heritage. Our conception of a gentleman and of the ideal state of matrimony are largely based on the ethical ideas of the feudal class. And the literature in which they were expressed, especially the Arthurian legends, still stirs the imagination of writers of both prose and poetry.

The term feudal has a curious and complicated history. All the Germanic languages had a word for cattle. As cattle were the only moveable goods of any importance among the early Germans, these words soon took the wider meaning of chattels. The Gallo-Roman language of the West Frankish state adopted such a term from the Franks and made it into "fie" or "fief." In the tenth century we find it used for arms, clothing, horses, and food. The man of wealth who kept a warrior in his household supplied him with these things. Hence when he decided to give the warrior land to support him, what was then called a "benefice," some called this land a fief. For a while we find such expressions as "a benefice vulgarly called a fief" and then the word "fief" triumphed and "benefice" disappeared.

"Fief" became "feudum" in Latin. In the seventeenth century "féodale" and "feudal" appear in France and England respectively as legal terms to refer to anything connected with fiefs and fiefholders—the mediaeval nobles and their lands. In the eighteenth century the meaning of these words was extended to cover the relations between the fief-holder and the non-noble peasants who tilled his fief. This usage appears in full force in

1789 in the famous decree of the National Assembly abolishing the "régime féodale.". . .

CHARLES MARTEL GIVES LAND TO HIS SOLDIERS

In discussing the beginnings of feudalism one must distinguish between feudal institutions and a feudal system. Feudal institutions appeared in early Carolingian times. Charles Martel needed a reliable and effective military force to stabilize his power in the Frankish state and to check the inroads of such external foes as the Moslems and the Saxons. The economy of Western Europe had fallen to a point where there was little money in circulation. Charles could support soldiers only by giving them land and the labor to work it. The Frankish church had an immense amount of land—scholars have guessed that it held about one third of the land in the state. To get its land cultivated, the church had long used an institution called a benefice. A benefice was a grant of land for a fixed term, often for the grantee's lifetime, in return for certain services. Charles used church land to grant benefices to his warriors. But Charles wanted not merely soldiers but soldiers who would stick by him through thick and thin. Now from the time when they had left the dank forests of North Germany to enter Gaul the Frankish kings had had a band of chosen men bound to them by special oaths—their *comitatus* or trustee. Charles Martel combined this institution with the benefice. The men to whom he gave benefices swore to be ever faithful to him. As the term *vassus* was in common use for dependents of various kinds, Charles applied it to his new soldiers. They became *vassi dominici*, vassals of the lord.

The granting of benefices became a general practice in the Carolingian Empire. The kings gave them from church lands, from territories conquered from their neighbors such as the March of Barcelona, and from estates belonging to the crown. Great Frankish landowners copied the king and granted benefices from their proprietary lands, their allods.

FEUDALISM AS A SOURCE OF STABILITY

As the Carolingian government decayed in the ninth and tenth centuries under the stress of internal strife and fierce attacks by Vikings, Moslems, and Magyars, the personal relationship between lord and vassal became one of the few stable elements in society. Though it never entirely replaced the far more ancient tie of kinship, it gradually gained priority over it. Hence there was a tendency for all political relationships to become feudal. The king's deputies in the various regions, the dukes and counts, became his vassals and their offices were considered to be benefices.

The early Carolingians—Charles Martel, Pepin, and Charlemagne—granted benefices and took them back at will. Their weaker successors undoubtedly found it extremely difficult to deprive an able warrior of his benefice. In fact, when a vassal died leaving a son who was an effective soldier, there was little point in attempting to prevent him from succeeding to his father's benefice. Thus while benefices were never recognized as hereditary during the Carolingian period, by the tenth century they usually were in practice when the heir was a male of full age. By the end of the eleventh century only the lord's right to a money payment called "relief," when the son succeeded his father, bore witness of earlier custom. Moreover, custom was beginning to demand that a lord safeguard the hereditary rights of a daughter or a son who was under age. The development of the principle of the hereditability of fiefs was obviously a most important stage in the history of feudalism. A temporary delegation of property or power had become an established proprietary right.

During the period when benefices or, as we shall now call them, fiefs were gradually becoming hereditary, another important change was taking place. In the ninth century most of the great landowners who had fiefs held them directly from the king—were, in short, the successors of the *vassi dominici.* But bit by bit the dukes and counts persuaded or forced the royal vassals in their territories to become their men. In 1025 Hugh IV de Lusignan was not quite sure whether he and his neighboring fiefholders were primarily vassals of the king or of the count of Poitou, but their successors were clearly the count's men. Thus there developed a feudal hierarchy on a territorial basis.

By the end of the ninth century feudal institutions were common in every part of the Frankish Empire except Saxony. In all probability a large percentage of the great landholders held benefices and were vassals. But these fief-holders usually had allodial lands as well, and in most cases they were more extensive than the fiefs. Moreover, there were many great men who held *only* allods*. At this point the history of the West and East Frankish states diverged sharply. The tenth and eleventh centuries saw the East Frankish state, modern Germany, ruled by strong kings who maintained their power and gave no encouragement to the development of a complete feudal system. But during this same period the West Frankish state, modern France, fell into almost complete anarchy. Every man who could afford the military equipment was a knight, and every knight's sword was turned against

*An allod was land that was held independently, rather than a fief, which had been granted by a lord.

his neighbors. Public authority broke down completely, and feudal institutions were too scattered to take its place. Even if a count wanted to maintain order and could secure the obedience of his vassals, the great allodial holdings escaped all superior authority.

During the course of the eleventh, twelfth, and in some regions the thirteenth centuries, the dukes, counts, and barons of France gradually brought the allods within the system of fiefs. The process is not entirely clear to us. In some cases it was done by force of arms, in others by the grant of privileges, and in others by money payments. Thus by the eleventh century the dukes of Burgundy were strong enough to forbid anyone to build a castle on an allod in the counties they controlled. If a man wanted to build a fortress, he had to turn its site into a fief held of the duke. In the thirteenth century the Burgundian dukes were giving lump sums of money to holders of allods to persuade them to do homage for their allodial lands. The allod never entirely disappeared in France. Only in those countries where feudalism was introduced by a conqueror—England, Sicily, Palestine, and Greece—did the feudal system become complete and all embracing. But by 1200 Northern France was almost completely feudalized, and the feudal bond became a reasonably effective political cement.

THE KNIGHT ON HORSEBACK WAS THE CENTER OF FEUDAL RELATIONS

I can only describe the feudal *system* in the briefest possible manner. Its base was the fully armed warrior—the knight. He had a fief which consisted of enough land and labor to support him. When he received his fief, the knight did homage to a lord. The lord was bound to protect the knight, his family, and his fief. In return the knight was bound to be faithful to his lord and do him service. When the lord needed soldiers for war in the field or to garrison his castle, the knight had to appear in full armor. When the lord summoned his vassals to court, the knight was bound to attend. When a vassal died, his heir owed the lord a money payment called relief and the vassal was expected to aid the lord financially on certain occasions such as the wedding of his eldest daughter or the knighting of his eldest son. The rights and duties of lord and vassals were set in the lord's court—an assembly of vassals presided over by the lord. These definitions of rights and duties were feudal law or custom and differed from fief to fief. Thus for example two fiefs lying side by side might have entirely different laws governing inheritance.

The feudal system provided for military and political cooperation between members of the knightly class with the least possible restraint on individual liberty. A knight had certain definite personal obligations toward his lord and his own vassals. He had rather more vague ones toward other vassals of his lord. But toward all other men he was a free agent who could do what he pleased. Thus it was a serious offence for him to rape the daughter of his lord or of one of his own vassals, but he could rape anyone else's daughter with impunity if he was powerful enough to ignore the ire of her relatives. Outside the bounds of feudal custom, the vassal was unrestrained. And within the feudal class the system was completely democratic—custom was set and enforced by the vassals.

Thus the feudal relationship was essentially a contract between lord and vassals which was defined and enforced by mutual agreement. The system operated in the same manner. It was assumed that lord and vassals had a common interest—the welfare of the fief. No lord was expected to make a serious decision, such as choosing a wife or going to war, without asking counsel of his vassals.

As a political system pure feudalism was little removed from anarchy. It assumed a more-or-less permanent state of war. While it provided machinery for the peaceful settling of most disputes, it did not *compel* men to settle their disputes peacefully. Thus if two knights quarrelled, they could always find a feudal court competent to hear the case, but if they preferred to wage war on each other, and they usually did, feudal custom did not hinder them. France in the eleventh and early twelfth centuries, and parts of Germany in the fourteenth and fifteenth, are prime examples of feudalism uncontrolled by public authority. In England from the beginning, in France after 1150, and in Germany before the downfall of the Hohenstaufen dynasty, royal authority based on the traditions of Germanic monarchy, mingled vaguely with those of Imperial Rome, curbed feudal anarchy to some extent. Because these kings ruled through a combination of royal and feudal institutions—were both kings and feudal suzerains—historians call them "feudal monarchs."

THE TANG DYNASTY USHERS IN CHINA'S GOLDEN AGE

C.P. FITZGERALD

After centuries of fragmentation and invasion, China was reunified in 583 by the short-lived Sui dynasty. The Sui was followed by the Tang dynasty, which governed China from 618 to 907. Under the second Tang emperor, Tang T'ai Tsung, China regained not only its geographical unity but much of the glory, security, and strength of the earlier Han dynasty. T'ai Tsung and later emperors, including the Empress Wu, one of China's few female rulers, conquered an empire; expanded trade; patronized scholarship, religion, and the arts; and helped turn China into one of the wealthiest and most influential empires on earth.

In the following selection, C.P. Fitzgerald describes how the early Tang emperors solidified their rule while opening Tang China to outside contact and influence. The capital, Chang'an, attracted merchants and scholars from Europe, the Middle East, Southeast Asia, and Japan. Indeed, along with Constantinople and Baghdad, Chang'an was one of the great cities of the world, boasting a population of more than 1 million. Under the Tang, Christianity and other world religions thrived, although the Tang emperors preferred Buddhism.

C.P. Fitzgerald was the author of many books on Chinese history and a scholar at the School of Pacific Studies in Canberra, Australia.

From *The Empress Wu*, by C.P. Fitzgerald (Melbourne: F.W. Cheshire, for the Australian National University, 1955).

A t this time [the early seventh century] China was on the threshold of a glorious age, the T'ang dynasty, which has always been held to have been the most brilliant epoch in her history. Li Shih-min, posthumously known as the Emperor T'ai Tsung, was the architect of this glory and the true founder of the dynasty. He had instigated the revolt of his father against the misrule of the Sui Emperor and had himself commanded the T'ang armies which reduced the warring confusion of his times to order and peace. He had repelled the inroads of the nomad Turks which threatened to overrun the Empire, and had remodelled the system of government and defence. The unity which T'ai Tsung had restored was something which China had not known for centuries, until the brief Sui dynasty which preceded the T'ang. That first restoration of unity had failed and fallen in ruin and revolt before the T'ang dynasty was founded. It had seemed that all hope of ending the wars which had divided China for four centuries was once more lost.

A Revitalized China

Thus, when in six years this new disunion was brought to an end by a series of brilliant campaigns, T'ai Tsung appeared to the men of his time as the saviour of the world. Not since the end of the Han dynasty in the third century had China been so strong, so populous or so peaceful. The refounding of the centralised united Empire by the T'ang was a turning point in Chinese history only comparable in importance to the first foundation of that Empire by the ruthless conqueror, Shih Huang Ti, first Emperor of the Ch'in dynasty. The Ch'in conquest, like the Sui, had proved transitory, but had been followed by the great Han dynasty, which had consolidated the united Empire and spread the power of China and her culture far to the south and west.

All that had been lost, or seemed to be lost, in the long period of division, and foreign conquest in the north, which had followed the downfall of the Han in A.D. 220. Weak and short-lived dynasties had succeeded one another in the southern half of China, which remained unconquered by the nomad invaders. Turbulent and equally transitory regimes were established by these invaders in the region north of the Yangtze River. Of these the Wei (A.D. 424–554) alone could claim to have contributed something to the heritage of Chinese civilisation, and that was more in the realms of art than in political skill or peaceful administration.

With the Sui, a Chinese family, although one with some Tartar blood, had regained the Throne, and, arising in the former domain of the Tartar northern dynasties, had easily overcome the feeble ruler of the southern empire (A.D. 587). Sui Yang Ti, the second sovereign of that line, had brought the dynasty to ruin by his extravagances, his cruelties and his repeated and uniformly unsuccessful attempts to conquer the kingdom of Korea. It was from the chaos that closed his reign that T'ai Tsung hammered out the T'ang Empire in six years of furious war.

That Empire, which was soon to rival the Han in extent and power, and perhaps to surpass it in cultural achievements, was still smaller and far less populous than the modern Republic of China. To the north the Chinese frontier was marked by the Great Wall, first linked together by the Ch'in Emperor Shih Huang Ti, and always maintained by Chinese sovereigns in later centuries. To the northeast the frontier indeed extended beyond the Wall to the Liao River in what is now South Manchuria, then the frontier of the Korean kingdom. Beyond the Wall to the north and west were the Turkish tribes, whom T'ai Tsung had repulsed and subdued so that a fringe of tributary tribes lay between the Chinese frontier and the Gobi Desert.

In Central Asia, north-west of China, the ancient dominion of the Han was re-established by the conquest of the oases and their petty kingdoms, which at that time were the links and route between China and the Middle East. Westward Tibet was then emerging from the mists of prehistory to become a powerful and warlike state, not yet the Buddhist theocracy of later centuries. The T'ang Empire was later to encounter much formidable hostility from this state.

The south of China was then a colonial region, as yet thinly peopled, and still largely in the hands of native tribes, who although akin to the Chinese, were on a lower level of civilisation. Chinese authority had been established in Canton and the valley of the West River by the Ch'in and Han emperors, and maintained fitfully by the southern rulers during the Partition, but it was only under the T'ang that this region really became firmly incorporated in the Chinese Empire and its people were made to feel themselves truly Chinese. Thus the men of Canton speak of themselves as "Men of T'ang" while the other Chinese are "Men of Han". Even in the T'ang period the southern provinces were still largely uncolonised by Chinese. The river valleys which run north into the Yangtze, the Siang in Hunan and the Kan in Kiangsi, were settled, but the hill country which lies between them, and the mountainous coastal provinces of Fukien and Chekiang were still but sparsely occupied. The south-west, the modern Yunnan and Kweichou, were mainly beyond Chinese jurisdiction; and in the former province the powerful Shan state of Nanchao flourished in defiance of Chinese power.

T'ai Tsung was the first ruler to divide China into provinces, some of which have retained the same names and much the same areas to the present day. He had only ten provinces, the whole vast area south of the Yangtze being divided between only two: Kiangnan, which covered all of what are now Hunan, Kiangsi, Chekiang and Fukien, with the parts of Kiangsu and Anhui south of the river; and Lingnan, which comprised the modern Kuangtung and Kuangsi. This division is itself a proof of the undeveloped state of south China at the time.

FOREIGN INFLUENCES AND CONTACTS

Beyond the sea, to the east, China was then in contact with the nascent Japanese empire, which eagerly borrowed the manners and forms of the great continental civilisation, as ten centuries later she was to borrow those of the West. To the south-east the Chinese traded with the island states of Indonesia, and through the intermediary of the Arabs, with India and the Moslem world, then rising on the ruins of the Persian and Roman empires.

From these foreign contacts the T'ang Empire derived important influences, especially in the realms of art and religion. Nestorian Christianity was introduced to China in the reign of T'ai Tsung by monks from Syria, and during the next two centuries was a flourishing creed counting many influential converts. The Persian refugees who fled to China before the Moslem conquest of their country also brought with them their own Zoroastrian worship, which was permitted in China, although it does not seem to have made many converts among the Chinese themselves. The Persians were an important part of the foreign population; after the death of Yesdegerd, the last Sassanian King, his son Firouz, who had appealed to the T'ang court for aid, fled to China in A.D. 672 and was given the rank of general in the Imperial Guards. The exiled Persian royal house continued to live in China and in A.D. 679 received the assistance of the T'ang Court in a fruitless attempt to recover the Persian throne.

Buddhism, which was originally also a foreign creed, was at this time at the height of its power in China. Introduced at the end of the Han dynasty, some four hundred years before, the Indian religion had gradually spread throughout China, north and south alike, and had gained a position and influence which no other foreign religion has ever acquired in China. Throughout the T'ang period Buddhism was really the religion of the Chinese people, even though it never ousted Confucian doctrine from the study of the scholar or ancestor worship from the homes of the people. At that time Buddhism, as the surviving examples of T'ang art show, was not the gentle and over-refined religion which it later became. The Buddha in T'ang art is often a stark figure, potent and awe inspiring, a dynamic incarnation of spiritual force.

In the deep impression which Buddhism in the T'ang and immediately preceding age left on the art and popular literature of China one can catch an echo of the fervour of belief in that time. The Court and the scholars might still find it right to pay traditional respect to the non-Buddhist systems of Confucianism and Taoism, but it is obvious that it was Buddhism which dominated the religious life of the age and penetrated every aspect of T'ang culture. Yet although Buddhism seemed so strong it was never able to capture the commanding position which Christianity secured in the civilisation of Europe. The Chinese people never repudiated their past beliefs in order to submit to Buddhism; there was no wholesale rejection of the gods and theology of the pre-Buddhist age comparable to the downfall of the pagan gods and philosophies of Greece and Rome. The Chinese made room for the Indian newcomer in their pantheon and in their mental attitudes, but they still maintained the old unbroken traditions of the most ancient past; ancestor worship, the imperial cult of Heaven, and the numerous local polytheisms which Taoism had gathered up into its comprehensive fold. It is this continuity, rather than the changelessness often imputed, which is the real outstanding character of the Chinese civilisation.

The Great Capital City

It was above all in the capital, Ch'ang An, that foreigners resided and made their influence felt in the fashions and amusements of the Court. Ch'ang An was then one of the greatest cities in the world, having an area of over thirty square miles enclosed by a rectangular wall which contained in the northern section, the Imperial and Palace cities, both walled cities in themselves. No exact figures for the population exist, but judging from the figures for the Metropolitan District given in the census of A.D. 742 which amounted to 1,960,188, the population of the city cannot have been much less than one million. Nor was Ch'ang An the only city of China at that time. At Lo Yang, some 200 miles to the east in Honan province, the T'ang had their Eastern Capital, a city certainly as large and magnificent as Ch'ang An. It was here that throughout the greater part of Wu Chao's life the Court resided. Both these capitals had in addition to the main Palace cities, detached imperial palaces, vast imperial parks and pleasaunces covering an area larger than that of the city itself. In Peking, the last of the long series of Chinese Imperial capitals, one may still see the type perfectly preserved. Ch'ang An and Lo Yang were such cities as Peking is today, or rather was, in the Ming and Manchu periods.

A TANG DYNASTY POET: LI PO

Li Po

The Tang dynasty is considered one of the richest periods of Chinese culture. Scholars produced numerous works of Confucian, Taoist, and Buddhist commentary, architects and sculptors built huge numbers of temples, and artisans produced intricate works of porcelain and silk. Furthermore, the works of Tang dynasty poets are still considered among the world's greatest literature.

Li Po, who lived from 701 to 762, is one of the best known Tang poets. He is said to have written more than two thousand poems and to have lived a raucous life as a brawler and drinker. Some of his poems, such as the following, suggest that the pleasures of life are as fleeting as fantasy or dreams.

T'IEN-MU MOUNTAIN ASCENDED IN A DREAM

A seafaring visitor will talk about Japan,
   Which waters and mists conceal beyond approach;
   But Yüeh people talk about Heavenly Mother Mountain,
Still seen through its varying deepnesses of cloud.
In a straight line to heaven, its summit enters heaven,
Tops the five Holy Peaks, and casts a shadow through China
With the hundred-mile length of the Heavenly Terrace Range,
Which, just at this point, begins turning southeast.
... My heart and my dreams are in Wu and Yüeh
And they cross Mirror Lake all night in the moon.
And the moon lights my shadow
And me to Yien River—

With the hermitage of Hsieh still there
And the monkeys calling clearly over ripples of green water.
I wear his pegged boots
Up a ladder of blue cloud,
Sunny ocean half-way,
Holy cock-crow in space,
Myriad peaks and more valleys and nowhere a road.
Flowers lure me, rocks ease me. Day suddenly ends.
Bears, dragons, tempestuous on mountain and river,
Startle the forest and make the heights tremble.
Clouds darken with darkness of rain,
Streams pale with pallor of mist.
The Gods of Thunder and Lightning
Shatter the whole range.
The stone gate breaks asunder
Venting in the pit of heaven,
An impenetrable shadow.
. . . But now the sun and moon illumine a gold and silver terrace,
And, clad in rainbow garments, riding on the wind,
Come the queens of all the clouds, descending one by one,
With tigers for their lute-players and phoenixes for dancers.
Row upon row, like fields of hemp, range the fairy figures. . . .
I move, my soul goes flying,
I wake with a long sigh,
My pillow and my matting
Are the lost clouds I was in.
. . . And this is the way it always is with human joy:
Ten thousand things run for ever like water toward the east.
And so I take my leave of you, not knowing for how long.
. . . But let me, on my green slope, raise a white deer
And ride to you, great mountain, when I have need of you.
Oh, how can I gravely bow and scrape to men of high rank
    and men of high office
Who never will suffer being shown an honest-hearted face!

WAR AND REFINEMENT IN HEIAN JAPAN

CONRAD SCHIROKAUER

The strongly isolationist island nation of Japan was nevertheless heavily influenced by developments in China during the Tang dynasty. Confucian philosophy, the Buddhist religion, and even the Chinese written language became common features of Japanese culture by the eighth century and thrived alongside such native Japanese institutions as the Shinto religion. Moreover, Japanese landowning clans learned the importance of centralized authority from their much larger neighbor, although landowning nobles maintained a great deal of independence within an emerging imperial structure.

In the following selection historian Conrad Schirokauer describes some of the important aspects of Japanese civilization during the Heian period, from 794 to 1185. The Fujiwara clan dominated the islands during much of this era, Schirokauer points out, but was continually beset by small-scale conflicts with other clans as well as by political intrigue. Nonetheless, the Fujiwara appreciated a sophisticated and refined life, and the Heian court was the source of such works as *The Tale of Genji*, a novel written by Lady Murasaki, a courtier who, Schirokauer suggests, enjoyed a life of leisure and aesthetic delights.

Conrad Schirokauer was professor of history at the City University of New York.

From *A Brief History of Chinese and Japanese Civilizations*, 2nd ed., by Conrad Schirokauer. Copyright © 1989 by Harcourt, Inc. Reprinted by permission of the publisher, Harcourt, Inc.

The Fujiwara were a family of civilian aristocrats who preferred intrigue to war and shared the disdain for the military that was prevalent among the Heian aristocracy. No society seems able to dispense with force entirely, however. Prior to the introduction of conscription and peasant armies, most fighting had been done by *uji* fighting men, that is, trained clan warriors. This class of fighters never disappeared. As less and less land was administered under the "equal field" system, raising conscript armies became less and less practical. In 792, two years before the move to Kyoto, the conscription system was abolished. The central government no longer had the means to raise armies—except as the emperor or his ministers raised fighting men in their own domains—and military power and responsibilities passed to government officials and great families in the provinces.

Since fighting involved costly equipment, such as horse and armor, and training in special techniques, such as archery and swordsmanship, it remained the profession of a rural elite established in both the political and the estate system. Some warrior leaders were originally provincial officials to whom the government had delegated military responsibilities. Others rising within the *shoen* [private landholdings] system were entrusted with defense responsibilities on the estates. The pace of the development of local warrior organizations and their size varied according to local conditions. They were especially prominent in the eastern part of the Kanto region, still a rough frontier area, where formidable warrior leagues grew and clashed.

It was fighting men of this type who kept order in the provinces, performing police and military functions as well as fighting for various patrons as they jockeyed for power. For example, such warrior organizations fought on both sides during the rebellion led in 935 by Taira no Masakado, a fifth-generation descendant of Emperor Kammu. The practice was to keep the size of the imperial family within reasonable limits by cutting off collatoral branches after a given number of generations. At that time they would be given a family name and endowed with rich official posts in the capital or the provinces. Their wealth and distinguished ancestry made them the elite of the provincial elite. Two of the greatest warrior families in Japan had such ex-imperial origins: the Taira (also known as Heike) and the Minamoto (or Genji). The Masakado Rebellion was put down only with great difficulty. At the time of Masakado's Rebellion in the east, there was trouble also in the west. Sent to suppress piracy on the Inland Sea, Fujiwara no Sumitomo (d. 941) instead turned outlaw himself. In the restoration of order, Minamoto no Tsunemoto (d. 961) played a leading role. His son later established an alliance with the Fujiwara house. This branch of the Minamoto, the Seiwa branch or Seiwa Genji, became in effect the Fujiwara's military arm, its "claws and teeth," or, less complimentary, its "running dogs."

In the eleventh century there was more fighting in the Kanto area, with wars from 1028 to 1031, smaller scale fighting between 1051 and 1062, and another war from 1083 to 1087. These wars provided opportunities for building up the strength of the Minamoto in eastern and northern Honshu so that they became the strongest force in this area, while the Ise branch of the Taira was developing strength in the Inland Sea area and also around the capital. At the same time, in the second half of the eleventh century, the Fujiwara went into decline, their manipulation of marriage politics hampered by a shortage of daughters. Emperor Go-Sanjo (r. 1068–72) came to the throne because his brother's Fujiwara empress was childless. Although he was opposed by the Fujiwara regent, he enjoyed the support of another powerful Fujiwara noble, and this support insured his success.

Rule by "Cloistered Emperors"

The revival of the imperial family begun by Go-Sanjo was continued by his son Shirakawa, who became emperor in 1072. He abdicated in 1086 but continued to enjoy great power as retired emperor until his death in 1129. Two more vigorous heads of the imperial line followed, Toba and Go-Shirakawa.

The role of the retired emperor was not unlike that of the Fujiwara regent, except that in place of the paramountcy of the family of the emperor's mother, the paternal family now attained supremacy. The resemblance to the Fujiwara went still further, for, despite the ambivalence of Shirakawa, the general policy of the abdicated emperors was to acquire for the imperial family the same type of assets enjoyed by the Fujiwara. As a result the imperial house acquired a vast network of estates and was transformed into the largest landholder in Japan.

The political situation at this time could and did get very complicated when there was more than one retired emperor on the scene. The ambitions and machinations of the courts, the Fujiwara, and the temples (which had their own armed forces) all contributed to political instability and complicated the politics and the life of the capital. Much of the substance of power continued to shift to the provincial warrior organizations employed by both the imperial and the Fujiwara families to foster their causes, but which soon supplanted them.

The system came to an end under Go-Shirakawa. In 1156 military power was, for the first time, directly involved in capital political disputes; and once the warriors had been called in they could not readily be dismissed. By 1160 the Taira clan were in control of the government. Kyoto remained the political center until 1185, but the last 20 years or so do not really form part of the Heian period. Rather, they constitute an interlude of warrior power that can best be considered as an overture to the Kamakura period. Yet, for another 700 years, until 1869, the imperial family and the Fujiwara remained in Kyoto, and the Fujiwara still provided most of the regents. Indeed, the Fujiwara family grew so large that men came to be called by the names of the branch families, and even in the twentieth century a member of one of these Fujiwara branches (Konoe) became a prime minister.

THE LIFE OF THE HEIAN ARISTOCRACY

Literature is our best source for the study of Heian society, which produced some of Japan's greatest prose and poetry. Its art diaries and other literary works furnish details of the daily life of the upper classes and insights into their values and taste. Most Heian authors were court ladies, and their feminine view of life at the top is unique in the history of East Asia and perhaps the world. Japan's greatest prose work, *The Tale of Genji* was composed by one such woman, Murasaki Shikibu (978–ca. 1016).

The literary eminence of Heian ladies itself suggests something of their social status. Obviously they had ample leisure for reading and writing; *The Tale of Genji* is twice as long as Tolstoy's *War and Peace*. Often they suffered from an excess of leisure. They became bored with long days of inactivity spent in the dimly lit interiors of their homes and welcomed the chance to exchange pleasantries and gossip with an occasional caller. If the caller was a man, he had to conduct the visit seated in front of a screen behind which the lady remained demurely hidden. Fortunately, there were numerous festivals to break up the monotony of the daily routine, and pilgrimages to temples provided further diversion.

Although there were also men who had literary inclinations and the means to pursue them, prose literature was considered the woman's domain; so much so that when Ki no Tsurayuki (869–945) composed the *Tosa Diary*, he pretended that it was written by a woman. Conversely, men continued to be educated in Chinese, which enjoyed undiminished prestige and remained the official language. This Chinese erudition constituted a male preserve from which women were excluded. For them it was not considered a respectable pastime, and those who nevertheless indulged in Chinese learning made it a point not to broadcast the fact. Nor was it proper for women to write in Chinese—instead they wrote Japanese using a mixture of Chinese characters and the *kana* syllabary, which now made its appearance. This was a system of phonetic symbols, originally derived from Chinese characters. Each symbol represents a syllable. With this system there was no longer any need to employ Chinese characters to represent Japanese sounds, but they were retained nevertheless, since Japanese has numerous homonyms. In the modern language, the Chinese characters, used to write nouns and the stems of verbs and adjectives, float in a sea of *kana*, representing particles, endings, and certain other common words. (Foreign words, however, are today written in an alternate *kana* system.) In modern Japan everyone uses this mixed system of writing, but during the Heian period it was used by women. Excluded from writing in Chinese, they were left free to express themselves in their own native language, and in the process they composed the classic works of Japanese prose.

The world described in this literature is a small one for it concerns only a tiny fraction of the Japanese people, those at the pinnacle of society in the capital. Although there are descriptions of travel outside the capital area, the focus is very much on the capital itself. A provincial appointment, lucrative though it might be, was regarded as tantamount to exile. The provinces were viewed as an uncultured hinterland where even the governing classes were hopelessly vulgar. To these aristocratic ladies, the common people whose labor made society possible were so far removed in manners and appearance as to resemble the inhabitants of another world. At best, they seemed uncouth. At worst, they were regarded as not quite fully human, as when Sei Shonagon encountered a group of commoners on a pilgrimage and noted in her famous *Pillow Book*, "They looked like so many basket-worms as they crowded together in their hideous clothes, leaving hardly an inch of space between themselves and me. I really felt like pushing them all over sideways."

Geographically limited, constricted in social scope, the world of the Heian aristocracy was also narrow in its intellectual range. The last official Heian government mission to China was sent in 838, and when near the end of the ninth century it was proposed to send another and Sugawara no Michizane was chosen as ambassador, he successfully declined on the grounds that conditions in China were unsettled. Even after order had been restored in China with the establishment of the Song, relations were not resumed. The Japanese of the Heian period were steeped in the Chinese culture of the Tang and earlier but, except for some Buddhist monks, displayed a lack of concern for the China of their own time. Perhaps societies, like people, require a period of cultural digestion before they are ready for a new meal. Be that as it may, in the absence of stimuli from abroad, the Heian aristocrats also failed to respond creatively to the changes taking place at home. As we have seen, these changes were momentous, but they were also slow and did not stimulate a reexamination of the old or inspire new intellectual departures. Since the course of historical development went against the fortunes of the court aristocracy, their viewpoint became increasingly pessimistic. This pessimism found an echoing note in Heian Buddhism.

REFINEMENT AND SENSIBILITY

What ultimately saved this small world from cultural sterility, and gave meaning to the lives of its inhabitants, was that these people developed the greatest subtlety of refinement within the range of their experience and concerns. At its best, as in the ideal of the perfect gentleman depicted by Murasaki's Genji ("the shining prince"), they sought to fuse life and art through the cultivation of human sensibilities. At its worst, their conduct smacked of effeminacy, and an aesthetic of good taste led to overrefinement.

In this world where aesthetics reigned supreme, great attention was paid to pleasing the eye. Ladies dressed in numerous robes, one over the other (twelve was standard), which they displayed at the wrist in overlapping layers, and the blending of their colors was of the utmost importance in revealing a lady's taste. Often all a man saw of a lady were her sleeves, left hanging outside her carriage or spread beyond a screen behind which she remained invisible. The men were by no means to be outdone in the care they took over their own attire. The following description is from Sei Shonagon's *Pillow Book:*

> His resplendent, cherry-colored Court cloak was lined with material of the most delightful hue and lustre; he wore dark, grape-colored trousers, boldly splashed with designs of wisteria branches; his crimson underrobe was so glossy that it seemed to sparkle, while underneath one could make out layer upon layer of white and light violet robes.

This concern for appearance also extended to the features of the gentlemen and ladies. Both sexes used cosmetics, applying a white face powder, which in the case of the women was combined with a rosy tint. The ladies took great pride in their long, flowing, glossy hair but plucked their eyebrows and painted in a new set. Such customs are not unfamiliar to the modern world, but far more difficult for us to appreciate are the blackened teeth of the refined Heian beauty. Confined to the aristocracy during the Heian period, this practice, like so many features of Heian taste and sensibility, later spread to the lower classes of society. It became the sign of a married woman, and in the Tokugawa period was also adopted by courtesans.

Specific fashions change, but the concern for visual beauty remained a lasting legacy from the Heian period. Even today, for example, great care is taken over the appearance of food, and its impact on the eye is considered at least as important as its taste.

The emphasis on visual beauty did not mean the neglect of the other senses. Music played an important part in the lives of the Heian aristocracy, and aural and visual pleasure was often combined in courtly dances, at which Genji, of course, excelled. Nor was the sense of smell neglected. The Heian ladies and gentlemen went to great lengths to blend perfumes, and a sensitive nose was a social asset second only to a good eye and ear. Among the aesthetic party contests used to while away the time in polite society, there were even perfume blending competitions such as the one described in *The Tale of Genji*.

IDEALS OF COURTLY LOVE

The ideal Heian aristocrat was as sensitive in personal relations as in matters of aesthetics: feelings should be as beautiful as dress. Nowhere was this more important than in the love affairs that gave Heian literature its dominant theme, and in this respect, too, literature often mirrored life. Marriages were arranged by and for the family in a game of marriage politics at which the Fujiwara excelled. But for a noble courtier to confine himself to one wife was the rare exception. He was much more likely to have, in addition, one or more secondary wives while conducting still other, more or less clandestine, love affairs. Nor were the ladies expected to remain true to one love for their whole lives either, although few were as amorous as Izumi Shikibu (generally considered the author of the love diary that bears her name). Nevertheless, jealousy posed a recurring problem for a lady of the Heian age who might have to bear long waits between visits from her lover. For the less fortunate and less hardy waiting could become a torture. So unhappy was the author of *The Gossamer Diary* that her writing has been characterized by Ivan Morris as "one long wail of jealousy."

The qualities most valued in a lover were quite similar regardless of sex: beauty and grace, talent and sensibility, and personal thoughtfulness. A gentleman is always considerate. The paragon, Genji, was ever gallant to one lady even though he discovered that she was very unattractive. He found himself in this predicament because Heian men often had no clear idea of the appearance of the women they were wooing, hidden as they were behind screens with only their sleeves showing. (Rare was the thoughtful consideration of a guardian like Genji who provided a lamp of fireflies to shed some illumination for the benefit of his ward's suitor.) Men fell in love with a woman's sense of beauty, her poetic talents, and her calligraphy. As in China, the latter was all-important, since it was thought to reveal a person's character. The Heian version of love at first sight was a gentleman falling hopelessly in love after catching a glimpse of a few beautifully drawn lines.

At every stage of a love affair, and in other social relationships too for that matter, the aesthetics of writing were stressed. At least as important as the literary merits of the poems that were exchanged on all occasions were such matters as the color and texture of the paper, the way it was folded, and the selection of a twig on which to tie the note. Most critical and most eagerly awaited of these poetic missives were the "morning after letters" sent by a lover immediately upon returning home from a night of love, from which he had torn himself away just before dawn with a proper show of reluctance. The first such letter was particularly important as it would provide a good indication of the seriousness and probable duration of the relationship.

In this world of sensitive people, men and women were expected to respond as readily to sadness as to joy. Both sexes cried freely and frequently, and neither felt any hesitation about expressing self-pity. Tears were a sign of depth of feeling and of a genuine awareness of the ephemeral nature of beauty, the transient nature of all that is good and beautiful. Sentiments such as these were expressed in a special vocabulary, using words so rich in their associations as to defy translation, words which became part of the subtle and shifting language of Japanese aesthetics.

The Maya Civilization of Mexico and Central America at Its Height

John S. Henderson

According to anthropologist John S. Henderson, the Maya civilization reached its height during the period from approximately 600 to 1000. Although unaware of other civilizations, the Maya therefore flourished at the same time as the Byzantine Empire, the Holy Roman Empire, the Arab/Islamic Empire, and the Tang dynasty in China.

In that era, the Maya was the largest civilization of the Americas, in existence since approximately 300 B.C. The Maya inhabited a large area containing both jungle lowlands and mountainous regions, and they constructed numerous cities. Henderson asserts that the Maya population probably reached its peak in the seventh and eighth centuries. Compared with the civilizations of Europe, Africa, and Asia, however, little is known about the Maya. Though they had a written language, most of their documents were destroyed during the Spanish conquest of the Americas in the 1500s. Most modern knowledge, therefore, comes from archaeological excavations such as that conducted at the city of Tikal in modern-day Guatemala.

John S. Henderson is an anthropologist at Cornell University.

From *The World of the Ancient Maya*, 2nd ed., by John S. Henderson. Copyright © 1981 by Cornell University. Used by permission of the publisher, Cornell University Press.

Remarkable, almost uniform, growth and development took place throughout the Maya lowlands during the first two centuries of the Late Classic period. Settlement systems were transformed into complex hierarchies as more communities grew into civic centers, smaller centers became larger, and the largest centers amassed greater power. Civic centers were hubs of social, religious, economic, and political activity for extensive surrounding regions. A few of the most powerful were able to translate prestige and influence into real political power, fashioning states of regional scope. Northern centers, building on smaller, simpler Early Classic foundations, progressively came to rival their great southern lowland counterparts. Ubiquitous stelae and hieroglyphic texts testify to comparable social and political institutions throughout the lowlands. Aristocrats took on new managerial roles. Occupations became increasingly specialized, particularly in the realm of craft production and building trades. Subsistence, more varied than ever, involved intensive agricultural techniques. Trade networks expanded, embracing wider areas and handling a greater volume and diversity of materials. Populations grew, becoming particularly dense in the immediate environs of powerful civic centers.

Processes leading to intensified regional differences and to increased homogeneity were at work simultaneously in the Late Classic Maya world. Shared patterns went beyond the very basic similarity in the overall way of life that had always existed throughout the Maya world. Settlement systems, civic centers, and the social order they imply had always been generally comparable. Now monumental art, the stela complex, and writing had spread throughout the lowlands. A common basic belief system sustained social and political institutions everywhere. The symbol systems used to express these concepts were so similar from region to region that they almost imply a single Maya religion. Specific shared elements were confined to aristocratic segments of lowland Maya societies. They were mainly products of interaction among the ruling groups of the several regions of the Maya world. Monumental art and hieroglyphic texts document some of the social and political ties that linked the aristocracies of various centers. Similar interchanges took place in the intellectual sphere among priest-scientists devoted to astronomical, astrological, and other esoteric investigations. Between A.D. 687 and 756, for example, inscriptions at all lowland centers reflect the adoption of a new uniform system of tabulating lunar periods. Long-distance exchange, increasingly centralized in the hands of noble merchants and administrators, also promoted communication. The emergence of regional states with expanding spheres of influence was a powerful stimulus intensifying these connections.

On closer inspection, the apparent homogeneity of the Maya world dissolves into a kaleidoscopic picture of regional variations on the same set of basic themes. Late Classic Maya monumental art has stylistic coherence and stands apart from the art of other Mesoamerican peoples. At the same time, regional styles of sculpture and painting are readily apparent. No one could mistake modeled stucco decoration from Palenque for the work of a Copán artist, or confuse the stelae of Quiriguá and Tikal. Styles of public architecture and architectural decoration show the same pattern of diversity within a single basic tradition. The elaborate mosaic facades of Uxmal's temples and palaces do not obscure their relationships to homologous buildings in the south. Regional differences in crafts are still more pronounced. Pottery manufacture involved a tremendous array of regional styles, though symbolic scenes and designs on luxury vessels were comparable everywhere. . . .

Maya populations reached their greatest size and widest distribution during the seventh and eighth centuries. The distribution of swampy land, variable farming conditions and communication facilities, the clustering of people around major centers, and other factors produced considerable variation in population density. All of the best areas for settlement had been occupied for hundreds of years.

The basic unit of settlement everywhere was the domestic plaza complex with three or four or more small thatched wattle-and-daub buildings grouped around open courtyards. These one-room dwellings, each on its own low platform, correspond to the single-family dwellings of today's Maya. Each housed a couple with their unmarried children. Plaza complexes grew as sons married and established new households in adjacent buildings around the courtyard. Clusters of several domestic plazas form hamlets in rural areas and neighborhoods within larger centers. Kinship and marriage ties must have been especially strong within these communities of a hundred or a few hundred souls, and they must sometimes have corresponded roughly to lineages and other formal kin groups, though there are no solid grounds for assuming that they always did so. Houses and domestic plazas larger and more elegant than the norm must be the dwellings of family and lineage heads with local political, economic, and religious leadership roles. Minor civic structures—small temples and aristocratic residences—were focal points for several basic communities. They reflect the more formal minor offices of administrative systems. Even in outlying areas, these minor civic centers were usually subordinate to larger ones. At the apexes of these hierarchies were such great regional capitals as Tikal. . . .

The best data for population estimates come from Tikal. . . . Here only a sample of the many thousands of structures could be excavated. Unlike most lowland centers, where settlement thins out gradually away from the civic nucleus, house density at Tikal drops off sharply beyond the bank-and-ditch constructions that define the basic residential community on the north and south. Excavation of more than 200 small buildings showed that 80 percent were houses dating to the eighth and early ninth centuries, the period of Tikal's greatest florescence. As most houses had been remodeled, they appear to have been occupied continuously during most of this time span. Some were surely occupied for shorter spans, but inconspicuous and destroyed houses missed by the survey should compensate in part for this error. When these figures are extrapolated to the center as a whole and multiplied by 5 (the average number of people per family in the early colonial period), the result indicates about 10,000 people in central Tikal alone. This figure makes no allowance for the occupants of palaces and other large buildings. Estimates of the population of the community within the bank and ditch run as high as 50,000. "Greater Tikal," including the surrounding region under the center's direct influence, must have embraced many thousands more who came often to the civic center for markets, social events, and ceremonies. However imprecise these estimates may be, they eliminate the possibility that Tikal was a sparsely populated "ceremonial" center.

Tikal, if not the largest of all Maya centers, was certainly among the most populous. Even at its peak it remained relatively open, without the extreme density of structures and people usually associated with such urban centers as Teotihuacán. Still, at Tikal and the other great Maya centers, daily life and social relations must have had something of an urban flavor. Certainly Maya centers performed all the civic functions of central places.

The Emergence of Islam

CHAPTER 3

Muhammad Is Called to Be a Prophet of God

William Montgomery Watt

The Islamic religion emerged from the Arabian trade center of Mecca in the early seventh century. Mecca was a crossroads for the exchange of ideas and religions as well as goods. Many of the Arabs who lived there were well-traveled merchants who had been exposed to the cultures of North Africa and the Middle East. Muhammad, the founder of Islam, was himself a merchant, as William Montgomery Watt points out in the following selection.

When Muhammad was about forty years old he experienced the call to be a prophet of God ("Allah" in Arabic). As Watt indicates, this call took the form of a series of recitations from Allah and an intermediary, the archangel Gabriel. Muhammad received these recitations for the rest of his life. Although he and his followers first memorized the divine messages, ultimately the texts were written down and assembled into the Islamic holy book, the Koran (or Qu'ran).

William Montgomery Watt is professor emeritus of Arabic and Islamic studies at the University of Edinburgh.

M uhammad's birth is thought to have taken place in or around the year A.D. 570. He was at first in the care of his mother, but she died when he was aged six. For a time he had been given to a wet-nurse belonging to a nomadic tribe, because life in the steppe was thought to be healthier for infants than that in Mecca, and many Meccan women did this. After

Amina's death, Muhammad was looked after by his grandfather 'Abd-al-Muttalib, until his death when Muhammad was eight; and then an uncle, Abu-Talib, took charge of him. When he was old enough, Muhammad went on trading journeys to Syria with his uncle. As a result of the experience he had gained in this way, a wealthy widow named Khadija, herself a merchant, commissioned him to look after her goods on a journey to Syria. Well satisfied with his fulfilment of the commission, she offered him her hand in marriage and he accepted. He is said to have been twenty-five, while she was forty, but she is also said to have borne him six or more children, some boys who died and four girls, Umm-Kulthum, Zaynab, Ruqayya and Fatima. After the marriage, Muhammad was able to use his wife's capital to trade on their account along with a partner. Previously he had had no capital of his own because a person below a certain age was not allowed to inherit, and so nothing had come to him from his father or grandfather. Doubtless this custom originated among the nomads, since obviously a minor could not look after a herd of camels.

Muhammad was a thoughtful person and was in the habit of making a retreat each year in a cave on Mount Hira, close to Mecca. There he presumably meditated on religious matters and on the social problems which increasing wealth was creating in the Meccan community. Of these he was probably specially aware because of his own exclusion for a time from the main trading activities until he married Khadija. In a particular year, when he was about forty, he had a strange experience. He heard a voice saying to him, 'Recite.' He responded, 'What shall I recite?' and the voice went on, 'Recite, in the name of thy Lord who created—created man from a blood-clot. Recite, for thy Lord is bountiful, who taught by the Pen, taught man what he knew not.' This is the opening passage of Surat al-'Alaq (96) of the Qur'an. Muhammad was puzzled by this experience, but when he returned home and told Khadija about it, she talked to her kinsman Waraqa, who had some knowledge of the Bible and may have been a Christian, and Waraqa expressed the view that what had thus come to Muhammad was similar to what had come to Moses. Partly because of what Waraqa had said and perhaps partly for other reasons, Muhammad came to regard the words he had heard and then recited as a revelation from God. . . .

Muhammad himself firmly insisted that he had not composed the Qur'an, but it had come to him from beyond himself; and sound scholarship requires that this claim be accepted. He also believed that the Qur'an ultimately came from God; and this also should be accepted by non-Muslims in the inter-faith conditions of the end of the twentieth century. The earliest Christian critics of the Qur'an, however, such as John of Damascus, who did secretarial work for a Muslim governor, knew of the references in it to Biblical characters, and so thought that Muhammad himself had put it together using what he had learned from the Bible. It was to counter this assertion that the doctrine of Muhammad's illiteracy was elaborated by Muslim scholars. Actually it is not a good argument, because even if Muhammad could not read, he could have had the Bible read to him or the stories related to him; and presumably there were some people in Mecca, like Waraqa, who had a slight knowledge of the Bible. Careful examination of the Qur'an today, however, shows that its knowledge of Biblical stories and events is minimal, whereas it contains much deep truth about the being of God and his dealings with the human race. This is a strong reason why the non-Muslim should accept the belief that somehow or other the Qur'an comes from God.

There is another passage which is sometimes said to be the first revealed. It runs:

> O immantled one,
> Rise and warn;
> Thy Lord magnify,
> Thy raiment purify,
> The Wrath flee,
> Give not to gain more,
> For thy Lord endure.
>
> (74.1–7)

It seems probable that this was not the first of all revelations but that the words 'Rise and warn' mark the point at which Muhammad had to proclaim the divine message publicly, and thus was the beginning of his public ministry. Many commentators think that 'wrath' should be translated 'abomination' and in practice means idolatry. The word 'immantled' may mean that Muhammad had put on a mantle or cloak as a protection against the unseen powers, or else to induce a revelation.

Muhammad continued to receive revelations from God at intervals for the rest of his life with a short gap in the earlier years. These revelations were in the first place recited and memorized by Muhammad and the followers he came to have. Later they were collected, partly by Muhammad himself and partly also afterwards by others. Muhammad had some written down for him, and one or two followers wrote down revelations for themselves. These revelations constitute the Qur'an or 'recitation' as we have it. The revelations came in different ways at different times. Some of these ways are mentioned in a verse: 'It was not for a human being that God should speak to him except by revelation, or from behind a veil, or that he should send a messenger to reveal [to him] what [God] willed by his permission' (42.51).

The messenger mentioned here is the angel Gabriel, for in another verse the words are addressed to Muhammad: 'Say, Who is an enemy to Gabriel? It is he who brought down this [revelation] upon your heart confirming what was present' (2.97). (The last phrase refers to previous scriptures.) Muslim scholars made lists of 'the manners of revelation' and found several besides those mentioned in the verse, though their precise interpretation of details is sometimes different. They held that in Muhammad's later years the revelations were normally brought by Gabriel. The first revelation, however, as described above, seems to have been no more than the hearing of a voice.

A VERSE FROM THE HOLY KORAN

THE KORAN

The Koran, the holy book of Islam, is organized into 114 chapters, or "suras" as they are called in Arabic. The word *Koran* itself simply means "recitation"; Muslims believe that this collection of stories, guidelines, and messages is the direct and literal word of God. The recitations were received mostly by Muhammad, the Prophet, although some were received by a few other early followers. Although it is not known for certain, the suras may not have been assembled into a single book until after Muhammad's death.

The following selection is from Sura 25, verses 35–60 of the Koran. This sura, entitled "Light," indicates to Muslims that God knows all things. One of the sura's important messages is that those who believe in God, and who obey the words of the prophet Muhammad, have nothing to fear.

God is the LIGHT of the Heavens and of the Earth. His Light is like a niche in which is a lamp—the lamp encased in glass—the glass, as it were, a glistening star. From a blessed tree is it lighted, the olive neither of the East nor of the West, whose oil would well nigh shine out, even though fire touched it not! It is light upon light. God guideth whom He will to His light, and God setteth forth parables to men, for God knoweth all things.

In the temples which God hath allowed to be reared, that His name may therein be remembered, do men praise Him morn and even.

Men whom neither merchandise nor traffic beguile from the

From the Koran, translated by J.M. Rodwell (London: J.M. Dent, 1909).

remembrance of God, and from the observance of prayer, and the payment of the stated alms, through fear of the day when hearts *shall throb* and eyes shall roll:

That for their most excellent works may God recompense them, and of His bounty increase it to them more and more: for God maketh provision for whom He pleaseth without measure.

But as to the infidels, their works are like the vapour in a plain which the thirsty dreameth to be water, until when he cometh unto it, he findeth it not aught, but findeth that God is with him; and He fully payeth him his account: for swift to take account is God:

40   Or like the darkness on the deep sea when covered by billows riding upon billows, above which are clouds: darkness upon darkness. When a man reacheth forth his hand, he cannot nearly see it! He to whom God shall not give light, no light at all hath he!

Hast thou not seen how all in the Heavens and in the Earth uttereth the praise of God?—the very birds as they spread their wings? Every creature knoweth its prayer and its praise! and God knoweth what they do.

God's, the Kingdom of the Heavens and of the Earth: and unto God the *final* return!

Hast thou not seen that God driveth clouds lightly forward, then gathereth them together, then pileth them in masses? And then thou seest the rain forthcoming from their midst; and He causeth *clouds like* mountains charged with hail, to descend from the heaven, and He maketh it to fall on whom He will, and from whom He will He turneth it aside.—The brightness of His lightning all but taketh away the sight!

God causeth the day and the night to take their turn. Verily in this is teaching for men of insight. And God hath created every animal of water. Some go upon the belly; some go upon two feet; some go upon four feet. God hath created what He pleased. Aye, God hath power over all things.

Now have we sent down distinct signs.—And God guideth whom He will into the right path:

For there are who say "We believe on God and on the Prophet, and we obey"; yet, after this, a part of them turn back. But these are not of the faithful.

And when they are summoned before God and His Prophet that He may judge between them, lo! a part of them withdraw:

But had the truth been on their side, they would have come to Him, obedient.

What! are they diseased of heart? Do they doubt? Are they afraid that God and His Prophets will deal unfairly with them? Nay, themselves are the unjust doers.

50   The words of the believers, when called to God and His Prophet

that He may judge between them, are only to say, " We have heard, and we obey"; these are they with whom it shall be well.

And whoso shall obey God, and His Prophet, and shall dread God and fear Him, these are they that shall be the blissful.

And they have sworn by God, with a most solemn oath, that if thou give them the word, they will certainly march forth. SAY: swear ye not: of more worth is obedience. Verily, God is well aware of what ye do.

SAY: Obey God and obey the Prophet. Suppose that ye turn back, still the burden of his duty is on him only, and the burden of your duty rests on you. If ye obey Him, ye shall have guidance: but plain preaching is all that devolves upon the Prophet.

God hath promised to those of you who believe and do the things that are right, that He will cause them to succeed others in the land, as He gave succession to those who were before them, and that He will establish for them that religion which they delight in, and that after their fears He will give them security in exchange. They shall worship Me: nought shall they join with Me: And whoso, after this, believe not, they will be the impious.

But observe prayer, and pay the stated alms, and obey the Prophet, that haply ye may find mercy.

Let not the Infidels think that they can weaken *God on His own* Earth: their dwelling place shall be the Fire! and right wretched the journey!

O ye who believe! let your slaves, and those of you who have not come of age, ask leave of you, three times a day, ere they come into your presence;—before the morning prayer, and when ye lay aside your garments at mid-day, and after the evening prayer. These are your three times of privacy. No blame shall attach to you or to them, *if* after these *times,* when ye go your rounds of *attendance* on one another, *they come in without permission.* Thus doth God make clear to you His signs: and God is Knowing, Wise!

And when your children come of age, let them ask leave to come into your presence, as they who were before them asked it. Thus doth God make clear to you his signs: and God is Knowing, Wise.

As to women who are past childbearing, and have no hope of marriage, no blame shall attach to them if they lay aside their *outer* garments, but so as not to shew their ornaments. Yet if they abstain from this, it will be better for them: and God Heareth, Knoweth.

60   No crime shall it be in the blind, or in the lame, or in the sick, *to eat at your tables:* or in yourselves, if ye eat in your own houses, or in the houses of your fathers, or of your mothers, or of your

brothers, or of your sisters, or of your uncles on the father's side, or of your aunts on the father's side, or of your uncles on the mother's side, or of your aunts on the mother's side, or in those of which ye possess the keys, or in the house of your friend. No blame shall attach to you whether ye eat together or apart.

And when ye enter houses, salute one another with a good and blessed greeting as from God. Thus doth God make clear to you His signs, that haply ye may comprehend them.

Verily, they only are believers who believe in God and His Prophet, and who, when they are with him upon any affair of common interest, depart not until they have sought his leave. Yes, they who ask leave of thee, are those who believe in God and His Prophet. And when they ask leave of Thee on account of any affairs of their own, then grant it to those of them whom thou wilt, and ask indulgence for them of God: for God is Indulgent, Merciful.

Address not the Prophet as ye address one another. God knoweth those of you who withdraw quietly *from the assemblies,* screening themselves behind others. And let those who transgress his command beware, lest some present trouble befall them, or a grievous chastisement befall them, *hereafter.*

Is not whatever is in the Heavens and the Earth God's? He knoweth your state; and one day shall men be assembled before Him, and He will tell them of what they have done: for God knoweth all things.

MUSLIM DYNASTIES BUILT A VAST AND RICH EMPIRE

Dominique Sourdel

Despite its humble beginnings in the Arabian desert, Islam quickly became a major world religion as Arab believers, called Muslims, conquered an empire. First under Muhammad, until the Prophet's death in approximately 634, then under a series of successors, or caliphs, Islamic armies sought plunder and the expansion of the faith in the Middle East, North Africa, and southern Europe.

In the following selection, Dominique Sourdel describes how Arab Muslims integrated themselves into the more advanced cultures of Syria, Iran, Spain, and other areas while converting many of the local people to Islam. According to Sourdel, Islamic culture rose to glory under the Ummayad caliphs, who ran the empire from the Syrian city of Damascus. Under the Ummayads, the empire reached its greatest geographical extent, stretching from Spain in the west to Afghanistan in the east. In 750, the Ummayads were defeated by the Abbasids, who claimed to be direct descendants of the family of Muhammad. They moved their capital to Baghdad in Iraq, mainly because they wanted greater access to the wealth, culture, and education of Iran (Persia). Islamic civilization, Sourdel claims, reached its golden age under the Abbasids, when Baghdad was a global center of trade, science, and literature.

Dominique Sourdel is emeritus professor of history at the University of the Sorbonne in Paris.

From *Islam*, by Dominique Sourdel, translated by Douglas Scott. Copyright © 1949 Presses Universitaires de France. Translation © 1962 by Walker and Company. Reprinted by permission of Walker and Company.

Syrian in origin, the Ummayyad dynasty endowed the Muslim Empire with a solid administrative framework and, taking over the traditions of civilization already established in the country, it developed social life and the process of urbanization. It was this dynasty that initiated the characteristic Muslim architecture (the huge mosques of Damascus, Medina, and Jerusalem). Though an Arab dynasty, it integrated the Syrian converts and attached them to the solid core of the conquerors in the capacity of "clients", who were enabled to take an active part in the organization of the state. The Syrians very quickly learned Arabic, which soon became the official language and then became converted to Islam, which did not seem to them very far removed from the Christianity taught by the rival sects of the oriental Church, and which procured them in addition certain social advantages. This environment favored the blossoming of an intellectual movement, and it was at this time that the juridical sciences and theological controversies began to make their appearance. Thus there came into being the classic civilization of Islam, which the period of the Abbasids did no more than bring to fruition.

Under the Ummayyads the Muslim Empire attained its widest extension. In the west there was the expansion into Tripolitania, the methodical conquest of the Maghreb, the founding of Qairwan, the resistance of the Berbers, and finally the total surrender of North Africa. Then came the invasion and conquest of Spain in 712 by the governor of Barbary, Mousa b. Nosair, assisted by his "client" Tariq b. Ziyad (Gibraltar is Arab *Jabal Tariq*), followed by the invasion—halted at the Battle of Poitiers—of Merovingian France. In the east there was the subjugation of Persia, the occupation of Afghanistan and of Transoxiana, then the invasion of Chinese Turkestan, the penetration into Sind, the Punjab, and Oudh. Thus the frontiers of Islam stretched from China to the Atlantic Ocean, and although in the course of the following centuries it was destined to gain fresh territories, never again did one undivided Muslim Empire attain the same size.

FROM THE UMMAYYAD TO THE ABBASID DYNASTY

The dynasty eventually succumbed to an agitation fomented in Khurasan by the descendants of el-Abbas, an uncle of the Prophet; these rebels had chosen an area humiliated by the arrogance of the Arab conquerors in which to conduct a propaganda campaign based on the Shiite movement of the Hanafiya sects. An emancipated Persian called Abu-Moslim led the rising, which spread into Iraq, where the pretender Abu-l-Abbas had himself proclaimed caliph in the great mosque of el-Kufa. In August, 750, he defeated the last Ummayyad, whose family were hunted down and wiped out. Only one representative of the family succeeded in escaping, and he went off to found the Ummayyad dynasty in Spain.

Having installed themselves in Iraq with Baghdad as their capital, the Abbasid dynasty relied heavily on the Persians, who came to play the principal role in the administration—men such as the Barmekides, celebrated viziers of the caliphs. The latter, setting themselves up as restorers of the tradition that had been broken by the Ummayyad usurpers, claimed to unite in their own person, more closely than had their predecessors, the temporal and spiritual powers. In actual fact, very far from reverting to the original customs, they did no more than augment the court ceremonial that had already been initiated by the caliphs of Damascus, and went even further in the matter of hiding themselves from the gaze of the crowd.

THE GLORIES OF ABBASID BAGHDAD

The administrative machinery was strengthened, and the succession was assured, in principle, by the caliph's nominating, while he was still alive, an heir presumptive chosen from among his sons. But intrigues and seditions were bound to imperil the stability of power. It was then that Islam entered its Golden Age; under the caliphs Harun al-Rashid (786–809), whose relations with Charlemagne seem to bear out legend, and el-Mamun (813–33), Baghdad was the center of intense intellectual activity, in which both native Arabs and Persian converts were able to participate. This was the full flowering of the urban civilization prepared by the Ummayyad period: it involved progress in religious studies, breadth of theological discussion, the formation of prose style, a renewal of poetic themes, and the introduction of secular sciences derived from India and Greece. This flowering of culture was accompanied by a very active economic life—the manufacture and export of silks, carpets, embroidered materials, the manufacture of paper from rags (a Chinese invention) at Baghdad and Samarkand, and an important commercial trade with the Far West and the Far East.

THE ABBASID EMPIRE DISINTEGRATES

The external causes mostly resulted from the dislocation of the Empire, from which the most distant provinces were gradually tending to become detached, whether, in the last resort, they did or did not remain nominally linked to the caliphate at Baghdad. In the west there was the independence of the Andalusian emirate, founded in 756, and the appearance in the Maghreb of certain kingdoms that were practically autonomous. . . . In the east, several Persian kingdoms made their appearance in Khurasan, . . . which fostered the renaissance in Persian literature and, by appealing to the Turkish mercenaries, occasioned the upsurge of the first Muslim Turkish dynasty, that of Mahmoud of Ghazna (999–1030), a Maecenas and military leader whose principal achievement was the conquest of North India for Islam. Then, in Egypt and Syria, several states were formed. . . .

At last, after 945, the caliphate itself fell under the dominion of Ahmad the Bouyid, a Shiite adventurer from the mountains of Dailam in Persia who claimed to be descended from the Sassanid kings and took for himself the title "Emir of Emirs." In 977 his successor Adod-ad-Daula succeeded in making himself master of an empire comprising two-thirds of Iran and Mesopotamia; adopting the old Persian title of *Shahanshah* (King of Kings) he succeeded, despite his Shiite principles, in ruling with justice over the Sunnite subjects of the caliph, who was now reduced to impotence. The dynasty disappeared with the arrival of the Seljuk Turks (1055).

MERCHANTS AND EXILES SPREAD ISLAM TO ASIA AND AFRICA

AUGUSTE TOUSSAINT

The Islamic world extends far beyond the Arabic and Persian Middle East. Countries from Indonesia in Southeast Asia to Nigeria in West Africa are primarily Islamic. India's population of 1 billion people includes over 150 million Muslims, and India's neighbors Pakistan and Bangladesh are among the largest Islamic countries on earth.

In the following selection, Auguste Toussaint describes how Islam spread throughout the Indian Ocean region during the Middle Ages. The conquests of Iran and Egypt, he suggests, gave Muslims control of ports that for centuries had conducted trade with India. It was only natural for Muslims to then take up the trade and export their religion at the same time. The entire Indian Ocean was connected by familiar trade routes, so Muslim merchants soon continued beyond India to the islands of Indonesia, and, ultimately, to China.

Toussaint also points out that political exiles as well as merchants brought Islam to the east coast of Africa. East African cities such as Mogadishu were already important trade centers, and the arrival of Arabs helped make them part of a larger Islamic economic network. Moreover, the Arab presence in Africa helped to produce a unique, multiethnic East African culture.

August Toussaint is the official archivist of the city of Port Louis, Mauritius, and the author of several books on the history and trade of the Indian Ocean.

From *History of the Indian Ocean*, by Auguste Toussaint, translated by June Guicharnaud (Chicago: University of Chicago Press, 1966). Copyright © 1961 Presses Universitaires de France. Translation © 1966 by The University of Chicago. Reprinted by permission of the University of Chicago Press.

It was natural that the first leaders of Islam, in fear of dispersing too widely the already scattered forces they had so rapidly acquired, should refuse to give their approval to plans for expeditions to distant lands. It was also natural that they should prefer to attack the Byzantine Empire and that of the [Iranian] Sassanids, which they could easily reach by land, rather than become involved in a struggle on the sea against the [African] Axumites or the Indians.

Iran was conquered within a few years, and became a province of the [Ummayyads] whose capital was at Damascus, in Syria, from 661 to 749. When they were overthrown by their rivals, the Abbassids, the seat of the caliphate was removed to Baghdad on the Tigris, which for five centuries was to remain the great capital of Islam in the countries of the Indian Ocean, until its conquest by the Mongols in the thirteenth century. Its port was Basra, which soon supplanted Apologos (Obollah) and continued to be the main port of the Persian Gulf until the eighteenth century. Under the Abbassids, the port of Masqat (Muscat), on the Arabian side of the gulf, and that of Siraf, on the Iranian side, also attained importance.

At almost the same time that they conquered Iran, the Arabs also subjugated Egypt. Having thus become masters of the countries of the Red Sea and the Persian Gulf, they re-established the unity of Alexander [the Great's] former empire which, as we have seen, had been divided up between his successors. Under their dominion, the two arms of the Erythraean Sea were no longer rival routes, but on the contrary became seaways leading to the same goal: India and its riches.

BOTH MUSLIMS AND EUROPEAN JEWS TRADED WITH INDIA

In the relations between Islam and India there is good reason to distinguish between military operations on the one hand and commercial operations on the other. The military conquest of India, begun early in the eighth century and not brought to a close until the end of the sixteenth, was a long series of land operations on a limited scale, in which the sea played no part. The conquest had no influence on the organisation of Indian trade, in which the Muslim conquerors never had any part.

In the ninth century, according to the Arab historian Baladhuri, there were, if not real colonies, at least notable settlements of Muslim merchants on the Malabar coast and in several cities on the seacoast as far north as the Indus. There was also at that time a large colony of Muslims in Ceylon, which the Arabs called Serendip, or Island of Rubies. The Maldive and Laccadive Islands, known to the Arabs as Robaihat, also received them as immigrants.

At about the same period we find a flow of trade becoming established, for the first time, between the countries of the western Mediterranean and India, initiated by Jewish merchants whose curious itinerary is described by the Arab geographer Ibn Khurdadhbih.

> These merchants (he wrote) speak Persian, Roman [Greek and Latin], Arabic, and the Frankish, Spanish, and Slav languages. They travel from West to East and from East to West, sometimes by land, sometimes by sea. From the West they bring back eunuchs, female slaves, boys, silk, furs, and spices. They sail from the country of the Franks, on the Western Sea, and head towards Farama [near the ruins of ancient Pelusium]; there they load their goods on the backs of beasts of burden and take the land route to Qulzum [Suez], a five days' journey, at a distance of 20 parasangs. They set sail on the Eastern Sea [the Red Sea] and make their way from Qulzum to Al Jar and Jidda; thence they go to Sind, India, and China. On their return they load up with musk, aloes, camphor, cinnamon, and other products of the Eastern countries, and come back to Qulzum, and then to Farama, where they again set sail on the Western Sea. Some head for Constantinople to sell their goods; others make their way to the country of the Franks.

These European Jews were apparently the only inhabitants of the Mediterranean region to trade in the Indian Ocean during the period of Arab ascendancy. The Venetians and Genoese did not arrive there until much later. . . .

MUSLIM VOYAGES TO SOUTHEAST ASIA AND CHINA

Muslim navigation in the west-east direction did not stop at India; it extended to distant China and to Indonesia. The 'route to China', opened up at the end of the seventh century, and used until the end of the ninth, is of very special interest. It was described in detail in an Arab nautical guidebook entitled *Silsilat-al-Tawarikh*, written in the year 851 by a traveller called Suleiman. After the *Periplus of the Erythraean Sea*, this is the first guide to navigation in the Indian Ocean that we possess. It was also the source for all the Arab travellers who wrote after Suleiman.

From the Persian Gulf, the vessels on their way to the Far East first went direct to Quilon, on the Malabar coast. From there they rounded the island of Ceylon and set sail from the Nicobar Islands, where they took on fresh provisions. They then called at

Kalah Bar (probably Kedah) on the Malay coast, whence some sailed on towards Sumatra and Java, and others headed for China. The latter went through the Strait of Malacca, known to the Arabs by its Malay name, Salaht—that is, 'strait'—and stopped first at Tiuman island, then at the ports of the Champa kingdom (Annam), then at Luqin (Hanoi), the last stop before reaching Kanfu (Canton), in southern China, the terminal point of the journey.

From Basra or Siraf the voyage took about six months, counting the stopovers: they left from the Persian Gulf at the beginning of winter, spent the summer at Canton, and came back with the monsoon of the following winter, making in all an expedition of a year and a half.

[Historian George] Hourani dates the first unquestionable Muslim expedition to Canton in the year 671. Less than a century later, in 758, the Arab colony was large enough to attack the port, which led to its being closed to foreign trade. Reopened in 792, Canton continued to be steadily visited by the Muslims until 878. In that year a frightful massacre put an end to the Muslim settlement. Subsequently, the Arab merchants merely met the Chinese merchants at the port of Kalah Bar in Malaya.

The Jews, however, though they had also suffered from the massacre of 878, continued to send expeditions to China in the tenth century and even later. As we have seen, they set out from the ports of Yemen to reach the Far East. Now in the tenth century, with the decline of the Abbassids in Iran and the rise of the Fatimids in Egypt (Cairo was founded in 972), the centre of Islam in the Indian Ocean shifted from the Persian Gulf to the Red Sea. According to Hourani, it is therefore probable that Jidda and Aden had by then supplanted Basra and Siraf as the main ports for sailing to China.

EXTENDING THE ISLAMIC WORLD TO AFRICA

The relations between the Islamic countries and the east coast of Africa were very different in nature. For once, the determining factor was not the attraction of profitable trade but the desire to escape religious or political persecution. In the seventh century the inhabitants of Oman, in revolt against the Caliph Abdul Malik (685–705), were forced to flee to the African coast, where they settled in the vicinity of Patta. In 739, following a new conflict, the vanquished, whom the chronicles refer to as Emozeides, also set off for Africa, where they settled on the Benadir coast.

Two centuries later, about the year 917, other 'political refugees', from a region in Arabia or Iran referred to as Al Hasa, came to the Benadir coast. These newcomers are said to have developed the ports of Mogadiscio (Mogadishu) and Brava, where there is a considerable Arab population even today. Finally, in 975, a certain Hasan ibn Ali, son of a sultan in Shiraz, Iran, and perhaps a sultan himself, left his country for unknown reasons, with a fleet of seven ships and a great number of 'colonists', and settled in Mombasa, Pemba, and Quiloa. One of the vessels went as far as the island of Johanna in the Comoros, a name derived from the Arabic *Komr*.

With the arrival of Hasan ibn Ali, the colonisation—for it was indeed a true colonisation—of the African coast entered on an imperialistic phase, as it were. The ancient land of Punt, from the Somali region to Sofala, then became known as the country of the Zanj—a word the Arabs used to designate the natives. The name is to be recognised in modern times in the island of Zanzibar, actually a corrupt form of *Zanjebar*.

Muslim navigation along the coast of Africa does not seem to have gone beyond Sofala. The region today referred to as South Africa remained unknown to the Arabs, and there is no proof that the dhows ever tried to enter the Atlantic by rounding the Cape of Good Hope.

A MUSLIM TRAVELER VISITS WEST AFRICA

IBN BATTUTA

In the ninth and tenth centuries, Arab merchant caravans crossed the Sahara desert from Egypt to the area around the Niger River in West Africa. There they found large cities, an advanced culture, and a thriving trade in gold. Over the next several centuries, traffic between West Africa and the Islamic heartland of the Middle East became regular, and many West African leaders and merchants converted to Islam.

The following selection contains observations of West Africa made by the chronicler Ibn Battuta, one of the most intrepid travelers of the Middle Ages. In the fourteenth century Ibn Battuta, who originally came from Tangier in Arabic North Africa, visited nearly every center of Islam in the world. He traveled to Sumatra and Java in Southeast Asia, to India and Persia, to the trade cities of East Africa, and finally to the gold-producing areas of West Africa.

The largest empire in West Africa at that time was Mali (here spelled Malli). Ibn Battuta notes the considerable deference the Africans pay to their king, or "Mansá." Moreover, he thinks it important to point out how observant Africans are of Islamic rituals and customs. While he finds many praiseworthy qualities among the citizens of Mali, he cannot approve of all their habits.

T he negroes are of all people the most submissive to their king and the most abject in their behaviour before him. They swear by his name, saying *Mansá Sulaymán kí*. If he summons any of them while he is holding an audience in his

From *Travels in Asia and Africa, 1325–1354*, by Ibn Battuta (London: Routledge & Kegan Paul, 1929). Reprinted with permission from Routledge.

pavilion, the person summoned takes off his clothes and puts on worn garments, removes his turban and dons a dirty skullcap, and enters with his garments and trousers raised knee-high. He goes forward in an attitude of humility and dejection, and knocks the ground hard with his elbows, then stands with bowed head and bent back listening to what he says. If anyone addresses the king and receives a reply from him, he uncovers his back and throws dust over his head and back, for all the world like a bather splashing himself with water. I used to wonder how it was they did not blind themselves. If the sultan delivers any remarks during his audience, those present take off their turbans and put them down, and listen in silence to what he says. Sometimes one of them stands up before him and recalls his deeds in the sultan's service, saying "I did so-and-so on such a day" or "I killed so-and-so on such a day." Those who have knowledge of this confirm his words, which they do by plucking the cord of the bow and releasing it [with a twang], just as an archer does when shooting an arrow. If the sultan says "Truly spoken" or thanks him, he removes his clothes and "dusts." That is their idea of good manners.

Ibn Juzayy adds: "I have been told that when the pilgrim Músá al-Wanjarátí [the Mandingo] came to our master Abu'l-Hasan as envoy from Mansá Sulaymán, one of his suite carried with him a basketful of dust when he entered the noble audience-hall, and the envoy 'dusted' whenever our master spoke a gracious word to him, just as he would do in his own country."

A ROYAL CEREMONY IN MALI

I was at Mállí during the two festivals of the sacrifice and the fast-breaking. On these days the sultan takes his seat on the *pempi* [throne] after the midafternoon prayer. The armour-bearers bring in magnificent arms—quivers of gold and silver, swords ornamented with gold and with golden scabbards, gold and silver lances, and crystal maces. At his head stand four amírs driving off the flies, having in their hands silver ornaments resembling saddle-stirrups. The commanders, qádí, and preacher sit in their usual places. The interpreter Dúghá comes with his four wives and his slave-girls, who are about a hundred in number. They are wearing beautiful robes, and on their heads they have gold and silver fillets, with gold and silver balls attached. A chair is placed for Dúghá to sit on. He plays on an instrument made of reeds, with some small calabashes at its lower end, and chants a poem in praise of the sultan, recalling his battles and deeds of valour. The women and girls sing along with him and play with bows. Accompanying them are about thirty youths, wearing red woollen tunics and white skull-caps; each of them has his drum slung from his shoulder and beats it. Afterwards come his boy pupils who play and turn wheels in the air, like the natives of Sind. They show a marvellous nimbleness and agility in these exercises and play most cleverly with swords. Dúghá also makes a fine play with the sword. Thereupon the sultan orders a gift to be presented to Dúghá and he is given a purse containing two hundred *mithqáls* of gold dust, and is informed of the contents of the purse before all the people. The commanders rise and twang their bows in thanks to the sultan. The next day each one of them gives Dúghá a gift, every man according to his rank. Every Friday after the *'asr* prayer, Dúghá carries out a similar ceremony to this that we have described.

On feast-days, after Dúghá has finished his display, the poets come in. Each of them is inside a figure resembling a thrush, made of feathers, and provided with a wooden head with a red beak, to look like a thrush's head. They stand in front of the sultan in this ridiculous make-up and recite their poems. I was told that their poetry is a kind of sermonizing in which they say to the sultan: " This *pempi* which you occupy was that whereon sat this king and that king, and such and such were this one's noble actions and such and such the other's. So do you too do good deeds whose memory will outlive you." After that, the chief of the poets mounts the steps of the *pempi* and lays his head on the sultan's lap, then climbs to the top of the *pempi* and lays his head first on the sultan's right shoulder and then on his left, speaking all the while in their tongue, and finally he comes down again. I was told that this practice is a very old custom among them, prior to the introduction of Islám, and that they have kept it up.

The negroes disliked Mansá Sulaymán because of his avarice. His predecessor was Mansá Maghá, and before him reigned Mansá Músá, a generous and virtuous prince, who loved the whites and made gifts to them. It was he who gave Abú Isháq as-Sáhilí four thousand *mithqáls* in the course of a single day. I heard from a trustworthy source that he gave three thousand *mithqáls* on one day to Mudrik ibn Faqqús, by whose grandfather his own grandfather, Sáraq Játa, had been converted to Islám.

IBN BATTUTA REPORTS ON WEST AFRICAN CHARACTERISTICS

The negroes possess some admirable qualities. They are seldom unjust, and have a greater abhorrence of injustice than any other people. Their sultan shows no mercy to anyone who is guilty of the least act of it. There is complete security in their country. Neither traveller nor inhabitant in it has anything to fear from robbers or men of violence. They do not confiscate the property of any white man who dies in their country, even if it be uncounted wealth. On the contrary, they give it into the charge of some trust-worthy person among the whites, until the rightful heir takes possession of it. They are careful to observe the hours of prayer, and assiduous in attending them in congregations, and in bring-ing up their children to them. On Fridays, if a man does not go early to the mosque, he cannot find a corner to pray in, on ac-count of the crowd. It is a custom of theirs to send each man his boy [to the mosque] with his prayer-mat; the boy spreads it out for his master in a place befitting him [and remains on it] until he comes to the mosque. Their prayer-mats are made of the leaves of a tree resembling a date-palm, but without fruit.

Another of their good qualities is their habit of wearing clean white garments on Fridays. Even if a man has nothing but an old worn shirt, he washes it and cleans it, and wears it to the Friday service. Yet another is their zeal for learning the Koran by heart. They put their children in chains if they show any backwardness in memorizing it, and they are not set free until they have it by heart. I visited the qádí in his house on the day of the festival. His children were chained up, so I said to him "Will you not let them loose?" He replied "I shall not do so until they learn the Koran by heart." Among their bad qualities are the following. The women servants, slave-girls, and young girls go about in front of everyone naked, without a stitch of clothing on them. Women go into the sultan's presence naked and without coverings, and his daughters also go about naked. Then there is their custom of putting dust and ashes on their heads, as a mark of respect, and the grotesque ceremonies we have described when the poets re-cite their verses. Another reprehensible practice among many of them is the eating of carrion, dogs, and asses.

Trade Expands Across the Old World: 600–1400

CHAPTER 4

THE SILK ROAD TO THE TANG DYNASTY

PETER HOPKIRK

Although it originated during the Roman Empire, the Silk Road was the greatest overland trade route of the Middle Ages. In the following selection, Peter Hopkirk traces the Silk Road from its source in China across the deserts and mountains of Central Asia until it reached trade centers in the Middle East, from where goods could easily be transported to Europe and the Mediterranean. The route, which took its name from the most desirable of all Chinese goods, was actually a network of roads dotted with oases and trading posts.

The Silk Road helped turn Chang'an, the capital of Tang dynasty China, into a cosmopolitan city. As Hopkirk notes, the city contained a number of communities of foreign merchants. Others had traveled to China in search of religious freedom. Many of these travelers brought with them a wide variety of exotic products, from perfumes and spices to rare and unusual animals, which appeared in the markets of Chang'an.

Peter Hopkirk is a journalist and the author of a number of books on the history of Central Asia.

T he Silk Road (sometimes known as the Silk Route) started from Ch'ang-an, present-day Sian, and struck north-westwards, passing through the Kansu corridor to the oasis of Tun-huang in the Gobi desert, a frontier town destined to play a dramatic role in this story. Leaving Tun-huang, and passing through the famous Jade Gate, or Yu-men-kuan, it then divided, giving caravans a choice of two routes around the perimeter of the Taklamakan desert.

THE ROUTE THROUGH THE DESERTS AND MOUNTAINS OF CENTRAL ASIA

The northern of these two trails struck out across the desert towards Hami, nearly three weeks distant. Then hugging the foothills of the T'ien Shan, or 'celestial mountains', it followed the line of oases dotted along the northern rim of the Taklamakan, passing through Turfan, Karashahr, Kucha, Aksu, Tumchuq and Kashgar. The southern route threaded its way between the northern ramparts of Tibet and the desert edge, again following the oases, including Miran, Endere, Niya, Keriya, Khotan and Yarkand. From there it turned northwards around the far end of the Taklamakan to rejoin the northern route at Kashgar. From Kashgar the Silk Road continued westwards, starting with a long and perilous ascent of the High Pamir, the 'Roof of the World'. Here it passed out of Chinese territory into what is now Soviet Central Asia, continuing via Khokand, Samarkand, Bokhara, Merv, through Persia and Iraq, to the Mediterranean coast. From there ships carried the merchandise to Rome and Alexandria.

Another branch left the southern route at the far end of the Taklamakan and took in Balkh, today in northern Afghanistan, rejoining the west-bound Silk Road at Merv. An important feeder road, this time to India, also left the southern route at Yarkand, climbed the hazardous Karakoram passes, the 'Gates of India', to the towns of Leh and Srinagar, before beginning the easy ride down to the markets of the Bombay coast. There was yet another branch at the eastern end of the trail known to the Chinese as 'the road of the centre'. After leaving the Jade Gate, this skirted the northern shore of [explorer Sven] Hedin's 'wandering lake' at Lop-nor and passed through the important oasis town of Loulan before rejoining the main northern route.

GLACIER-WATERED OASES MADE THE SILK ROAD VIABLE

The Silk Road was entirely dependent for both its existence and survival upon the line of strategically situated oases, each no more than a few days' march from the next, which hugged the perimeter of the Taklamakan. In turn, these depended for their survival upon the glacier-fed rivers flowing down from the vast mountain ranges which form a horse-shoe around three sides of the great desert. As the Silk Road traffic increased, these oases began to rank as important trading centres in their own right and no longer merely as staging and refuelling posts for the caravans passing through them. Over the centuries the larger and more prosperous oases gained sway over the surrounding regions and developed into independent feudal principalities or petty kingdoms.

This made them an increasingly attractive target for Huns and others greedy for a share of the Silk Road profits. Because this trade was beginning to bring considerable wealth to Han China, a ceaseless struggle now ensued between the Chinese and those who threatened this economic artery. Periodically the Chinese would lose control of the Silk Road and it would temporarily fall into the hands of the barbarian tribes or to some independent feudal ruler. The new overlord would then demand tribute for allowing the safe-passage of goods in transit, or simply pillage the caravans, until the Chinese managed to regain control of the route by force of arms, treaty or savage reprisals. Even when the Silk Road was firmly under Chinese control, caravans rarely travelled unarmed or unescorted for there was also always the risk of being attacked by brigands (particularly Tibetans skulking in the Kun Lun) on one of the more lonely stretches of the trail. All this made the journey a costly one, ultimately encouraging the development of sea routes, but in the meantime adding greatly to the price of the goods. Nonetheless, despite these hazards and interruptions, the Silk Road continued to flourish. . . .

CHINA'S COSMOPOLITAN CAPITAL, CH'ANG-AN

The art and civilisation of the Silk Road, in common with that of the rest of China, achieved its greatest glory during the T'ang Dynasty (618–907), which is generally regarded as China's 'golden age'. During the long periods of peace and stability which characterise this brilliant era, prosperity reigned throughout the empire. Its capital Ch'ang-an, the Rome of Asia and point of departure for travellers using the Silk Road, was one of the most splendid and cosmopolitan cities on earth. In the year 742 its pop-

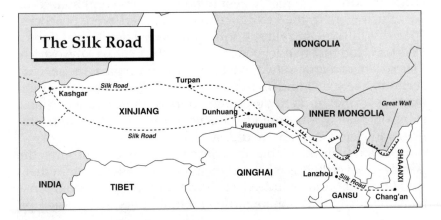

ulation was close on two million (according to the census of 754, China had a total population of fifty-two million, and contained some twenty-five cities with over half a million inhabitants). Ch'ang-an, which had served as the capital of the Chou, Ch'in and Han dynasties, had grown into a metropolis measuring six miles by five, surrounded by a defensive wall. The gates were closed every night at sunset. Foreigners were welcome, and some five thousand of them lived there. Nestorians, Manichaeans, Zoroastrians, Hindus and Jews were freely permitted to build and worship in their own churches, temples and synagogues. An endless procession of travellers passed through the city's gates, including Turks, Iranians, Arabs, Sogdians, Mongolians, Armenians, Indians, Koreans, Malays and Japanese. Every known occupation was represented: merchants, missionaries, pilgrims, envoys, dancers, musicians, scribes, gem dealers, wine sellers, courtiers and courtesans. Dwarfs, gathered from all over Asia, were particularly popular among the Chinese as jugglers, dancers, actors and entertainers. Entire orchestras were brought from distant towns along the Silk Road and from elsewhere in Asia to entertain the imperial court.

A remarkably accurate record of the origins and occupations of these foreigners is found in the terracotta tomb figures discovered around Ch'ang-an (today called Sian) in graves dating from that era. Many of these *ming-chi,* or tomb furnishings, clearly depict foreigners whose race or country of origin scholars have been able to determine from their physiognomy or dress. In addition to the continuous procession of travellers, a cornucopia of luxuries and everyday goods emptied itself daily into the capital's many bazaars. Among the more exotic commodities, many of which arrived via the Silk Road, were cosmetics, rare plants (including the saffron crocus), medicines, aromatics, wines, spices, fragrant woods, books and finely woven rugs. In addition to the 'heavenly horses' from Ferghana, some of which were trained to dance to music, there were peacocks, parrots, falcons, gazelles, hunting dogs, the occasional lion or leopard, and that two-legged marvel (to the Chinese) the ostrich. These latter creatures, two of which reached China in the seventh century, were first known to the Chinese as 'great sparrows' and later as 'camel birds', a description borrowed from the Persians. One of these was reputed to be able to run three hundred Chinese miles in a day, and to digest copper and iron.

Despite their insatiable appetite for these exotic imports, the Chinese nevertheless regarded the foreigners who brought them as *Hu,* or barbarians. Indeed, such was their deeply rooted sense of superiority that they regarded all foreigners with contempt.

Gifts from foreign rulers were accepted by the imperial court as tribute and visiting princes and envoys received as vassals.

Under the T'ang Dynasty the Silk Road may have enjoyed a golden age, but the fortunes of both the dynasty and its principal trade route were firmly bound together. When the dynasty began to decline, so too did the civilisation of the Silk Road. It was a process which was to end in the ultimate disappearance, together with their monasteries, temples and works of art, of many flourishing towns. Indeed, so completely did all traces of this once-glorious era vanish that it was not until the nineteenth century that it was rediscovered. The reasons for its disappearance are complex, and the process was spread over several centuries. But there were two principal causes. One was the gradual drying up of the glacier-fed streams which supplied the oasis towns. The other was the sudden arrival, sword in hand, of the proselytising warriors of Islam from far-off Arabia.

TRADE AND RELIGION TRAVELED TOGETHER

RICHARD C. FOLTZ

In the following selection, Richard C. Foltz describes how religion moved just as easily as trade goods along the Silk Road across Asia. While Islam took hold in the oases of Central Asia, transported by Arab and Persian merchants and holy men, a number of other religions were transported to Tang dynasty China at the eastern end of the route. Holy men, scholars, and pilgrims all experienced the same hardships that merchants faced in the harsh climate and terrain of the Silk Road.

Manichaeism, which emerged in third-century Persia, greatly appealed to travelers since it was a combination of religious ideas from the Middle East and India. Unwelcome in Islamic areas, many Manicheans followed the trade caravans to China. Nestorian Christians, who had been declared heretics for their belief that Jesus was human rather than divine, found freedom to worship in Chang'an, China's capital. Moreover, Foltz asserts, certain Buddhist sects were strengthened by the new connections between China and India, where Buddhism had emerged.

Professor of history Richard C. Foltz is the author of three books on India and Central Asia.

T he Silk Road was more than just a conduit along which religions hitched rides East; it constituted a formative and transformative rite of passage. No religion emerges unchanged at the end of that arduous journey. Key formative influences on the early development of the Mahayana and Pure Land movements, which became so much a part of East Asian

From *Religions of the Silk Road*, by Richard C. Foltz. Copyright © 1999 Richard C. Foltz. Reprinted with permission of St. Martin's Press, LLC.

civilization, are to be sought in Buddhism's earlier encounters along the Silk Road. Manichaeism,[1] driven underground in the West, appears in the eighth century as a powerful political force in East Turkestan, then gradually blends into the amorphous mass of Chinese popular religion. Nestorian Christianity,[2] expelled as a heresy from the Byzantine realm, moves eastward, touches hundreds of thousands among the Eurasian steppe peoples, and appears centuries later like a bad dream to the first Catholic missionaries in China, who find it comfortably entrenched there as the recognized resident Christianity of the East.

Islam, carried along by the momentum of the Arabs' military success, makes its appearance on the Silk Road in the eighth century but comes to a temporary halt halfway, following the Battle of Talas in 751. Directly and indirectly, Islam would be carried east through trade, just like its predecessors. Nor would the new tradition remain Arab property: It would belong instead to the Persians, the Turks, the Chinese—and it would feed from their cultures. Ideas, after all, like individuals, need to acquire new tastes and new sponsors if they are to thrive in foreign climes.

The existence of trade routes and constant commercial activity linking diverse cultures from ancient times meant that religious ideas (like technology and other aspects of culture) could spread easily along trade networks which spanned Eurasia. Indeed, like running water finding open channels, this spread was probably inevitable. But the religion-trade relationship was mutually reinforcing. For example, the expansion of Buddhism brought an increased demand for silk, which was used in Buddhist ceremonies, thereby further stimulating the long-distance trading activity that had facilitated the spread of Buddhism in the first place.

THE CARAVAN EXPERIENCE

If one needed or wanted to travel from one place to another in premodern Asia, the most prudent way (indeed, virtually the only way) of ensuring one would survive the trip was to join up with a caravan heading in the direction one wished to go. Travel was an exceedingly expensive and dangerous proposition, especially the farther one got from areas of dense population.

Inner Asia contains vast tracts of inhospitable land, often with little water and sparse human settlements frequently separated by great distances. The road from the Mediterranean to China is barred by some of the world's highest and most rugged moun-

1. A religion that developed in third-century Persia that combined aspects of several religions, including Christianity, Judaism, and Zoroastrianism 2. Adherents believed that Jesus was fully human rather than divine.

tain ranges, some of its driest, most expansive deserts, and an extreme continental climate which makes either winter or summer
travel extremely difficult. The most physically challenging regions also tended to be those farthest from the reach of governmental administrations, making them prime grounds for ban-
ditry. And where there was local government, it might be hostile
to outsiders.

Caravans coped with all of these problems in a variety of ways.
There is safety in numbers, and caravans could be made up of
anywhere from several dozen to several thousand travelers at a
time. They followed established routes, so were unlikely to get
lost, and traveled in set daily stages, stopping in places where the
locals expected them and were prepared to meet their needs. Usually they were led by professional caravaneers who had made the
trip before, and attempts were made to secure the approval and
protection of all the authorities through whose lands the caravan
was to pass. Occasionally caravans would receive military escorts
through particularly dangerous or unruly areas.

The oases of the Silk Road—Marv, Balkh, Bukhara, Samar-
qand, Kashgar, Turfan, Khotan, and others—owed their prosperity and often their very existence to the regularity of passing
caravans. They offered way stations, or *caravansarays*, where large
numbers of travelers could stop and rest for a night or more,
stock up on food and supplies, buy local goods and sell the locals imported ones. Travelers would also often exchange their
beasts of burden, either to obtain fresh, healthy, and rested animals or to trade in one type of animal for another more suitable
for the next stage of the journey.

Caravan travelers transported their goods and personal be-
longings mainly on horses, mules, and donkeys. For desert regions camels were used: dromedaries in southwestern Asia and
Bactrians in the colder, higher elevations of Inner Asia. In the
most extreme conditions the choice was rather a yak or a *hainag*,
which was a cross between a bull yak and a cow. Donkeys and
mules carried packs, while horses, oxen, and camels often drew
carts. The pace, set by the camels, was tediously slow: four miles
an hour unloaded and two and a half to three miles an hour
when loaded up. The average load was around three hundred
pounds per camel. At this pace, a caravan might cover thirty
miles a day.

Even with the protection and regularity provided by a caravan, disasters were not uncommon. Dehydration, starvation, and
exhaustion could befall even the best-planned expedition. Snow-
storms or sandstorms could make a caravan lose its way, and
even large caravans were not immune to attack from highway-

men. All in all, to travel was to assume an immense amount of risk, not to mention the expense. Exotic tales notwithstanding, a reasonable person would hope as much as possible to *avoid* romance and adventure, and pray just to arrive home again safely one day!

Clearly caravan traffic existed primarily by and for long-distance trade. For the most part no one but a merchant would have the means, the motivation, or the mettle to undertake travel when its conditions were so rigorous and its outcome so uncertain. This also explains why it was mainly goods of high value in proportion to their bulk that were carried along the Silk Road: one had to stand to make a considerable profit from his wares for such a daunting endeavor to seem at all worthwhile.

RELIGIONS MOVED ALONG THE CARAVAN ROUTES

Even so, there were people who joined caravans for other than purely commercial reasons. Diplomatic missions attached themselves to caravans. Sometimes people who had some special talent, or thought they had, would travel to distant courts in hopes of receiving patronage. A few hardy souls traveled merely to satisfy their own curiosity. Others had scholarly interests and traveled for purposes of research.

With the appearance of proselytizing religions came missionaries. First Buddhists, then Christians and Manichaeans, and finally Sufi Muslims latched onto caravans which would take them and their "spiritual goods" into new lands. As new religious traditions carried by the Silk Road disseminated eastward and took root along the way, travelers were increasingly able to find coreligionists in even the most far-flung and out-of-the-way places who could provide them with assistance and fellowship and to whom in return they could bring some contact from the outside world.

The spread of religious traditions across Asia also stimulated religious pilgrimage. For example, once Buddhism had established itself in China, Chinese Buddhists began to feel the need for direct contact with the sources of their tradition in India. Chinese monks, the most famous of whom are Fa-hsien in the fifth century and Hsüan-tsang in the seventh, traveled the Silk Road through Central Asia and down into the Indian subcontinent. Over time Korean and Japanese Buddhist pilgrims also appeared. And by the thirteenth century Christian Turks from Mongolia such as Rabban Sauma and his disciple Markos were undertaking the pilgrimage west to Palestine.

From the tenth century or even earlier, Sufi masters attached

themselves to Silk Road caravans in order to spread their interpretations of Islam eastward into Inner Asia and China. They frequently won large local followings, converting people perhaps
more by their own personal charisma than through the canonical teachings of the faith. Often such figures were attributed with
miraculous powers, and when they died their disciples typically
would erect a shrine in their honor which might later become a
focus of pilgrimage.

It was not only, or even primarily, through missionary activity
that religious ideas spread along the Silk Road, however. The earliest of the "mobile" religious systems to take this eastward path,
the Iranian and the Hebraic, were not proselytizing faiths. Even
the later so-called missionary religions won converts at least as
much through their prestige as foreign, cosmopolitan traditions
as they did through active proselytization.

This is a phenomenon that historian Jerry Bentley has aptly
characterized as "conversion by voluntary association." According to this interpretation local communities, especially in remote
areas, would tend to see foreign traders as being their link to the
outside world, a world that wasn't hard to imagine as being far
more advanced and civilized than the isolated settlement one
lived in. Likewise, any local who adopted the cultural trappings
of the foreigners (religion being a particularly visible example)
could feel and might be considered by others as being more connected to that greater outside world.

A significant aspect of this tendency for anyone involved in
commerce was the practical consideration of maintaining the
strongest and broadest connections possible with one's business
associates. Numerous cases in world history serve as illustration.
For example, the spread of Islam through the Sahara and around
the Indian Ocean Basin is generally attributed to the success of
Muslims in dominating the trade networks of those regions, with
the resulting dominance of shari'a law in the marketplace and fa-
vorable concessions and taxation terms being extended to Muslim traders in areas under Muslim control. The same pattern applies to Central Asia beginning in the eighth century, but even
before Islam a similar process was at work there. It is surely no
coincidence that the periods in which Buddhism, Manichaeism,
and Nestorian Christianity experienced their most active spread
through Inner Asia were connected with the adoption of those
traditions by merchant communities.

Indian Ocean Trade Connects China with the Islamic World

K.N. Chaudhuri

During the Middle Ages, overseas as well as overland trade expanded widely. Indian Ocean sailors learned to take advantage of the seasonal monsoon winds, and beginning in the seventh century, many trade vessels sailed quickly and easily along the coasts of East Africa, Arabia, Persia, India, Southeast Asia, and China. The expansion of Indian Ocean trade helped create a network of important ports throughout the region, from Kilwa and Mogadishu on the African coast to Calicut in India to Canton in China, which was the final destination of many ships. Canton, indeed, supported large communities of Arab and Indian merchants.

According to K.N. Chaudhuri, author of the following selection, the emergence of wealthy, creative civilizations at opposite ends of the Indian Ocean provided the impetus for the expansion of Indian Ocean trade. The Tang dynasty of China established itself in the seventh century, at virtually the same time as the Islamic Arabian empire. The Chinese produced the most desirable products worldwide and provided a huge market for imported goods. Muslims traveled widely as conquering armies expanding the faith and, Chaudhuri points out, developed an appetite for Chinese porcelain and silk in the process.

K.N. Chaudhuri is professor of the economic history of Asia at the University of London.

I n 618 Emperor Li Yüan succeeded to the Celestial throne after the murder of the last of the Sui, Yang Ti. The High Progenitor, as he was entitled later, and his son Li Shih-min, the Grand Ancestor, were the joint founders of the T'ang dynasty, one of the greatest in the long history of China. Four years later, on 16 July 622, in the far-distant and arid coastland of Arabia, Prophet Muhammad abandoned his birthplace and fled to the oasis town of Medina. It was from there that his followers were to prey on the caravans of the wealthy merchants of Mecca, on their way to the Mediterranean markets of Gaza and Busra (Bostra). For commerce and civilisation in the Indian Ocean, these separate and unconnected events mark out a fresh beginning, a new order. The two geographical divisions of the great sea, the western and the eastern, meeting together in the massive under-water volcanic cliffs of the Java seas, were now gradually brought closer in a long chain of trans-oceanic trade. The administrative unification and the economic achievements of T'ang China, while they were responsible for the creation of new consumer demands and social tastes for luxuries within the limits of the empire, also led in the Far East to the emergence of a larger zone of Chinese cultural influence. In spite of cyclical periods of civil war, political disintegration, and foreign invasion, the Celestial empire continued to act from the seventh century to the fifteenth as an area of economic high pressure, attracting to itself overland caravans, tributary missions from foreign princes, and large ocean-going vessels engaged in a two-way traffic. The Sinicisation of a large part of Asia and its people was as much connected with the political and military expansion of China as a general economic and social acceptance of her cultural values and standards of life.

The expansion and the new activities which became faintly evident in the rhythm of both caravan and trans-oceanic trade from the seventh century onwards in northern and southern China received a great deal of their impetus from the domestic aspirations and developments of the T'ang and Sung empires. However, in the West it was joined by the second and most powerful of the historical forces of the time, the rise of Islam and its expansion across the fertile lands of the Near East and South Asia. Movements of people by definition involve the exchange of ideas, economic systems, social usage, political institutions, and artistic traditions. The spread of Islam subsumed all these things. It may be

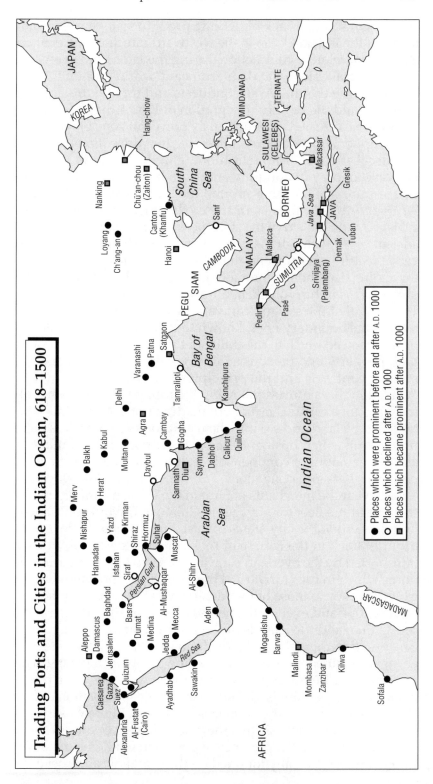

Trading Ports and Cities in the Indian Ocean, 618–1500

- ● Places which were prominent before and after A.D. 1000
- ○ Places which declined after A.D. 1000
- ▪ Places which became prominent after A.D. 1000

an exaggeration for lack of definite proof to state that the commerce of the Indian Ocean in the westward direction had entered a period of relative contraction during the later Roman empire with the weakening of a Mediterranean "world economy". It is certainly true that the Arab conquests and rapid demographic diffusion and the political integration of Egypt, Syria, Iran, and North Africa created an enormously powerful zone of economic consumption. It was an expanding area that drew its commercial and fiscal strength from refashioning in the West the Mediterranean economy of antiquity and from harnessing the productive resources of the lands around the Indian Ocean in the East. Arab economic success in the early caliphate period was achieved with the aid of the skills possessed by the people of the ancient Near East. But the growth of great urban centres, a universal feature of Islam, and the new capital cities gave rise to an expanding demand for commodities of all kinds and for precious objects. This in turn quickened the pace of long-distance trade. The revival of the sea and caravan routes across the famous international boundary lines, known to merchants since Hellenistic times, owed much to the ability of the Islamic rulers to protect their property and persons against violence. The laws of commercial contracts and the principles of juridical rights which evolved in the centuries following the foundation of Islam took into account a cardinal fact of pre-modern trade. Merchants who travelled by land and sea into the realms of foreign princes were prone to take their business elsewhere without the guarantee of a certain amount of commercial freedom secured by reciprocal political rights and obligations. . . .

Each year the merchants of Siraf in the Persian Gulf organised their maritime fleet for voyages to China, to Daybul and Calicut in India, and to the city-states of East Africa. Some of the goods brought back in the course of these journeys were obviously transported by the overland caravan routes to the Mediterranean ports, which in turn forwarded the cargo to the northern Frankish markets or to those of the Muslim Maghreb. But a large part of the exotic and even of the necessary imports from Africa, India, China, and the islands of the Indonesian archipelago was consumed within Islamic lands. In many ways, the articles exchanged retained their original use and symbolic meaning. The demand for Chinese porcelain in western Asia was not a transplanted taste for chinoiserie but an evolving appreciation of fine shape, material, colour, and glazes in pottery. There was even a widespread belief in Asia that the pale sea-green celadonware of China could reveal the presence of poison in food. The medieval trade of Asia was really founded on the economic and social acceptance of the four great products of eastern civilisation—silk, porcelain, sandalwood, and black pepper—which were exchanged for incense (Arabian gum resins), thoroughbred horses, ivory, cotton textiles, and metal goods. It should not of course be forgotten that the Indian Ocean possessed two faces, the sea itself and the arid plateau beyond the Himalayan heights. Just as the monsoon winds obeyed a global climatic law evident in the annual expansion and contraction of the pressure areas over the entire Asian landmass, so the sea-lanes of the Indian Ocean were supplemented all through history by the northern caravan routes with sturdy two-humped camels, horses, and mules as transport.

THE SIXTH VOYAGE OF SINBAD THE SAILOR

THE THOUSAND AND ONE NIGHTS

During the seventh and eighth centuries, Arab Islamic conquerors turned their attention to the conversion of Persia. Among
Persia's many attractions was its rich tradition of literature and
culture; indeed, Persian quickly became the primary literary language in the Islamic Middle East.

Persian-language writers and storytellers drew inspiration
from a large number of sources. As Islam expanded beyond Persia to India and East Africa, and as Islamic traders came in contact with peoples from China to Africa, folklore from these lands
was mingled with traditional Middle Eastern tales. The results
include some of the greatest works of world literature, from
Omar Khayyam's *Rubaiyat* to the collection from which the following selection is taken, *The Thousand and One Nights*, or *Arabian Nights*.

The Thousand and One Nights takes place at the court of Harun
al-Rashid, an Abbasid caliph who reigned in the early ninth century. In the story, he threatens to kill a slave girl, Sheherezade,
[here Shahrazade], if she fails to entertain him with stories night
after night. Sheherezade accordingly tells captivating stories of
romance, intrigue, and adventure for 1001 nights, until the caliph
finally allows her her freedom. Among her stories are descriptions of the seven voyages of Sinbad the Sailor, who, judging
from the following passage, roamed the Indian Ocean in search
of trade and adventure.

From *The Book of the Thousand Nights and One Night*, vol. 3, from the literal and complete
version of Dr. J.C. Mardrus; and collated with other sources; translated by E. Powys Mathers (London: Casanova Society, 1923).

Companions and dear guests, I was sitting one day taking the air before my door and feeling as happy as I had ever felt, when I saw a group of merchants passing in the street who had every appearance of returned travellers. This sight recalled to me how joyful a thing it is to return from journeying, to see the birth land after far voyage, and the thought made me long to travel again. I equipped myself with merchandise of price, suitable for the sea, and left the city of Baghdad for Bassora. There I found a great ship filled with merchants and notables as well provided with goods for trading as myself; so I had my bales carried on board and soon we peacefully set sail from Bassora. . . .

We sailed from place to place and from city to city buying and selling and rejoicing in the new sights which met our gaze. But one day, as we were lying on the deck with a feeling of perfect safety, we heard despairing cries and, looking up, saw that they were uttered by the captain, who also threw his turban far from him and, beating himself in the face, pulled out handfuls of his beard.

We clustered round him, asking what the matter was, and he answered: "All good folk here assembled, learn that we have been driven from the seas we knew into an unknown ocean where we shall surely perish, unless Allah sends something to save us. Let us pray to Him!"

So saying the captain climbed the mast and was about to trim the sails, when a great wind rose and, striking us full in the face, broke our rudder to pieces just as we were passing a high mountain. The captain swarmed down the mast, crying: "There is no power or might save in Allah! None can arrest the force of Destiny! My friends, we are altogether lost!"

While the passengers were weeping and saying farewell to each other, the sea rose in her fury and broke our vessel into fragments against the mountain of which I have spoken. We were all thrown into the water, where some were drowned and others, among whom was myself, were able to save themselves by clinging to the lower crags.

Now this mountain rose straight up from the strand of a large island, the beaches of which were covered with the remains of wrecked ships and every kind of jetsam. The place where we landed was strewn with a multitude of bales from which rich merchandise and costly ornaments had escaped.

I walked among these scattered treasures and soon found a little river of fresh water which, instead of flowing into the sea, as do all other rivers, came from a cleft in the mountain and, running inland, at last plunged into a cave at the foot of it and disappeared.

Nor was that all; the banks of this stream were thick underfoot with rubies and other coloured precious stones, and all crumbling with diamonds and pieces of gold and silver. Also its bed was littered with gems beyond price, instead of pebbles; and the whole region, beneath and beside the water, blazed with the reflected light of so much riches that the eyes of the beholder were dazzled. Chinese and Comarin aloes of the first quality grew about the water. In this island there was a stream of raw liquid amber, of the colour of tar, which flowed down to the sea shore, being melted to the consistency of boiling wax by the rays of the sun. Great fish would come out of the sea and drink greedily of this substance, which heated their bellies, so that after a certain time they would vomit upon the surface of the water. There it became hard and changed both its nature and colour; at last it was carried back to the beach in the form of ambergris, which scented the whole island. The liquid amber, which the fish did not swallow, also spread a perfume of musk about the shore.

All these riches were useless to man because none might touch upon that island and leave it alive, seeing that every ship which came near was dashed to pieces by the force of the waves.

Those of us who had been saved remained in sorrowful case upon the beach, desolate in the middle of great wealth and starving among the material for many feasts. Such food as we had we scrupulously divided; but my companions, who were not used like myself to the horrors of starvation, ate their shares in one or two meals and began to die off in a few days. I was more careful, eating sparsely and only once a day. Also I had found a separate supply of provision of which I said nothing to my friends.

We who lived washed those who died and, wrapping them in shrouds made up of the rich fabrics which strewed the shore, buried them in the sand. To add to the hardships of the survivors, a sickness of the belly broke out among us caused by the moist air of the sea. All but myself of those who had not starved died of it, and I dug with my own hands a grave for the last of my companions.

In spite of my prudent abstention, very little of my food remained; so, seeing that death was not far off, I wept and cried aloud: "Ah, why did you not die while there remained comrades who would have washed you and given you to the earth? There is no power or might save in Allah!" Then I began to bite the hands of my despair.

WORLD HISTORY BY ERA

Science and Technology Develop in Asia: 800–1300

CHAPTER 5

THE INVENTIONS AND IDEAS OF TANG AND SONG CHINA

STEPHEN F. MASON

China enjoyed a golden age under the Tang dynasty, which ruled from 618 to 907, and the Song dynasty, which governed from 960 until 1279. During those six centuries, China's influence spread across East Asia, Chinese products were traded from Japan to Africa, and cities such as Chang' An and Hangzhou were among the largest and most vibrant on earth. Tang and Song scientists and craftsmen reflected the creativity of China during the Middle Ages.

In the following selection, Stephen F. Mason summarizes some of the important technological innovations of the Tang and Song eras. Chinese Buddhist monks invented block printing and the book. Scholars and magicians, searching for ways of prolonging life and predicting the future, invented the magnetic compass, which soon became a necessary instrument on ocean voyages. As Mason also points out, the Chinese invented gunpowder in this era. The Arabs, who learned about gunpowder from merchants and travelers, called it "Chinese snow." These inventions, and many others, had a lasting impact on the world.

Stephen F. Mason is a professor of chemistry at the University of Exeter, England.

Porcelain manufacture, which had started with the crude proto-porcelain of Han times, came to a high level of perfection under the Tang, an imperial bureau for its manufacture being set up in 621. The wheelbarrow had been invented

From *A History of the Sciences*, by Stephen F. Mason (London: Routledge & Paul, 1953).

during the fifth century, and in the seventh appeared tread-mill-operated paddle boats, fitted with water-tight bulkheads and a stern-post rudder. During the Tang period, the first block printing began in the Buddhist monasteries of China. The earliest printed book is the Diamond Sutra, dated A.D. 868, found in the Caves of the Thousand Buddhas at Kansu. The printing of books soon became general throughout China, the Confucian classics being printed from 932 and the official dynastic histories between 994 and 1063. Block printing spread to the border tribe of the Uigurs some time before 1206, the year in which they were overrun by the Mongols. The Uigurs printed the Buddhist works, with Sanskrit notes and Chinese page numbers, in their own Turkish language, using an alphabetic script that had originated in Syria. Movable type of clay was invented in China by Pi Sheng in the 1040's. Wooden movable type came into use some time later, specimens dating from c. 1300 being found in the Caves of the Thousand Buddhas. Finally, movable type of cast metal was developed, specimens of fonts dating from 1403 being found in Korea, and books printed from such type dating from 1409.

THE CHINESE INVENT GUNPOWDER

By the end of the Tang period, gunpowder had been developed in China, whilst firearms appeared before the end of the Song. Saltpetre occurs as a natural efflorescence of the soil in China and India. It is first mentioned in Chinese texts of the first century B.C. The Chinese alchemists of the third century A.D. mixed sulphur and saltpetre in the correct proportions for gunpowder, and exposed the mixture to high temperatures. Such experiments may have been the origin of the fireworks mentioned in seventh-century texts. In the wars of the Tang period, fire arrows were used, but they were probably only burning pitch attached to an arrow head. In 969 a new type of fire arrow appeared, which seems to have been a kind of rocket. A record of 1040 states that gunpowder was used in the new fire rockets, the record giving the correct formula for gunpowder, together with the details of its preparation. A Chinese edict of 1067 prohibited the export of sulphur and saltpetre to foreign lands, which is an indication of how valuable gunpowder was considered to be in China at the time.

Marco Polo, who obtained a high position in the Chinese bureaucracy under the Mongols, said that the Chinese had firearms by A.D. 1237. Chinese records of the time tell of several different kinds of gunpowder weapons. The first reference to a firearm projecting bullets occurs in 1259 when the Song armies repelled the Tartars with firearms made of bamboo tubes. The Tartars in turn used gunpowder weapons against the Mongols. In 1231 they used a weapon called 'The Heaven Shaking Thunder', which appears to have been a grenade, an iron vessel filled with gunpowder and fitted with a fuse, that was hurled from a catapult. The Mongols captured a Chinese ammunition works in 1233, the general commanding, Souboutai, leading the Mongol invasions of Europe a few years later. During their invasion of Japan, 1274–81, the Mongols used iron cannon according to three different accounts, one of which adds that they used iron cannon balls. The oldest existing Chinese cannon that can be dated are A.D. 1354, 1357, and 1377, the oldest European cannon that can be so dated are A.D. 1380, 1395, and 1410.

THE MAGNETIC COMPASS

Another Chinese development of the Song period was the use of the magnetic compass for land and sea travel. In 1086 Shen Kua, a scholar-director of waterworks, wrote a work in which he described the various wonders he had seen in his time, such things as fossils, relief maps, and actual cases of transmutation of metals, and a magical means of finding direction. The transmutation he described was the conversion of iron into copper by means of a solution of copper sulphate, which was long regarded in the west as a real change of one metal into another. As regards the magnetic compass, he said that when magicians want to find direction, they rub a needle on a lodestone and then hang it up by means of a thin thread. The needle will usually point to the south, but sometimes, he adds, it will point to the north. By 1150 such compasses were used regularly for sea voyages and land travel, the declination of the compass from the true north and south being recognized by this time.

The Song dynasty, like the Han, was rich in mathematicians, astronomers, calendar makers and surveyors. The official Chinese biography of such men, published in 1764, lists thirty-eight eminent mathematicians from the Han period, and twenty-nine from the Song, whilst the highest number from the dynasties between was nine from the Sui. In 1247 the *Nine Sections of Mathematics* was published by Ch'in Kui Shao, in which place value and a sign of zero were introduced into Chinese numerals. He gave algebraic methods of solving trigonometrical problems, and dealt with higher numerical equations and indeterminate equations. Chon Huo, 1011–75, president of the bureau of astronomy, solved the problem of summing a series of squares over a given number of terms, and Chu Shi Kie, c. 1280, gave the first description of Pascal's triangle of binomial coefficients.

CHINA FAILED TO TAKE ADVANTAGE OF ITS TECHNOLOGY

ARTHUR COTTERELL

During the Tang and Song dynasties, Confucian scholar-bureaucrats dominated Chinese life. These high-level officials had passed a series of extremely difficult examinations in Chinese history and Confucian philosophy, among other subjects; any candidate who passed the highest level of examinations was entitled to a powerful government job with correspondingly high status and prestige. They tended to control scientific and technological research and, as Arthur Cotterell suggests in the following passage, favored invention and research over the commercial development of new products.

Cotterell points out that Song China had many elements necessary for the sort of industrial revolution that Europe underwent in the eighteenth and nineteenth centuries. China failed, however, to exploit such innovations as the printed book, blast furnace, stern-post rudder, and other devices that first appeared in China. While Song officials patronized learning and invented such intriguing items as the world's first mechanical clock, they adapted these innovations to industrial applications only indirectly, from seventeenth-century European inventions with Chinese origins.

Arthur Cotterell is the author of several books on early civilizations and the editor of the *Encyclopedia of Ancient Civilizations*.

From *China: A History*, by Arthur Cotterell (London: Pimlico, n.d.). Reprinted by permission of The Random House Group Limited.

L earning, as enshrined in the civil service examinations, formed the basis of the Song achievement. The adminis- tration was modelled on the Tang and the recruitment of officials aided by government-sponsored universities and colleges. Not only were more students allowed to pass their final examinations and take up an official appointment, but also there was a significant widening of the curriculum. During the ascendancy of the reformer Wang Anshi (1021–86), technical and scientific subjects could be offered. Previously the questions set, though concerned with administrative, governmental and economic problems, were expected to be answered within the context of orthodox Confucian literature and philosophy. Although subjects such as engineering and medicine did not long survive the fall of Wang Anshi in 1076, this extension of official knowledge is an indication of the contemporary rise in scientific consciousness among the educated classes. Wang Anshi's humble background may account for his interest in labour-saving devices, but no country could then compare with China in the application of natural knowledge to practical human needs.

CHINA'S CONTRAST WITH EUROPE

During the Song dynasty the empire reached the edge of modern science and underwent a minor industrial revolution. The world's first mechanised industry was born at the same time that the printing of books facilitated the exchange of scientific knowledge derived from observation and experiment. But it remains an intriguing historical fact that China, far ahead of other cultural areas in scientific and technical understanding between the first century BC and the fourteenth century, did not generate modern scientific method. Nor was the commercial development under the Song emperors followed by anything which faintly resembled the rise of capitalism in Europe, for China was to continue on its own distinct course, a society dominated by the scholar-bureaucrat. Only in the late nineteenth century were the educated classes convinced that the country needed to import modern technology, the early stages of which had been acquired by the West, albeit indirectly, from China.

Western debts to Chinese science are now admitted. The major information flow occurred after the end of the Southern Song, when Mongol conquest of all between the Don and the Mekong rivers encouraged overland trade and travel. Yet the fundamental ideas of Chinese science were largely neglected in favour of specific inventions or processes. An instance of this short-sightedness is Marco Polo. His *Travels* hardly touch upon scientific topics though in the 1280s he had been governor of Yangzhou, a centre specialising in the production of armaments and military supplies in Jiangsu province. By the thirteenth century Europeans were using the magnetic compass, the stern-post rudder and the windmill, and in the fourteen century mechanical clocks, water-powered textile machinery, blast furnaces, gunpowder, segmental-arch bridges, and block printing are recorded. Whilst the exact origin of these inventions was unknown to the inhabitants of Europe at this time, their significance as agents of social and economic change was not unnoticed. In the early 1600s Francis Bacon was fully aware that the metamorphosis of the continent stemmed from the applications of these inventions. He wrote:

> It is well to observe the force and virtue and consequences of discoveries. These are to be seen nowhere more conspicuously than in those three which were unknown to the ancients, and of which the origin, though recent, is obscure: namely, printing, gunpowder, and the magnet. For these three have changed the whole face and state of things throughout the world, the first in literature, the second in warfare, the third in navigation: whence have followed innumerable changes: insomuch that no empire, no sect, no state seems to have exerted greater power and influence in human affairs than these mechanical devices.

The clue to this acute observation was Bacon's own scientific activities. What he was pointing out was a crucial watershed in European history, the divide between medieval and modern times. Knowledge became readily available in printed form, whereas previously only the very rich layman could afford the long, tedious and expensive process of hand-copied manuscripts. The Renaissance and the Reformation followed. Gunpowder eclipsed both knight and castle, besides in the Thirty Years' War inaugurating conflict on a continental scale, while the magnetic compass had sent Columbus to America in 1492 and helped Magellan circumnavigate the globe in 1520.

CHINESE BUREAUCRATS CONTROLLED SCIENCE AND INDUSTRY

Nothing like this transformation occurred in China. Despite the commercial activities of the great cities—Marco Polo was stunned by the sheer size of the economy—the merchants were never permitted to acquire any lasting influence in state affairs. Neither were cities free as in the mercantile centres of Europe, where a charter granted privileges to the burghers not enjoyed by those in the surrounding countryside; nor had the merchant guilds any social standing. The merchants, victims of sumptuary laws and state regulation, sought admission for their sons to the official class, which by tradition disdained commerce. Because of his unchallenged authority and the intimate relation of mankind with Nature in Chinese thought, the scholar-official was interested in the benefits of technology, so that the imperial government acted as an important stimulus to advance. Its own direct revenues were therefore enhanced by the introduction of advanced metallurgical bellows, which worked through the conversion of longitudinal motion by crank, connecting-rod and piston-rod.

Another remarkable water-powered machine was capable of spinning thirty-two threads simultaneously; in different versions it was used for silk-reeling and hemp-spinning. The leather driving belt of this piece of textile machinery had an interesting parallel in the chain-drive belonging to Su Song's astronomical clock. Su Song (1020–1101) and other engineers applied the principle of regular and controlled water flow to an armillary sphere, a model of the heavens used in astronomy. It allowed the sphere to move in accordance with the apparent movements of the planets and the stars. Though the hours were struck on a gong, it was not seen as the perfection of the water clock, which essentially it was.

Imperial patronage also extended to medicine, in 1111 the twelve most eminent practitioners at the throne's behest compiling an encyclopedia of current knowledge. This work was part of a general movement towards the codification of medical disorders—symptoms, diagnosis and treatment. Its novel concern to standardise medical practice and reassess early theory in the light of new evidence reached its culmination in the comprehensive study of diet and health undertaken by the Ming doctor Li Shizhen (1518–93), whose work is still used by Chinese doctors today.

Indian Mathematics Transformed Europe

A.C. Crombie

Modern science was made possible by many developments, among the most important of which is the arrival in Europe of what are known as "arabic numbers." This now-familiar number system includes nine single digits that can be arranged in any combination, as well as a symbol for the concept of zero. Over a period of several centuries beginning in the 1100s, as A.C. Crombie points out in the following selection, the straightforward "arabic" system replaced the older system of Roman numerals in Europe.

The arabic system, however, originated neither in Arabia nor the Islamic world but in India. Arabs learned of the system as Islamic influence spread in India and as Indian scholars gravitated toward Islamic cultural centers such as Baghdad. Europeans learned of the system from their contact with Arabs. According to Crombie, this contact ranged from the exchange of scholarship, especially among the Muslims and Jews of Spain, to the activities of merchants operating in Muslim North Africa, or Barbary as it was also known.

A.C. Crombie was a senior lecturer in the history of science at Oxford University.

In the field of mathematics the Arabs transmitted to Western Christendom a body of most valuable knowledge which had never been available to the Greeks, though here the Arabs were not making an original contribution but simply making more widely known the developments in mathematical thought which had taken place among the Hindus. Unlike the Greeks, the Hindus had developed not so much geometry as arithmetic and algebra. The Hindu mathematicians, of whom Aryabhata (b. 476 A.D.), Brahmagupta (b. 598 A.D.) and later Bhaskara (b. 1114) were the most important, had developed a system of numerals in which the value of a digit was shown by its position. They knew the use of zero, they could extract square and cube roots, they understood fractions, problems of interest, the summation of arithmetical and geometrical series, the solution of determinate and indeterminate equations of the first and second degrees, permutations and combinations and other operations of simple arithmetic and algebra. They also developed the trigonometrical technique for expressing the motions of the heavenly bodies and introduced trigonometrical tables of sines.

ARABIC NUMBERS ACTUALLY CAME FROM INDIA

The most important mathematical idea which the Arabs learnt from the Hindus was their system of numerals, and the adoption of this system in Christendom was one of the great advances in European science. The great merit of this system, which is the basis of the modern system, was that it contained the symbol for zero and that any number could be represented simply by arranging digits in order, the value of a digit being shown by its distance from zero or from the first digit on the left. It had very great advantages over the cumbrous Roman system. In the system which the Arabs learnt from the Hindus the first three numbers were represented by one, two and three strokes respectively, and after that 4, 5, 6, 7, 9 and possibly 8 were probably derived from the initial letters for the words representing those numbers in Hindu. The Arabs had learnt something of this system from the Indians, with whom they had considerable trading relations, as early as the 8th century, and a complete account of it was given by al-Khwarizmi in the 9th century. It was from a corruption of his name that the system became known in Latin as 'algorism.'

The Hindu numerals were introduced into Western Europe gradually from the 12th century onwards. It was symptomatic of the practical trend among mathematicians that al-Khwarizmi himself, whose work on algebra was translated by Adelard of Bath, said . . . that he had limited his activities

> to what is easiest and most useful in arithmetic, such as men constantly require in cases of inheritance, legacies, partition, law-suits, and trade, and in all their dealings with one another, or where the measuring of lands, the

digging of canals, geometrical computation, and other objects of various sorts and kinds are concerned.

Later in the same century Rabbi ben Ezra, by origin a Spanish Jew, fully explained the Arabic system of numeration and specially the use of the symbol 0. Gerard of Cremona reinforced this exposition. But it was not till the 13th century that the Arabic system became widely known. This was due very largely to the work of Leonardo Fibonacci, or Leonardo of Pisa (d. after 1240). Leonardo's father was a Pisan merchant who was sent out to Bugia in Barbary to take charge of a factory, and there Leonardo seems to have learnt a great deal about the practical value of Arabic numerals and about the writings of al-Khwarizmi. In 1202 he published his *Liber Abaci* in which in spite of the name he fully explained the use of the Arabic numerals. He was not personally interested in commercial arithmetic and his work was highly theoretical, but after his time Italian merchants generally came gradually to adopt the Arabic, or Hindu, system of numeration.

EUROPEANS REPLACE ROMAN NUMERALS WITH ARABIC NUMBERS

During the 13th and 14th centuries the knowledge of Arabic numerals was spread through Western Christendom by the popular almanacs and calendars. As the dates of Easter and of the other festivals of the Church were of great importance in all religious houses, one almanac or calendar was usually found in these establishments. A calendar in the vernacular had been produced in France as early as 1116, and Icelandic calendars go back to about the same date. This knowledge was reinforced in the West by popular expositions of the new system by mathematical writers such as Alexander of Villedieu and John Holywood or, as he was called, Sacrobosco, and even in a surgical treatise by Henry of Mondeville. About the middle of the 13th century two Greek mathematicians explained the system to Byzantium. The Hindu numerals did not immediately drive out the Roman ones and in fact until the middle of the 16th century Roman numerals were widely used outside Italy, but by 1400 Arabic numerals were widely known and generally understood at least among men of learning.

THE ADVANCED KNOWLEDGE OF ARAB PHYSICIANS

PHILIP K. HITTI

Baghdad, the capital of the Arab Empire during the period of the Abbasid caliphate (750–1055), was one of the world's great cultural and intellectual centers. There, Arab and Persian scholars and scientists painstakingly collected the classic texts of Greece and Rome, the Christian Near East, Egypt, and China as well as Arabia, Persia, and India. Using these varied sources, Arabs derived new scientific knowledge, notably in medicine. Arab doctors were respected throughout the Old World and Arab medical texts, such as Ibn Sina's *Canon of Medicine*, were still in use centuries after the decline of the Abbasids.

In the following selection, Philip K. Hitti describes the important Arab physicians and their innovations. He notes the significance of Arab recognition of medicine as a practical science to be addressed by practical means, rather than as a magical or religious matter. Arab physicians learned, for example, that disease could be spread by stagnant water, that blood was circulated by the heart, and that many medical problems could be solved through simple, pragmatic means.

Philip K. Hitti is the author of many books on Arabic history and Islamic civilization.

O nly after they had been exposed to the influence of Islam and of other cultures did the Arabians become aware of the existing body of scientific knowledge. It was the Muslim conquests of the early century that established vital contact between them and the rich cultural tradition represented by Greeks, Syrians, Persians, and Egyptians. In medicine and other sciences, in philosophy, and in art and architecture the sons of the desert had little to teach and much to learn. It is to their credit, however, that they appreciated that fact and encouraged their subjects to preserve and promote their local traditions so long as they did not conflict with Islam. Throughout the caliphal period the bearers of the torch of learning were first Christians and then new converts from Persia, Syria, and other conquered territories. . . .

ARAB MEDICINE WAS INFLUENCED BY THE ANCIENT GREEKS

Arab knowledge of scientific medicine probably began in al-Ma'mun's time [the mid–ninth century] when the Christian Hunayn ibn-Ishaq translated Galen [a court physician of the Roman Empire who wrote in Greek]. For centuries Galen's works became as authoritative in Arab medical practice as they were earlier in Roman and Greek practice. Galen in Arabic provided the Muslim practitioner with the first opportunity to become "modernized." By the end of the ninth century the Christian monopoly on the field was broken, passing before long into the hands of Muslims, mostly Persians, who wrote, of course, in Arabic.

The series of distinguished Muslim physicians is headed by al-Razi (Nuh ibn-Zakariya, 865–925), whose last name is derived from his birthplace al-Rayy outside the modern capital of Persia. Al-Razi began his career studying alchemy under Hunayn and ended it as a physician and surgeon. Like his predecessor al-Kindi and his successor ibn-Sina he was also a philosopher but, unlike them, he made no attempt to reconcile Greek philosophy and Islamic religion. To him the two were irreconcilable. In fact he was a radical thinker, a rationalist who rejected the concept of prophecy, challenged Koranic dogma, and subordinated theology to philosophy. In this respect he was rare if not exceptional in Islam.

In medicine as in philosophy this physician was original. He was one of the first to exercise a measure of empirical spirit and reject occultist explanations. In surgery he was one of the first to use the seton [animal hair or linen used to repair torn tissue]. His method of choosing a site for a new hospital building in Baghdad—by hanging up shreds of meat in different places of the city to determine the degree of putrefaction—indicates originality in thinking. Of the two hundred works ascribed to al-Razi—half of which have been lost—thirteen are about alchemy. Two of his medical works may be singled out: *al-Hawi* ("the comprehensive book") and *al-Judari w-al-Hasbah* ("smallpox and measles").

True to its name *al-Hawi* was a veritable medical encyclopedia summing up what the Arabs knew of Greek, Syriac, Persian, and Hindu medicine and enriched by the addition of the author's experiments and experiences. The author spent fifteen years compiling it and used probably more words than ibn-Sina in *al-Qanun*. A publisher in Hydarabad has already issued eighteen volumes of it (1955–65) and promises more. The book was first translated into Latin (1279) under the auspices of Charles, king of Naples and Sicily, by the Jewish physician Faraj ben-Salim, translator of other Arabic medical works. Under the title *Continens* it soon established itself as a standard text and was repeatedly printed from 1486 onward. A fifth edition appeared in Venice in 1542. The invention of printing from movable type in the mid-fifteenth century facilitated the distribution of al-Razi's and other Arab scholars' works. It made the name Rhazes familiar in medical schools.

Al-Razi's monograph on smallpox and measles, an ornament of Arab medical literature, is considered the earliest of its kind. In it the author gave the first clinical account of smallpox and distinguished it from measles. Translated into Latin, it was printed about forty times between 1498 and 1866; it was translated into a number of modern languages including English (1848). It confirmed the author's reputation as one of the keenest thinkers and greatest clinicians not only of Islam but of Christendom.

It was not long before *al-Hawi* had a competitor in *al-Kitab al-Maliki* ("the royal book," *Liber regius*) by 'Ali al-'Abbas (Haly Abbas) al-Majusi (d. 994). The book was dedicated to the author's patron, a Buwayhid sultan. Like its predecessor it was a treasure house of the science and practice of medicine, but this latter work was more concise. It advanced medical knowledge by presenting a number of points, then new, including a rudimentary conception of the capillary system, and evidence that in the act of delivery the baby does not come out by itself but is pushed by the muscular contraction of the womb. A Damascene physician who served as dean of the Mamluk hospital in Cairo, ibn-al-Nafis (d. 1288), added a clear conception of the pulmonary circulation of the blood. That was two and a half centuries before the time of Harvey, the Englishman who is generally credited with the discovery. What makes ibn-al-Nafis' discovery especially remarkable is the fact that it was arrived at by deduction rather than by dissection. The thirteenth-century physician has been described as one "who would not prescribe medicine when diet sufficed."

Earlier than the comprehensive encyclopedia, "the royal book" was translated in part into Latin by Constantine the

African (d. 1087) and wholly by the Pisan Stephen of Antioch. It was the only major Arabic work the Crusaders carried back with them to Europe.

IBN SINA: THE MOST INFLUENTIAL PHYSICIAN OF THE MIDDLE AGES

The works of al-Razi and al-Majusi were in due course superseded as textbooks and outlived in usage by those of ibn-Sina, titled by his people *al-shaykh al-ra'is* ("the dean of the learned and the chief of courtiers"). The title was well deserved. Ibn-Sina distinguished himself as a physician, philosopher, scientist, and vizir. He is generally considered the greatest physician of the early Middle Ages.

Al-Husayn, to use his first name, was born in 980 near Bukhara (Transoxiana) and wrote primarily in Arabic except for a few works in Persian. When he was sixteen years old, according to his autobiography, he had mastered a number of the then-known sciences, including medicine which he "found easy." He then started on his career as a teacher and a practitioner. The fame of the prodigy reached the ailing Samanid governor of Bukhara, and when the young physician cured him he was granted the privilege of using the well-stocked royal library. In eighteen months he reportedly had devoured the contents of the entire library.

Of the forty-three medical works authored by ibn-Sina his masterpiece was *al-Qanun fi al-Tibb* ("the canon in medicine"), which he completed in the course of a turbulent career at Hamadhan. The book summarized in a million words the Hippocratic and Galenic traditions, synthetized with Syro-Arabic and Indo-Persian sources and supplemented by the author's experience and experimentation. He made even old material in it look new and usable: more methodical in arrangement, classification, and presentation than *al-Hawi, al-Qanun* represented the culmination of Arab systematization of medical science. It established itself as the supreme medical authority in the world of Islam until the nineteenth century. Its success in the West was almost equally spectacular. Translated by Gerard of Cremona, the *Canon* in the last third of the fifteenth century appeared in three Latin editions and one Hebrew edition. Gerard, the Italian counterpart of Hunayn, the Arab translator, is credited with translating no fewer than eighty Arabic works, about three-fourths of the total number of Arabic works translated into Latin. The *Canon* was used as a text in the universities of Paris and Louvain till the mid-seventeenth century. In the words of a modern historian of medicine, it "remained a medical bible for a longer period than any other work."

The book covered general medicine, pathology, and pharmacology, told how to treat diseases affecting all parts of the body from head to foot, recognized the importance of dietetics, the effect of climate on health, and the close relation between emotional and physiological conditions. Alchemy was denounced. Among other features were its discussions of the contagious nature of consumption, and the spreading of disease by soil and water. In surgery it recommended medicated wine as an oral anesthetic.

AN ARAB PHYSICIAN IN EUROPE

Surgery was not one of the fields in which Arabs made a distinct contribution. Islam, as interpreted by its ulama, discouraged dissection, a prerequisite for understanding the body's anatomy. It was Western Islam, where traditional ties were loose, that produced the greatest Arab surgeon and one of the greatest of medieval Europe, abu-al-Qasim (Abulcasis) al-Zahrawi (d. ca. 1013).

Al-Zahrawi was the court physician of al-Hakam, under whom the Umayyad caliphate of Cordova enjoyed its heyday. Al-Zahrawi's claim to distinction rests on his *al-Tasrif fi Man 'Ajaz 'an al-Ta'lif* ("an aid to him who lacks ability to use large treatises"). The book included a detailed surgical section, the first of its kind, summarizing the surgical knowledge of the time. This part was translated first into Latin by the indefatigable Gerard and then into Provencal and Hebrew. In the mid-fourteenth century a distinguished French surgeon incorporated that part into his book. It passed through many editions including one in Venice (1497), another in Basel (1541), and a third in Oxford (1778). For centuries al-Zahrawi's book was used as a text in the medical schools of Salerno, Montpellier, and elsewhere. It either introduced or emphasized cauterization of wounds and it described crushing of stones inside the bladder. It also brought out the necessity of dissection and even vivisection. A feature of the book was illustrations of instruments used by the author, instruments which served as models in Asia and Europe.

The Mongols Conquer the Largest Empire in History

—— | CHAPTER 6 | ——

Genghis Khan and the Mongol Empire

Franz Michael

The Mongols, warlike nomads from the dry, cold regions (or steppe) of Central Asia, conquered a vast empire in the thirteenth century. Mongol possessions stretched from eastern Europe in the west to China in the east. In addition to China, Mongol warriors defeated Russia and Persia and threatened India, western Europe, and Japan. Although the Mongol Empire held together for less than a century, it was at its height larger than any other land empire ever assembled.

In the following selection, Franz Michael claims that the reason the Mongols were able to conquer such huge territories and such powerful peoples was the capability of their leader, Genghis Khan. Brutal and brilliant, Genghis Khan was able to unite various tribes under his authority and devise effective military tactics suited to his small but mobile armies. Moreover, he was willing to use outside help and advice when necessary. Michael also notes that, although Genghis Khan began the conquest of the greatest prize of all, China, the conquest was completed by Kublai Khan, Genghis Khan's grandson.

Franz Michael is emeritus professor of history at George Washington University in Washington, D.C.

S teppe society was always mercurial. The nomad life of constant movement from summer to winter pastures and back again demanded capable leadership for organized migration by whole communities. Clashes over pasture rights were common. The nomads were armed people; the leader who could guarantee protection as well as conquest could rapidly increase his following; conversely, if he failed, his following would break up. This importance of leadership and its success in warfare can explain the rapidity with which steppe empires rose and fell apart.

The Mongol empire, the greatest of these steppe empires and the largest of all land empires in history, was forged by one leader in a few decades through the unification of all the steppe people in Central Asia under one clan. The empire was created in one generation; it broke apart two generations later, first splitting into four separate empires, each of which collapsed when its military cohesion ended. . . .

The Mongols were steppe people par excellence; they detested agricultural labor for themselves and believed in the freer life of the steppe, of animal husbandry, and of the warrior. Their primary goal was the creation of a great steppe empire that would extend its conquests in all directions to neighboring countries.

THE RISE TO POWER OF GENGHIS KHAN

This steppe empire was the creation of one man, one of the greatest and most brutal and fearful leaders of all time, Temuchin (1167–1227), who received the title Genghis Khan, the Great Khan of all steppe people. Like most of the rising steppe leaders, Temuchin started as a small tribal chieftain, a man skilled in tribal warfare who was challenged in his position, had to fight for survival and recognition, and moved on from success and conquest to more conquest until he had unified all the people of the steppe, who received under him the name of Mongols.

In his strategy Genghis Khan differed from the leaders of the Hsi Hsia, the Liao, and the Chin states who had all started at the Chinese frontier but had immediately turned into China to set up Chinese dynasties that were open to further attack from the tribal world of the steppe. Genghis Khan took Peking—from the Chin—in 1215 but then returned to the steppe, attacking and uniting the peoples of Mongolia, Central Asia, and the tribes along China's western frontier, creating a base from which he could carry the Mongol advance in all directions: Russia, Europe, the Near East, Iran, and China. This rapid expansion introduced a centrifugal factor that eventually ended the Mongol unity based on control from the steppe.

Europe was saved from conquest when the successful Mongol armies, having heard of the death of Ogotai, son and successor of Genghis Khan, turned back in 1241 to Karakorum, the capital of the Mongol empire, to participate in the election of his successor. The conquest of Iran ended at the Persian Gulf with the establishment of the khanate of Il-Khan. Russia remained under the khanate of the "Golden Horde" until the fifteenth century, Central Asia under the khanate of Chagatai. But the final dilution of the centripetal cohesion of the Mongol polity, as established by Genghis Khan, came with the conquest of China, and the shift of the capital from Mongolia to Peking, then called Khambalik (Cambulac). China became the most important of the Mongols' domains, altering the character of the steppe empire, and accelerating its disintegration.

Genghis Khan's steppe empire was based on military organization. Through local wars, negotiated submission, and asserted authority, Temuchin joined together some fifty tribes and was elected by them as khan. Other tribes were attached to this core, and in 1206 Temuchin was elected Genghis Khan—Genghis meaning "limitless strength"—by a general assembly of all the tribes, the Great Kurultai.

The Great (Genghis) Khan's first task was to organize his tribal adherents into a unified "national" force. The various tribal groups of fighting men were formed into an imperial army in units of 10, 100, 1,000, and 10,000 men under appointed officers chosen from existing leaders. Genghis Khan's main instrument of power, which he founded at the same time, was an imperial guard, selected from the best fighters of each larger unit, as a privileged loyal force to control the army and the nation at large. . . .

In contrast to founders of other tribal kingdoms, Genghis Khan did not borrow his governmental structure from the Chinese tradition but created his own out of the military order of the steppe. This difference in the basic concept and structure of the Mongol empire remained valid even after Kublai Khan, grandson of Genghis Khan, had moved his capital to Peking and his forces had conquered all of China. The Mongols remained in China an alien people of conquerors whose aim was to exploit and enjoy the products of the labor of the conquered population. To rule they employed mostly alien people, Central and Inner Asians, Persians, Arabs, and Europeans. Only at a lower level and especially in South China was it unavoidable to use Chinese officials, who in turn shared in the exploitation of their countrymen. When dissatisfaction exploded, the Chinese collaborators became as much the target of popular fury as did the Mongols and their foreign officials.

THE MONGOL ARMY WAS THE MOST FORMIDABLE OF ITS TIME

For the purpose of conquest, the military machine that Genghis Khan created was the most formidable of the time. The cavalry formations of mounted archers were the most mobile force known and were feared by all. The stirrup, which had come into use in the fourth century A.D., permitted greater control of the horse when massed columns of cavalry were maneuvered, a tactic fully developed by the Mongols. The powerful compound bow, made of horn and wooden pieces, could be used from the galloping horse in attack as well as in feint retreat—the so-called Parthian shot. In their blitzkrieg strategy the Mongols overran the more traditional armies of their enemies. But for the siege and capture of walled cities, the Mongols had to dismount and needed special new techniques of warfare, and these they obtained from the Chinese, from whom the Mongols learned the use of large catapults and explosive missiles. Their greatest weapon, however, was psychological: They spread before them fear of terror and slaughter. Their declared rule was that any town that resisted, if only shortly, would be totally destroyed, all inhabitants, men, women, and children massacred, and all structures leveled to the ground, so that a horse galloping over the ground at night would not stumble. It was sheer lust of conquest that fired the Mongols. Genghis Khan is known to have claimed that the greatest joy in life was to kill one's rivals, sleep with their wives and daughters, and ride their horses.

Self-sufficient within their steppe economy in the essentials of life, the Mongols depended on external input only for agricultural products and the ware of craftsmen. To obtain such wares the Mongols favored foreign traders and artisans who provided them with luxuries, as well as the goods they wanted or needed. In their own nomadic social system, no special merchant or artisan class was possible or permitted, but trade caravans, merchants, and artisans from foreign countries were supported, protected, and patronized. And because the steppe was the traveling route for the caravans that linked the West with East Asia, the Mongols, in command of the steppe, profited greatly from their monopoly control over the trade routes.

One other area of human aspiration in which this ruthless power proved to be most tolerant was religion. The Mongol's own early faith was shamanism, but since they sought for their administrative organization and conquests trained foreign experts, they had to accept the religions and educational systems of their many foreign functionaries. Among their officials and merchants were Muslims, Buddhists, Nestorians, Manichaeans, and European Christians, and as far as acceptance of foreign religious faiths was concerned, the Mongols were the most cosmopolitan and tolerant power of the time. Kublai Khan corresponded with the pope and had plans to invite several hundred Catholic priests to his country. Though this invitation was disregarded, several Franciscan and Dominican monks visited China during Mongol rule, and some left important records of their observations.

GENGHIS KHAN AND KUBLAI KHAN IN CHINA

The Mongol conquest of China was accomplished at a tremendous cost both in lives and physical destruction. When Genghis Khan took Peking, he followed the rule of slaughtering the total population and laying waste to the city, as he did wherever he met with any defiance. Yet exceptions began to be made. It was a Khitan aristocrat, Yeh-lü Ch'u-ts'ai (1190–1244), formerly an official under the Chin Dynasty and captured by the Mongols, who advised the Great Khan that the slaughter of the whole population of cities would mean the loss to the Mongols of the skill of the craftsmen and artisans who lived there, and the destruction of the population of the rural areas would deprive them of tax income. The Mongol ideal of turning conquered territory into grazing land for their horses was impractical in China. China had to be governed by Chinese administrative methods. In the words of Yeh-lü Ch'u-ts'ai, "You can conquer China on horseback but you have to dismount to rule her." Yeh-lü Ch'u-ts'ai's advice saved the inhabitants of K'ai-feng after it had fallen and may have prevented wholesale slaughter in other Chinese cities, although the populations of some cities along the conquest route to Nanking and Hangchow were not spared by the conqueror.

Kublai Khan (1215–1294), Genghis Khan's grandson, who was elected Great Khan in the Mongol capital of Karakorum in 1260, moved his capital from there to Peking (Khambalik) in 1263, and in 1271 assumed the Chinese dynastic name of Yüan Dynasty after capturing most of North and Central China. The remainder of the Sung empire fell between 1272 and 1279, when the Mongol conquest of China was completed. Nominally Kublai Khan remained the head of the whole Mongol empire, but he had to fight wars against some of his brothers and cousins who led parts of it. Even the nominal unity ended after Kublai's death in 1295, when the three western khanates that had accepted Islam as their faith and ideology refused to recognize the authority of Kublai's successor in Peking. The latter favored Lamaist Buddhism and was in their eyes an infidel. The cohesion of the Mongol continental empire thus lasted less than ninety years and the Mongol Yüan Dynasty in China came to an end in 1368.

MONGOL CONQUESTS INVOLVED GREAT BRUTALITY

HAROLD LAMB

In the following selection, Harold Lamb describes the Mongol conquest of the Kwaresm-shahs in 1218. The Shahs, converts to Islam
of Turkish descent, controlled lands from Baghdad in modern-day
Iraq to Samarkand in Central Asia. Though this territory was
heavily populated and wealthy, and the Turks, Persians, and
Arabs who inhabited it were strong fighters, they proved to be
no match for the armies of Genghis Khan. The Mongol leader decided to attack after a peaceful attempt to open trade relations
with the Shah resulted in the humiliation and murder of the
Mongol trade envoy.

According to Lamb, Genghis Khan sought to impose Mongol
ways on the Islamic Middle East. He disliked cities, and often
simply destroyed them. Preferring the empty steppes of Central
Asia to settled agriculture land, he depopulated regions through
brutality and genocide. Lamb goes on to point out that the Mongols employed psychological terror so effectively that many
Muslims saw Genghis Khan and his armies as "a scourge of the
supernatural."

Harold Lamb, one of the most popular nonfiction authors of
the first half of the twentieth century, was the author of many
works of history and travel.

From *The March of the Barbarians,* by Harold Lamb (New York: Literary Guild of America). Copyright © 1940 by Harold Lamb.

The Muslim forces had expected to meet a horde of barbarians. They met, instead, disciplined divisions, maneuvering in silence with amazing speed, according to a plan carefully prepared by the old Mongol. These divisions appeared out of the night, striking with blasts of steel-tipped arrows and heavy bows. Although they outnumbered the Mongols, the armies of the Khwaresm-shah were scattered in a few weeks. The Shah himself became a fugitive, like his former rival of Black Cathay, with a Mongol man hunt at his heels. His life ended in an island of the Caspian where the Mongol horsemen could not reach him—he died of exhaustion and terror.

The scattered armies were given no chance to reform. Genghis-Khan was trusting to speed of movement; he had brought the tactics of the hunt into warfare in the west. Cities were stormed, or tricked into surrender, and demolished in a few days.

THE MONGOLS EMPLOYED PSYCHOLOGICAL WARFARE

For the first time the Mongols devoted themselves to inspiring terror. Confronted by superior numbers of a warlike race utterly alien to the steppes, they waged a war of extermination against the multitudes. They led out the peoples of walled towns, examining them carefully and ordering the skilled workers—who would be useful—to move apart. Then the soldiers went through the ranks of helpless human beings, killing methodically with their swords and hand axes—as harvesters would go through a field of standing wheat. They took the wailing women by the hair, bending forward their heads, to sever the spine the more easily. They slaughtered, with blows on the head, men who resisted weakly.

In some places, the Muslims say, not even the dogs and cats survived the passing of the Mongol horsemen. Terror fell on the cultivated lands of Islam like a pall, interrupting communications, sending the living into hiding. It paralyzed the will to resist. And it lasted for years.

"A man of Nisapur," the historian Ibn Athir relates, "told me that he watched, hidden in a house, through an opening. When the Mongols appeared to kill someone, they cried each time, 'Allah-ilahi!' [in the name of Allah] (in mockery of the Muslim cry). When the massacre was over, they led away the women after pillaging the houses. I watched them mount their saddles. They laughed, chanting in their speech, and shouting 'Allah-ilahi.'

"So great was the dread that Allah put into all hearts," Ibn Athir continues, "things happened that are hard to believe. Someone told me that a Tatar rode alone into a village with many people, and set himself to kill them, one after the other, without a person daring to defend himself. I heard also that one Tatar, wishing to kill a prisoner of his and finding himself without a weapon, ordered his captive to lie down. He went to look for a sword, with which he killed the unfortunate, who had not moved.

"Someone said to me: 'I was on the road with seventeen other men. We saw a Tatar horseman come up to us. He ordered us to tie up our companions, each man to bind the other's arms behind his back. The others were beginning to obey him, when I said to them, "This man is alone. Let us kill him and escape." They replied, "We are too much afraid." "But this man will kill you," I said. "Let's do for him, and perhaps Allah will preserve us."

"'Yet, by my faith, not one of the seventeen dared do it. So I killed the Tatar with a blow of my knife. We all ran away and saved ourselves.'"

DESTRUCTION AND GENOCIDE IN THE ISLAMIC WORLD

The systematic slaughter went on. And the Muslims began to whisper that Genghis-Khan was a scourge of the supernatural, an implacable being, the Accursed.

From one city all the inhabitants were led out, separated into groups and told to bind each other's arms. When they were all trussed up, the Mongol soldiery surrounded them and killed the masses with arrows—men, women and children, without discrimination. Then the Mongols retrieved their arrows.

The prisoners taken at the siege of Bokhara were not slain. They were conducted to Samarkand, and tied in groups, to be driven toward the walls to form a human shield for the first ranks of the Mongol attack on that city. And the captives of Samarkand were led off, to serve in the assault of Urgench, the city of the Khwaresm-shahs.

These captives were driven to the task of filling up the ditch around the great city, and then to undermining the walls. The Mongols stormed the walls and fired the outer quarters of the Muslim metropolis with naphtha [fire-arrows]. But the multitudes penned up within the city defended each street, until the Mongol dead lay piled between the buildings.

The Mongols then drove their horde of captives to dam the Amu River that flowed past Urgench, and divert its course. They forced their way into the streets from the bed of the river, and the defenders of the city surrendered.

These survivors were driven out into the fields and separated into three groups. The artisans and skilled workers were sent east, to labor for the conquerors; young women and children were kept to become slaves; the rest were killed methodically. The chroniclers say that each Mongol soldier put to death twenty-four of the inhabitants of Urgench. There were about 50,000 Mongols at this siege.

Many Muslims had hid themselves among the ruins and the piles of the slain. They did not escape, because the Mongols destroyed the dam before leaving. The river water flooded the ruins, wiping out all trace of life.

Here, the chronicles relate, the two eldest sons of Genghis-Khan quarreled. Juchi, the first-born, wished to keep the city un-demolished, since it might belong to him thereafter. Chagatai insisted that no city could be spared after causing the death of Mongols. Urgench vanished, in actuality, from the face of the earth, and two centuries passed before the Amu River found its way back to its old bed, flowing again into the sea of Aral.

At times, after the Mongols sacked a town, they rode off, only to appear suddenly a few days later, to put to death the survivors who had returned to the ruined houses. So the people of Islam who lived through the terror learned to avoid all town sites, leaving them to the scavenger birds and dogs that fed for a while on the decaying bodies.

Along the belt of Arabic-Iranian civilization, four fifths of the population was eradicated. The slaughter was methodical, without evidence of sadistic torment. At times men who were known to have wealth were tortured to make them give up their treasures—whether real or imagined. No towers of skulls were built as monuments to the Mongol terror.

Genghis-Khan deliberately turned the rich belt of Islamic civilization into a no-man's-land. He put an end to the agricultural working of the land, creating an artificial steppe here, on the frontier of his new empire. Making it, he thought, suited to the life of his own people.

GENGHIS KHAN ORGANIZES HIS STATE

PETER BRENT

Genghis Khan began his military career as Temujin, one of many Mongol tribal chieftains. Both his mother and tribal shamans had predicted great accomplishments from the young man. After many military successes, particularly against rival groups of Central Asian nomads in northern China, Temujin was named the leader of a combined Mongol force in 1206. He was given the title of Great Khan, or Genghis Khan, the "Lord of All Men."

In the following selection, Peter Brent describes this conqueror, giving a few human qualities to a historical figure whose reputation is that of an inhuman monster. Brent points out that Genghis Khan sought to create a fair, if firm, system of laws for all his people. In addition, he tried to maintain a constant readiness for war and movement; both men and women had specific responsibilities in the Mongol war machine.

Peter Brent is the author of many works of popular history, including books on the Vikings, Charles Darwin, and T.E. Lawrence.

W ho was he, this Khan, sitting on the threshold of history in his great white tent, its wooden pillars bright with gold, his nine-tailed standard flicking in the cool upland winds? He was tall, it is said, with a noble beard and eyes that were described as like a cat's. He was, clearly, a man of resource and resolution. He was not afraid of hardship himself, nor of inflicting it on others. He was cruel, when diplomacy demanded it, magnanimous when he could see the profit in it. He had smashed the Kereits, because their treachery had to be punished in a manner all would remember; he had pardoned the defeated Naimans, had handed back their weapons, married the widow of their chieftain, accepted one of their princesses as wife for his son Tuli, in this way settling his western frontiers with friends. He was a man who could not read or write, but when his men captured the Uighur scribe, Tatatungo, Tayang Khan's chief minister, he learned from him the significance of a royal seal and the value of writing; Tatatungo became his own Keeper of the Seal, the teacher of his children and the children of the *orloks* [generals], and the channel through which the Uighur script became that of the Mongols. He was a man who despised the urban culture of his Chinese neighbours and the mercantile culture of the Islamic lands far to the west; at the same time, he was often to use those who had their roots in these civilizations as his own advisers, and he would show a religious tolerance that makes the Christian Europe of his day seem barbarous by comparison. Yet he was ruthless: the destruction of cities, of territories, of whole peoples, seems never to have caused him a moment's concern. His loyalty to those who served him, and those who entered into friendship or alliance with him, was absolute; his vengeance on those who broke their obligations terrible.

Unlettered, untutored, come from poverty and blighted hope by way of force and fantasy, his empire resting on the inspired giving of one sable coat, he had nevertheless a world-encompassing

A tenacious warrior and shrewd ruler, Genghis Khan maintained a well-organized military and a strict code of law throughout his empire.

vision. From a long line of swift, improvisatory tacticians had sprung this one colossal strategist. And yet the question remains— was he ambitious for conquest, at this moment, with the many peoples of the grasslands gathered about his tent in unified commitment? Were his conquests piecemeal, each based on its own logic, yet each one setting the next inevitably in motion? For the moment, perhaps, as Gokchu, the 'Trusted of Heaven', Gokchu the *shaman*, proclaimed him Khan of all the peoples, and as the princes of those peoples carried him on a sheet of black felt towards his throne, he was content. He was the 'Godsent', uniter of nearly half a million people, lord of another million and a half, overlord of the steppe from the Altai to the Khingan, utterly dominant, his status marked by the gifts of the great chieftains piled before him—brightness of gold, dark radiance of furs, glitter of silks, brilliance of brocades. The hundred cauldrons of the feast raised an obeisance of steam to the sky, that sky whose blue would by his decree henceforth be part of the name of those he led: the Koko-Mongols, the Mongols of the Blue Heaven. But it may be, too, that despite his forty or so years of age, he glanced once or twice towards the women where, in placated state, sat the only person he seems ever to have feared—Yulun, his mother.

A Code of Law for the Mongol Empire

While the people were still gathered and the weeks of feasting passed, the work of organization began. It was now that he gave Tatatungo, his Uighur adviser, the task of writing down the *Yasak*, that code of laws that he proposed for the Mongols. Stating, 'There is equality', it was to apply to everyone: 'Each man works as much as another. . . .' These laws have survived only in fragmentary form, but ranged from matters of detail, like the prohibition against washing in a running stream or against cattle drinking from a well—probably simple measures of public hygiene—through such moral precepts as the one urging men not to be drunk more than three times in a month, to matters of State—for example, the death penalty was decreed for any prince or *orlok* discovered in communication with a foreign monarch. The *Yasak* also included such general exhortations as the commandment to treat all religions with equal respect. The laws limited the ruler as much as the people—he should take no grand titles, but be known simply as Khan; he should not seize the property of a man dying without heirs, but see that it went to those who had looked after him; his soldiers should not be less than twenty years old. On the other hand the people should supply the Khan's needs from their surplus, and each tribe was obliged to send for his use horses, rams, milk and wool or woollen goods; and any man who left the military unit to which he was assigned was to be executed. Regulating all functions and duties, the *yasak* bound the Mongols into a single controlled unity. Of great importance historically was the law laying it down that on the death of the Khaghan (a title Genghis, of course, never used of himself) all the princes of the family should gather in a *kuriltai* [a meeting of Chiefs] to decide on the successor. The obligation to do this became a political focus of an intensity affecting not only Mongols but also at times their most distant neighbours.

To administer these laws a judge was needed, some man whom all could trust, whose uprightness and disinterestedness would be manifest to everyone. Genghis Khan picked Shigiku-tuku, grown into a man from the gold-braceleted orphan he had picked up so many years before among the tents of the defeated Tatars. It was he who, under the Khaghan, was responsible for the new ideals of honour and disciplined conduct that now spread astonishingly among these unlettered and superficially uncivilized tribes. Violence, robbery and theft all diminished, as did adultery, considered among these many-wived patriarchs to be a crime equal to any of the others. This was partly due to the stringency of the new juridical procedure: only those were found guilty who had been caught red-handed or had freely confessed. It may be that this diminished not so much the incidence of crime as that of criminals caught and punished, but it seems indisputable that for the ordinary tribesman, travelling across those endless pastures with his tent, his wagon, his family and his flocks, a new peace now brought him comfort. . . .

SEPARATE SPHERES FOR WOMEN AND MEN

To release his men for war (Genghis knew where his power lay) he gave women new and far-reaching responsibility over everything the family owned. Their bodies, on the other hand, belonged as before to their husbands; to take a lover was to court death as well as pleasure. The men, for their part, had at all times to be ready for war; their chieftains were to use peace as periods of training and the hunt as their training scheme, seeing to it that their men were prepared at any time to reach for weapons and horses and gallop away to the Khan's battles. It was the men's responsibility to see that their weapons were always keen, their bow-strings ready to be tautened, their quivers full of good straight arrows. It was the women who had to make sure of the rest of the war equipment—the sheepskin cloaks, the riding boots with their felt overshoes—and who saw to it that saddle bags were always filled with dried milk, curds and *koumiss* [fermented mare's milk]. The *touman* [army unit] of one tribe would then link with that of its neighbours into an army group, to which the Khaghan would appoint an *orlok* as commander. Because these groups knew one another and trained together, they answered swiftly to the orders they received. As to those orders, they were passed through a permanent committee of trusted leaders, what may be termed a general staff, and administered by lesser officers. Ordinary laws were enforced by a sort of police force that kept the highways safe and saw to it that lost or stolen beasts were restored to their owners—and also that such thieves as still took the sheep, cattle, camels or, perhaps worst of all, horses of their neighbours were punished, as the law decreed, by death.

MARCO POLO REPORTS ON THE GREAT KHAN

MARCO POLO

In 1271, a young Venetian merchant named Marco Polo traveled with his father and uncle across Asia to China. China was then ruled by the Mongol, or Yuan dynasty, and the emperor of China was also the Great Khan. Known as Kublai Khan, he was Genghis Khan's grandson. Marco Polo found favor with Kublai Khan, and for many years he worked as an official in the Chinese government. He did not return to Europe until 1295. While a prisoner of war for a brief period, Marco Polo told the stories of his travels to fellow inmates. One of them later published the stories as *The Travels of Marco Polo*. The book was to have a huge influence on European scholars and merchants, most of whom knew nothing of the Mongols or China aside from what they read in Marco Polo's account.

In the following selection, Marco Polo describes a court feast in Mongol China. Kublai Khan ruled from a huge palace in Kanbalu, a name Europeans later transliterated as "Xanadu," near modern-day Beijing. The palace was the setting for huge celebrations and lavish ceremonies, both of which involved elaborate rules of behavior.

W hen his Majesty holds a grand and public court, those who attend it are seated in the following order. The table of the sovereign is placed on an elevation, and he takes his seat on the northern side, with his face turned towards

From *The Travels of Marco Polo*, translated by W. Marsden, edited by Manuel Komroff (New York: Boni & Liveright, 1926).

the south; and next to him, on his left hand, sits the Empress. On his right hand are placed his sons, grandsons, and other persons connected with him by blood, upon seats somewhat lower, so that their heads are on a level with the Emperor's feet. The other princes and the nobility have their places at still lower tables; and the same rules are observed with respect to the females, the wives of the sons, grandsons, and other relatives of the Great Khan being seated on the left hand, at tables in like manner gradually lower; then follow the wives of the nobility and military officers: so that all are seated according to their respective ranks and dignities, in the places assigned to them, and to which they are entitled.

The tables are arranged in such a manner that the Great Khan, sitting on his elevated throne, can overlook the whole. It is not, however, to be understood that all who assemble on such occasions can be accommodated at tables. The greater part of the officers, and even of the nobles, on the contrary, eat, sitting upon carpets, in the halls; and on the outside stand a great multitude of persons who come from different countries, and bring with them many rare curiosities.

In the middle of the hall, where the Great Khan sits at table, there is a magnificent piece of furniture, made in the form of a square coffer, each side of which is three paces in length, exquisitely carved in figures of animals, and gilt. It is hollow within, for the purpose of receiving a capacious vase, of pure gold, calculated to hold many gallons. On each of its four sides stands a smaller vessel, containing about a hogshead, one of which is filled with mare's milk, another with that of the camel, and so of the others, according to the kinds of beverage in use. Within this buffet are also the cups or flagons belonging to his Majesty, for serving the liquors. Some of them are of beautiful gilt plate. Their size is such that, when filled with wine or other liquor, the quantity would be sufficient for eight or ten men.

Before every two persons who have seats at the tables, one of these flagons is placed, together with a kind of ladle, in the form of a cup with a handle, also of plate; to be used not only for taking the wine out of the flagon, but for lifting it to the head. This is observed as well with respect to the women as the men. The quantity and richness of the plate belonging to his Majesty is quite incredible.

KUBLAI KHAN'S RULES OF ETIQUETTE

Officers of rank are likewise appointed, whose duty it is to see that all strangers who happen to arrive at the time of the festival, and are unacquainted with the etiquette of the court, are suitably accommodated with places; and these stewards are continually visiting every part of the hall, inquiring of the guests if there is anything with which they are unprovided, or whether any of them wish for wine, milk, meat, or other articles, in which case it is immediately brought to them by the attendants.

At each door of the grand hall, or of whatever part the Great Khan happens to be in, stand two officers, of a gigantic figure, one on each side, with staves in their hands, for the purpose of preventing persons from touching the threshold with their feet, and obliging them to step beyond it. If by chance any one is guilty of this offence, these janitors take from him his garment, which he must redeem for money; or, when they do not take the garment, they inflict on him such number of blows as they have authority for doing. But, as strangers may be unacquainted with the prohibition, officers are appointed to introduce and warn them. This precaution is used because touching the threshold is regarded as a bad omen. In departing from the hall, as some of the company may be affected by the liquor, it is impossible to guard against the accident, and the order is not then strictly enforced.

The numerous persons who attend at the sideboard of his Majesty, and who serve him with victuals and drink, are all obliged to cover their noses and mouths with handsome veils or cloths of worked silk, in order that his victuals or his wine may not be affected by their breath. When drink is called for by him, and the page in waiting has presented it, he retires three paces and kneels down, upon which the courtiers, and all who are present, in like manner make their prostration. At the same moment all the musical instruments, of which there is a numerous band, begin to play, and continue to do so until he has ceased drinking, when all the company recover their posture. This reverential salutation is made as often as his Majesty drinks. It is unnecessary to say anything of the victuals, because it may well be imagined that their abundance is excessive.

When the repast is finished, and the tables have been removed, persons of various descriptions enter the hall, and amongst these a troop of comedians and performers on different instruments. Also tumblers and jugglers, who exhibit their skill in the presence of the Great Khan, to the high amusement and gratification of all the spectators. When these sports are concluded, the people separate, and each returns to his own house.

Medieval Europe Reaches Out: The Crusades

CHAPTER 7

THE CRUSADES REFLECTED EUROPEAN REVIVAL

JOSEPH R. STRAYER

Compared with China or the Islamic world, Europe was a backward civilization for much of the Middle Ages. Aside from a brief flowering of empire and culture under Charlemagne in the late eighth and early ninth centuries, Europe remained disunited, primitive, and mostly illiterate between the fall of the Roman Empire and the year 1000. The Roman Catholic Church and its leader, the pope, dominated much of European life, but even Christianity had yet to reach all people.

Beginning in the tenth century, however, European civilization began to revive. Stable kingdoms started to emerge in England, France, and Germany. Italian city-states such as Venice began to engage in trade with both the Islamic world and Byzantine Christians. Furthermore, as Joseph R. Strayer explains in the following selection, the Roman Catholic Church increased its influence, freeing itself from the control of warring Germanic nobles and asserting its authority over all Christians. Reformed monasteries, such as Cluny in France, led the way.

Pope Urban II's Call to Crusade in 1095 was a strong reflection of the new power of the church. The pope asked all Christians to forsake their homelands in order to save Jerusalem from Turkish Muslim conquerors. Thousands obeyed him, setting off nearly two centuries of Crusades to the Holy Land. Only the First Crusade, however, achieved significant success, establishing a string of crusader states in the Middle East and, in 1099, conquering Jerusalem. According to Strayer, intense faith allowed the cru-

From *Western Europe in the Middle Ages: A Short History*, by Joseph R. Strayer (New York: Appleton-Century-Crofts, 1955).

saders to take Jerusalem and, in turn, the conquest of Jerusalem gave Europeans a new sense of confidence.

Joseph R. Strayer was professor of history at Princeton University.

A religious revival accompanied and stimulated the political revival. The importance of this movement is easily overlooked, but it is one of the most significant developments of this transitional period. Europe had been nominally Christian since the Late Roman Empire, but the intensity of religious conviction was at first not very great. Barbarians who had been converted *en masse* and country-dwellers who seldom saw a priest were not much influenced by the teachings of the Church. The establishment of a parish system, which brought everyone into regular and frequent contact with the clergy, was the answer to these difficulties, but the parish system spread slowly, and was not fully established until the Carolingian period. Then the ninth-century invasions brought in new barbarians, and destroyed parish churches in many places. As a result, it was not until the late tenth century that the Church had steady, uninterrupted contact with most of the people of Western Europe, and it was only then that Christianity began to exert its full effect on Western men. It got under their skins; it was no longer a matter of external forms and ceremonies, but a matter of personal conviction. People began to worry more about making their behavior conform to Christian standards; they were more willing to follow the leadership of the Church. . . .

THE CHURCH REFORMED ITSELF WITH POPULAR SUPPORT

The reform movement in the Church, which attempted to free the clergy from worldly ties, could never have succeeded without popular support. The German emperors were forced to yield much of their control over the Church because public opinion turned against them. The peace movement, which attempted to suppress or mitigate the senseless violence of feudal war, was led by churchmen, but would have had no strength without the support of laymen of all classes. There was a great increase in gifts to churches and monasteries, and an equally large increase in the number of people taking religious vows. The old established monasteries were no longer strict enough to satisfy some of the converts; new orders were founded which made greater demands on their members. The first great reformed order was that of Cluny, founded in 910. With hundreds of monasteries scattered through Europe, it played an important role in the eleventh-century quarrel between Church and Empire. Later came the Carthusians, who lived as hermits in isolated cells and met only for religious services. The Cistercians, founded at the end of the eleventh century, refused to own serfs, and cleared waste land with their own hands. Fervor and piety gave the new orders great prestige; the most influential men in the West during the late eleventh and early twelfth centuries were the abbots of the great reformed monasteries.

The most spectacular result of the religious revival was the First Crusade. It was a demonstration of papal leadership, a manifestation of popular piety, and an indication of the growing self-confidence of Western Europe. Europe no longer waited in anguish for an attack from outside enemies. Now, for the first time, it took the initiative and sent its armies far into the lands of two great Eastern civilizations. It took courage to do this, and the courage was based on the absolute conviction that the Crusade was the will of God.

POPE URBAN II'S CALL TO CRUSADE

We shall never know with certainty why Urban II proclaimed the Crusade at Clermont in 1095. Many things distressed him, and the Crusade was a solution to many of his problems. The Mohammedan caliphate had broken up into a group of quarreling states, and access to Jerusalem was no longer easy to Christian pilgrims as it had been in the days of the great caliphs. A military expedition could take advantage of the fragmentation of Moslem power and end the scandal of infidel domination of the Holy Places. The Eastern Church had broken with Rome in 1054 and the Eastern Empire had been badly defeated by the Turks at Manzikert in 1071. A military expedition could strengthen the Byzantine bulwark, thus giving protection to the West, and the Eastern Emperor might show his gratitude by urging the reunion of the two Churches. In the West the struggle with Henry IV was still going on, and the German ruler was having considerable success in Italy. The Crusade could add to papal prestige; it could prove that the pope, not the emperor, was the leader of Western Christendom. Finally, it should not be forgotten that the Council of Clermont began with a discussion of the peace movement and that the Crusade had a very direct connection with the peace movement: it removed a large number of quarrelsome men from Europe.

Whatever the pope's calculations, the response to his appeal was based largely on simple piety. The Crusade was the greatest of all pilgrimages, the most efficacious of all penances, and most

Crusaders sought only spiritual benefits from the expedition. If a mere visit to Jerusalem were sufficient penance for the deepest sins, how much greater the reward for those who freed the Holy Places from infidel domination. Even the feudal adventurers who joined the Crusade hoping for lands and booty were not immune to these ideas. They gained their lands, but they too made the pilgrimage to the Holy Sepulchre and bathed in the waters of Jordan.

The Crusaders needed intense faith to attain their objective. Almost everything else was against them—their ignorance of the geography and politics of the Near East, their lack of experience in organizing large armies, their suspicions of each other and of their nominal allies, the Orthodox Christians of the East. The first Crusaders who reached Asia Minor—mostly unarmed pilgrims guarded by a handful of poor knights—were massacred by the Turks. The real armies, led by the great lords of France, western Germany, and Norman Italy, were not quite so helpless, but they suffered severely during the long years of fighting and marching. They were almost defeated by the Turks in crossing Asia Minor; they almost starved during the siege of the great fortress city of Antioch. They were saved by the fact that the feudal army was invincible when it had anything like decent leadership and by the sharp divisions among their opponents. A great victory over a Moslem army at Antioch opened the way to Jerusalem, and the Holy City fell to the Crusaders in July 1099—almost four years after the Council of Clermont and three years after the main armies had started their journey to the East.

THE FIRST CRUSADE CONQUERS JERUSALEM

The success of the Crusade had a tremendous moral effect on Europe. There were already some reasons for optimism, but they were based on small, local, unspectacular gains. Now an almost impossible task had been accomplished, and everyone in Europe was aware of it. God had set them the task, and God had given them the strength to perform it. It is not surprising that there was an increase in confidence, in self-assurance, in optimism in twelfth-century Europe.

Even more important, the successful Crusade, following the successful reform movement and the successful struggle with the Empire, firmly established the leadership of the Church. From the late eleventh well into the thirteenth century, the Church set the goals and fixed the standards for Western European society. This was leadership and not dictatorship; the Church did not and could not control all secular interests and activities. Loyalty to the Church was like patriotism today; it was taken for granted, and therefore ignored, in the ordinary transactions of daily life.

Men were selfish in the Middle Ages as they are selfish now; they sought power and profit for themselves without considering the general welfare. But, just as the most corrupt politician or predatory business man of today can hardly defy openly the national interest, so the barons and the townsmen of the Middle Ages found it difficult to defy the Church. They had to conform, at least outwardly; they could not pursue indefinitely lines of conduct which the Church condemned. And the completely selfish man was rare, then as now. Most people had some tincture of religious idealism, some generous impulses which they followed occasionally. They accepted the leadership of the Church, not because they feared hell, but because it made them feel better when they conformed to the ideals of their society. By conforming they could overcome their feeling of personal insignificance; they could become fellow-workers in the divine plan for the world. The leadership of the Church was accepted because it gave meaning to life. And it was because they had leadership and were sure that life had meaning that men of the twelfth century could achieve so much.

THE CRUSADES: A GREAT CLASH OF CULTURES

ALFRED DUGGAN

When western European Catholic nobles set out for the Holy Land on the Crusades, they could not know that they were bringing about a major clash of three cultures. Western Christendom was setting itself on equal terms with the Eastern Christendom of the Byzantine Empire, which had always looked on western Europe as barbaric and heretical. Meanwhile, the Turks who controlled Jerusalem, and whose successes against the Byzantines inspired the Crusades, were newcomers to both Islam and the Middle East, although they had proven their mettle against local Arabs on the battlefield.

In the following selection, Alfred Duggan traces the development of all three cultures—the western Christian, the eastern Christian, and the Islamic—focusing on political as well as religious change. Religious differences kept the Christians of east and west apart, particularly after the pope excommunicated the head of the eastern church in 1054. Nonetheless, political developments could trump religious ones, as Duggan notes. When the Byzantine emperor Alexius sought military help against the Turks, he recalled the fierceness of the Norman nobles of the west.

A historical novelist, Alfred Duggan is also the author of a number of nonfiction histories.

From *The Story of the Crusades, 1097–1291*, by Alfred Duggan. Copyright © 1963 by Alfred Duggan. Used by permission of Pantheon Books, a division of Random House, Inc., and of Faber & Faber, London.

Ever since the Church was founded at the first Pentecost there have been Christians in Jerusalem; though sometimes they took refuge in the countryside while the Holy City was attacked by hostile armies. In particular two Jewish revolts against Rome brought terrible retribution. In A.D. 71 the Temple was destroyed after a bitter and destructive siege; in A.D. 135 the Emperor Hadrian rebuilt captured Jerusalem as a normal Roman town, with temples in which the usual Roman gods were worshipped. But the Church endured. There has always been a Bishop, successor to St James; and a congregation, however small, for him to rule.

Therefore when the Emperor Constantine recognised Christianity as the official religion of the Roman Empire, some 300 years after the Passion [Christ's crucifixion], the sites of the main Holy Places were still remembered; just as we can still identify the sites burned in the Great Fire of London, 300 years ago. Constantine's mother, St Helena, could go straight to Calvary, where she dug up the True Cross. The well-remembered tomb where the Body of God had lain for three days is so near the place of Crucifixion that she was able to include both under the roof of a mighty Roman basilica, the Church of the Holy Sepulchre. A new city-wall was built out to the north to include this great shrine; for Calvary, like most places of execution, was originally outside the city. About the same time the Church of the Nativity was built at Bethlehem; and other Holy Places, some of less certain authenticity, were worthily commemorated. Pilgrims came to Jerusalem from all parts of the Roman Empire, as they have come ever since to this day.

The Emperor Constantine also founded a new capital at the city of Byzantium, renamed Constantinople in his honour. But by about the year 400 it was recognised that the troubles of the time were too grave to be dealt with by one sovereign, and the Empire was divided. The lands west of the Adriatic were ruled by an Emperor whose capital was nominally Rome, though in fact he lived at Ravenna; the Balkans and Asia Minor were ruled by the Emperor in Constantinople.

The western Empire was overrun by warlike barbarians, our ancestors. But the eastern Empire flourished until by the year 600 Constantinople ruled all the Greek lands of Europe and Asia, and in addition southern Italy and the north African coast right up to Morocco. The Emperor of Constantinople was by far the most powerful monarch in the known world; his only rival was the Emperor of pagan Persia, on his eastern frontier.

The east-Romans were devout Christians; though in Egypt and Syria the natives supported heretical sects because they disliked being ruled by Bishops sent from Constantinople. But the organisation of the eastern Church, whose liturgy was said in Greek, differed greatly from that of the west, whose Mass was said in Latin. In the west all Christians obeyed the Pope, who represented among other things the vanished civilisation of Rome; in Constantinople the unquestioned head of the Church was the Emperor, who bore among his official titles that of Isapostolos, Equal to the Apostles. He appointed the Patriarchs of Jerusalem, Antioch, Alexandria and Constantinople, and might dismiss them at his whim. The Greeks agreed that the Pope was the senior Patriarch, but they would not take orders from him alone. They held that doctrine should be settled by a General Council, or at least by an agreement of the five Patriarchs; and that in matters of discipline their Emperor was supreme. Unfortunately the Empire was not hereditary. In theory the Emperor was elected by the people and the army; in practice he was often a successful soldier who had seized power by murdering his superior officer. Fear of rebellion might make him a cruel tyrant; and the more competent soldier-Emperors knew little of Church affairs.

In 610 the Persians invaded the Empire. In 614 they captured Jerusalem, with help from the large Jewish community within the city. Sixty-five thousand Christians were massacred, and the thirty-five thousand survivors sold into slavery. The Persians burned the Church of the Holy Sepulchre, and carried off the True Cross as a trophy of victory. In 630, after years of bitter fighting, the Emperor Heraclius defeated them and forced them to return the True Cross. A large part of it was sent back to Jerusalem; though to avoid another such disaster portions were sent to Constantinople and Rome. From these fragments many tiny splinters have been taken, the relics now venerated in churches all over the world.

For his liberation of Jerusalem Heraclius was reverenced by posterity as the first Crusader. But the war had continued for nineteen years, with appalling devastation from the Bosphorus right up to Mesopotamia. Both Persia and the Empire were greatly weakened.

THE RISE OF ISLAM

Meanwhile, in 622, Mahomet [Muhammad] began to preach among the Arabs. When he died ten years later Islam was supreme in Arabia. The Moslems appointed as the successor of Mahomet a Caliph, a supreme temporal and religious ruler, and under his guidance set out to conquer the world.

They met with amazing success. Both the east-Romans and the Persians were too war-weary to undertake another long struggle. In 638 Jerusalem surrendered to the Caliph Omar. By 717 the Moslems had conquered the whole northern coastline of Africa, southern Spain, the Persian Empire and the eastern lands as far as India. But after the Moslem invasion had reached the very walls of Constantinople the east-Romans rallied; in Asia Minor the frontier of Christendom was fixed at the Taurus Mountains. Though the Caliph was now the most powerful ruler in the world the Emperor in Constantinople was still the most powerful Christian ruler.

In Jerusalem the Church survived. As well as a creed, Mahomet had laid down a code of laws for his followers, and in it he made provision for conquered peoples who would not accept Islam. For idolaters there was no mercy; conversion or death were the alternatives. But those who worshipped One God, the Peoples of the Book—Zoroastrians, Jews, and Christians—might live in peace under Moslem masters. Of course they must accept certain disabilities. They must pay an annual tax for the privilege of being left alive; they might never ride a horse nor carry a weapon; they might not convert a Moslem nor marry a Moslem girl, though Moslems might take Christian girls by force into their harems. Existing churches, including the Church of the Holy Sepulchre, remained Christian, but no new ones might be built. (This rule could be dodged by judicious bribery.) Disputes between Christians were judged by their own clergy, who were held responsible for the good behaviour of the laity and hanged if their flock rebelled. Such a life was not intolerable, and the Christians of Syria tolerated it; except for the mountaineers of Lebanon who became defiant Christian rebels. But these mountaineers had usually been in rebellion against the tax-collector from the plain.

The Christians of Syria and Palestine still regarded the Emperor in Constantinople as the head of their church. The Caliphs respected his military power, and heeded his protests on behalf of his fellow-Christians. Pilgrims continued to visit Jerusalem, welcomed by the Moslem rulers for the money they brought into the country.

CHANGES THROUGHOUT THE REGION

In 800 the Pope crowned Charlemagne as Emperor. This new Empire naturally annoyed the Greeks, as we may now call the east-Romans. So Charlemagne negotiated directly with the Caliph Haroun al Raschid, who recognised him as protector of Latin pilgrims and allowed him to set up Latin hostels in Jerusalem for their convenience.

In the 10th century the Greeks grew stronger. They reconquered Cilicia and in 969 took the great city of Antioch. By this time there was no single Caliph ruling the whole Moslem world. A Caliph in Baghdad reigned over Mesopotamia and the east, while a Caliph in Cairo was obeyed by Africa; but both these Caliphs were spiritual figureheads whose power was wielded by the commanders of their armies.

In 1004 the Caliph of Cairo, Hakim, went mad. In an effort to extirpate Christianity he ordered the destruction of the Church of the Holy Sepulchre. But soon after he proclaimed himself to be God, and his Moslem subjects got rid of him. The Greek Emperor was permitted to rebuild the Holy Sepulchre and all went on as before; except that the Druze community among the mountains of Syria still worship Hakim and wait for him to come again.

By 1050 western pilgrims were visiting Jerusalem in large numbers. The journey was reasonably safe, by the standards of those days. The Hungarians and the Poles had been recently converted. A German had only to travel down the Danube, among Christians, until he entered the Greek Empire at Belgrade; then the Emperor's police would guard him until he reached Antioch. At the Syrian frontier he bought a safe-conduct from the officials of the Egyptian Caliph, who policed the road as far as the Holy Places. From France or England the normal route was by way of Rome to Bari, the capital of the Greek province of Italy, and then across the Adriatic to Durazzo at the head of the great road to Constantinople. Of course such a long journey had its hazards, and the expense was very great. A pilgrimage to Jerusalem, imposed as a penance, got rid of a disturber of the peace for at least a couple of years; and by the time he came back he would be too poor to make trouble. Sweyn Godwinsson [brother of Harold, King of England] was ordered to make the journey as a penance for his many crimes; in 1052, on his way back, he died of exposure among the mountains of Asia. But Nature was the most dangerous enemy; both Greeks and Moslems welcomed Latin pilgrims.

THE NORMANS AND THE TURKS

Two migrations broke up this peaceful arrangement. The Normans had a particular devotion to the warrior-angel St Michael, whose most famous shrine is on Monte Gargano in southern Italy. They went there in great numbers and presently intervened in the struggle between the Italian cities and their Greek governors. By 1059 the Pope had recognised the Norman leader Robert Guiscard as Duke of Apulia and Calabria, and Robert's brother Roger was campaigning against the Moslem rulers of Sicily.

Later the Normans crossed the Adriatic to pursue the war against the Emperor from whom they had conquered southern Italy. In Greece they won no permanent foothold, but they showed themselves to be dangerous neighbours. In Constantinople, where no one had hitherto bothered about barbarous

Latins, the Normans were feared.

About the same time, the 1050s, the Turks appeared in Asia Minor. They were nomads from the steppe, moving south to pillage civilisation. They had recently become Moslems, though they were not yet strongly attached to their faith; they could sometimes be converted to Christianity, which could never be done with genuine Arab Moslems.

These uncouth Turks were awed by the superior culture of Baghdad. They could have overthrown the Caliph, but they preferred to be his servants; so long, of course, as the Caliph did what his servants told him. A Caliph who annoyed his Turkish advisers would be put away, and another Caliph chosen from the correct Arab family.

Turkish raids into the Greek Empire became more and more serious. All the raiders were mounted, usually driving a herd of spare horses, and the excellent Greek regular army seldom caught them before they had done grave damage. At last the Emperor Romanus Diogenes made up his mind that the only thing to do was to march east and fight a decisive battle with the Sultan of all the Turks wherever he might find him. In August 1071 the two armies met at Manzikert on the eastern frontier of the Empire near Lake Van.

THE BATTLE OF MANZIKERT

The Emperor brought all the soldiers he could scrape together, perhaps as many as 100,000 horse. About half were drilled and disciplined heavy cavalry; the other half were the private retainers of noble families. The great weakness of the Empire was the lack of a true royal house, so that any famous general might snatch at the crown. Romanus, himself a famous general, had married the widow of the last Emperor; his young stepson Michael Ducas would share the throne when he came of age, unless in the meantime Romanus won such a great victory that his subjects begged him to reign alone. That was one reason why he wanted to fight a decisive battle. His second in command was Andronicus Ducas, a noble so powerful that the Emperor dared not leave him behind in Constantinople, and so well born that if he were present with the army he must hold a high command.

After a morning of hard fighting the Greeks began to give ground. They might have got away in good order, but Andronicus thought more of the interests of the house of Ducas than of the well-being of the Empire. He ordered the second line to retire, leaving the Emperor and his regular cavalry surrounded by the Turks. Romanus was wounded and captured.

The Empire never recovered from Manzikert. The regular

army had been destroyed, and every surviving senior officer tried to win the throne for himself. Romanus bought his freedom, which made things worse by increasing the number of pretenders. Turkish bands roamed through Asia Minor, destroying the farms and killing the peasants until the richest and most populous part of the Empire had become a desert. For a time the great walled cities held out; but their garrisons no longer took orders from Constantinople, where rival Emperors continually rose and fell. The Turks entered Nicaea as mercenaries of a pretender; after he had been defeated they remained. Another Turkish chieftain gained possession of Smyrna and began to build a pirate fleet. The great fortress of Antioch was ruled by an Armenian general in the Greek army, who to keep it paid tribute to the Turks. In 1085 his son sold the city to the infidel. Other Armenian princes moved into the mountains of Taurus and took over the fortresses of Cilicia. The Armenians, a warlike race, were Christian heretics. The King of Armenia had established Christianity in his realm a few years before it became the religion of the Roman Empire, and the Armenians have never forgotten that theirs was the first Christian state. They would rather pay tribute to the infidel and keep their ancient creed than obey the Greek Orthodox Patriarch of Constantinople.

During all this chaos and destruction there occurred an odd little incident. Before Manzikert, Romanus had hired a band of Norman mercenaries from Italy, led by a knight named Roussel de Balliol. They escaped the battle because they were besieging a nearby fortress. After the disaster Roussel established himself as independent ruler of the city of Amasia in Pontus. His government was so just, orderly and cheap that his Greek subjects preferred him to their own Emperor. A young Greek noble, Alexius Comnenus, was sent to suppress him. Alexius had to give out that he had blinded his prisoner to stop the Amasians continuing to fight for their Norman lord. Roussel was not in fact blinded, because Alexius also admired and liked him. It seemed that Latins, especially Normans, might be a grave danger to the Empire. Given the choice, Greeks of the Orthodox faith would rather be ruled by Latin Normans than by their own extortionate governors.

In 1054 the Pope excommunicated the Patriarch of Constantinople, and the Orthodox Church has remained in schism ever since. At the time it was seen as a personal quarrel between two angry prelates, a quarrel that would soon be healed. It did not affect the other Patriarchates, Jerusalem, Antioch and Alexandria, whose subjects remained in communion with both Rome and Constantinople.

Asia Minor was infested with Turkish bands. In Syria every

city was ruled by a different Arab or Turkish chieftain. The mountains were held by Armenian nobles. Each of these rulers was at war with all the others. Jerusalem was fairly well governed by the officers of the Egyptian Caliph, but it was impossible for a pilgrim to get there from the west.

In 1081 Alexius Comnenus became Emperor of Constantinople. He had no soldiers except foreign mercenaries; in Asia Minor he held nothing but a few scattered seaports; the Normans of Italy menaced his European possessions. But he still had a great deal of money, and he was a very intelligent statesman. Above all, he was a patriot, who thought first of the welfare of his Empire. He was not interested in the fate of the Holy Places, save in so far as they might be useful to his own country.

In the spring of 1095 Pope Urban II held a council at Piacenza in northern Italy. . . .

A Plea for Help

Now that the mighty Turkish horde had split up into numerous bands the Emperor Alexius hoped to go over to the offensive. But he lacked soldiers. The trained regular army which had been destroyed 25 years ago at Manzikert had never been replaced because its recruits came from Asia Minor, now devastated by the Turks. Alexius, who had plenty of money, relied on foreign mercenaries, either heathen Patzinak horse-bowmen from the steppe, or the Varangian Guard of Scandinavians and English who fought on foot with two-handed axes. He had no heavy cavalry, and perhaps he remembered how formidable had been the Norman knights who followed Roussel de Balliol. He asked the Pope to proclaim to the council that knights would be serving God if they took service with the Greek army in defence of the oppressed Christians of Asia Minor. Alexius did not forget that he was the head of a church which had broken away from the Pope. He explained that he could not now heal the schism, for if he ordered his subjects to submit to Rome they would overthrow him. Of course after he had conquered the Turks he would be more powerful, able to compel even his bishops to do as he said. In the meantime his Latin mercenaries might bring their own priests. . . . Alexius was always quite willing to heal the schism if the Pope would meet him halfway. No Greek understood that the Pope cannot go halfway to compromise with error.

Urban promised to ask for recruits at a convenient opportunity. He was all the more willing because he feared that Constantinople was not so strong as its Emperor supposed. At any moment the Turks might break in; and then they would be on the borders of the Latin west, his own responsibility.

MOST CRUSADES WERE FAILURES

JOSEPH DAHMUS

After the First Crusade (1096–1099), which captured Jerusalem and established a number of crusader kingdoms in the Middle East, Crusades to the Holy Land were called at intervals for nearly two hundred years. As Joseph Dahmus points out in the following selection, most of the later Crusades were designed to either recapture or maintain control of Jerusalem, and virtually all of them failed. The last of the crusader kingdoms, Acre, was lost to the Turks in 1291.

Many reasons account for the failures of the Crusades. European nobles had been forced to pledge their loyalty to the Byzantine emperor, but they rarely observed the pledge. This led to constant conflicts over territory and tribute, and finally, in the Fourth Crusade, to crusaders meddling in Byzantine politics. More significantly, however, crusaders began to face revived Muslim armies, particularly those led by Saladin, an Egyptian noble who ultimately dominated the entire Middle East. As Dahmus points out, the Third Crusade led by, among others, King Richard the Lion-Heart of England, was unable to defeat Saladin.

Joseph Dahmus is professor emeritus of history at Pennsylvania State University.

During the course of the [First] crusade, Western leaders committed many errors, although none so great as the manner in which they disposed of the territories they conquered from the Turks and Fatimids. At Constantinople they had agreed to hold what territories they might conquer in the name of

From *The Middle Ages: A Popular History*, by Joseph Dahmus. Copyright © 1968 by Joseph Dahmus. Used by permission of Doubleday, a division of Random House, Inc.

the Byzantine emperor. And they had not objected when Alexius took over Nicaea. As they moved farther away from Constantinople, however, particularly following Alexius' failure to relieve them in their desperate straits before Antioch, the feeling grew general that the emperor had forfeited any hold he might have had over them. What lands they might seize they would keep for themselves. So they set up four states from the land they conquered. These included the County of Tripoli, the County of Edessa, the Principality of Antioch, and the Kingdom of Jerusalem. All four were held independently of the Byzantine emperor. The result was a deepening of the suspicion that had already existed between the emperor and the crusaders, which in turn sharply reduced the potential success of subsequent crusades.

THE SECOND CRUSADE FAILS

This friction between Constantinople and the crusaders contributed to the dismal failure of the Second Crusade. What prompted this crusade was the fall of Edessa to the Turks in 1144 and the threat which resurgent Turkish power held for the other Christian states to the south. Pope Eugenius took the lead in arousing Europe and prevailed upon St. Bernard, which was not easy, to preach the crusade. Bernard, who objected to the use of force, even against heretics, to bring men to the belief of the Christian God, must have gone through much soul-searching before agreeing to the assignment. And the failure of the crusade may have convinced him that he was right in the first place to oppose the idea. Two kings, Louis VII of France and Conrad III of Germany, hearkened to Bernard's eloquence. Only a saint like Bernard, so Conrad declared, could have persuaded him to go. He, too, must have had afterthoughts. The armies moved separately over the route followed by the First Crusade. At Dorylaeum the Turks mauled Conrad's army so severely that it ceased being an effective force. Conrad and what was left of his army joined Louis, then moved down to Attalia where the two kings took ship to Antioch. The ships that the Byzantine emperor Manuel should have supplied to ferry the army across never showed up, so the Turks cut them to pieces.

Western writers blame the perfidy of Byzantium for the failure of this crusade, although Manuel could argue that the crusaders were interested only in their own states; that open assistance would involve him with his Turkish neighbors; furthermore, that the Christian Normans were planning an attack on his own territories in Greece. A last desperate and foolhardy attack on Damascus by remnants of the crusading army and local Christian knights failed with heavy losses. The only positive consequence of the Second Crusade came over in Portugal. There a fleet of crusaders from England, the Low Countries, Germany, and Scandinavia stopped to assist a local Christian count to capture Lisbon and lay the foundations of modern Portugal.

RESPONDING TO SALADIN'S RECONQUEST OF JERUSALEM

The Third Crusade (1189–1192) was the Christian West's response to the fall of Jerusalem. The man responsible for the new threat in the East was Saladin, vizier of Egypt, who had overrun Syria after annihilating a crusading army at Hattin in July 1186. Jerusalem fell to him a year later. This crusade is the best known of the seven or more major expeditions which the West fitted out to take or hold Jerusalem, thanks to the presence of Saladin, three European kings who took part, and the manner Sir Walter Scott and other writers have woven the subject with romance. Frederick Barbarossa, king of Germany and Holy Roman emperor, led an army from Germany along the old pilgrim road through the Balkans. Richard the Lion-Hearted, king of England, and Philip Augustus, king of France, took ship directly to Acre. Religious motives may have warmed Frederick's soul. Philip Augustus went because it was the proper thing to do, while Richard hoped for military glory. Saladin was most concerned about the powerful army Frederick was bringing through Anatolia, and well he might. Had Frederick reached Syria, the Third Crusade would in all probability have gone down in history as the most successful of the crusades. But Frederick was drowned while crossing the Seleph River in Asia Minor, and only a portion of his forces ever reached Acre. There the two constantly quarreling kings, Philip and Richard, scored their greatest success when they captured the city in July 1191. Philip returned to France shortly after, and although Richard defeated Saladin on several occasions, he lacked the manpower and siege equipment to take Jerusalem. So the two finally drew up a treaty which reconstituted part of the kingdom of Jerusalem and permitted Christian pilgrims free access to the city.

The Fourth Crusade (1202–1204), which followed ten years after the Third, was the work of Pope Innocent III. No kings responded to his appeal. Richard and Philip were busily fighting over Normandy, while Germany had no king at all. Still, a good many knights indicated their willingness to take up the cross, and Innocent's hopes were high. According to plans, the crusaders were to gather in Venice, which had contracted to transport them to Egypt. Unfortunately, many knights took ship at other Italian ports, and only a third of the expected thirty-five thousand men showed up at Venice. These, Venice refused to transport to the

East until the full eighty-five thousand marks which had been promised were delivered. So the crusaders and Venetians argued and haggled. Finally, it was agreed that in return for the crusaders' assistance in capturing Zara, which belonged to the Christian king of Hungary, Venice would advance the necessary credit. After a few days of fighting, the crusaders and Venetians captured and pillaged Zara, much to the indignation of Pope Innocent, who excommunicated them all when he learned of it.

Meantime Alexius, son of the deposed Byzantine emperor, had been attempting to convince the crusaders that they should help him and his father to get back in control in Constantinople. He would contribute a huge amount of money to the cause, an army of ten thousand men, even heal the schism, if they would help him. Some of the crusaders refused to consider the offer and left directly for Syria. But the majority accepted Alexius' proposal, stormed Constantinople, and restored his father to his throne. Then during the winter months while the crusaders waited for spring before proceeding on to Syria, a revolt took place in the city, Alexius was strangled (his father had died), and a new emperor acclaimed. This provided the Venetians their opportunity. Under their prodding the crusaders attacked the city a second time, captured it, then for three days subjected it to one of the most savage lootings in the history of warfare. Pope Innocent, who was not wholly disappointed over the miscarriage of the crusade since the schism was now ended, accepted the new Latin empire as a papal fief and set about organizing a new expedition.

Although the cultural and economic impact of the Crusades was profound, the crusaders were often unsuccessful in their attempts to maintain or recapture Jerusalem.

THE CHILDREN'S CRUSADE

Before this Fifth Crusade materialized, the strange, tragic episode of the Children's Crusade intervened. During the summer of 1212 a shepherd boy by the name of Stephen came to Philip Augustus with a letter he claimed he had received from Christ. According to the letter Stephen was to lead a crusade of children to Syria, that God would show his favor by opening up the Mediterranean and provide them dry passage to Jerusalem. Philip told the boy to go back to his sheep, but he refused, stayed on and preached. Within a few weeks many thousands of children, perhaps as many as thirty thousand, most of them twelve years old and younger, had gathered at Vendôme. From there they trudged southward to Marseilles with Stephen riding along in his cart. When the sea did not open up, a fortunate few managed to make their way back home. The majority crowded into seven vessels and ended up in the slave markets of Islam. A similar movement in Germany, this one headed by a Nicholas, recruited somewhat older children, including a sprinkling of what the modern world might classify as juvenile delinquents. This group made its way to Genoa and Pisa, but again the sea refused to open up. Some of the youths stayed and made their home in Italy. Two shiploads of them left port and were never heard from again. A few made it back to Germany where irate parents hanged the father of Nicholas for having permitted his son to dupe their young ones.

Two years after Pope Innocent's death, the Fifth Crusade (1218–1221) began its equally futile course. The Fourth had planned to land in Egypt; this one did, and during the summer months of 1218 a powerful host gathered there recruited from many countries of Europe and from Acre as well. Egypt was in a weakened condition, and its sultan was old and tired. Had the crusading army possessed one capable leader in place of the half-dozen who aspired to that position, the crusaders might have been able to conquer the delta region and Cairo. But "sane counsel," as the chronicler wrote, "was far removed from our leaders," which was especially true of the papal legate Pelagius who usually had his way. They did occupy Damietta, which the sultan did not attempt to hold, but they turned down his offer of Jerusalem in return for their evacuating his country. Without the surrounding fortresses, the Templars and others argued, Jerusalem could never be held. In July 1221 an army of some fifty thousand men advanced up the Nile despite a warning that the river, which was nearing flood stage, would imperil their retreat should this become necessary. Within a few days the crusaders found themselves completely cut off by the Nile and the Egyptian fleet. The humane sultan agreed to let them go home.

Many people, including the pope, placed the onus for the failure of this crusade on Frederick II of Germany, who had kept promising to join the army in Egypt. In 1227 Frederick was finally ready to go, and in September an army of some forty thousand men embarked with him from Brindisi. Dysentery had already caused many of the knights who had gathered at Brindisi to succumb, so when Frederick became ill, he promptly turned back and retired to a spa to recuperate. When Pope Gregory IX, who had good reason to mistrust Frederick, learned of his action, he excommunicated him for again reneging on his promise. In 1228 Frederick did finally go, regardless of his excommunicate condition, less as a crusader, however, than as a claimant to the kingdom of Jerusalem through its heiress whom he had married. One of the reasons he had delayed going up to this time had been to permit negotiations to mature which he was conducting with the sultan of Egypt. The sultan had an admiration for Frederick and had also need for Frederick's alliance against the sultan of Damascus. So he promised him Jerusalem and other cities, but then the sultan of Damascus died, and Frederick found his bargaining value reduced to zero. However, the sultan agreed to honor part of his promise—had he done more his subjects would have overthrown him—and by the Treaty of Jaffa (1229) turned over Jerusalem and Bethlehem together with a corridor to the sea. Moslems were to retain free access to their shrines in Jerusalem.

THE END OF CRUSADES TO THE HOLY LAND

Christians retained control of Jerusalem until 1244 when the Khwarizmian Turks, in alliance with Egypt, captured the city. The fall of Jerusalem prompted Louis IX of France to undertake what proved the last major crusade (1248–1254). He landed a powerful army in Egypt, but there suffered the same fate that had ended the Fifth Crusade. Since the resources of the entire eastern Mediterranean had been drawn upon to the point of exhaustion to fit out this expedition, its destruction constituted a near-fatal blow to the Christian position in Syria. For four years after his release as a prisoner of the sultan of Egypt, Louis remained in the East in order to reorganize the defenses of what remained of Christian territories, even though there was desperate need for him back in France. In 1270 Louis undertook a second crusade which his Machiavellian brother, Charles of Anjou, persuaded him to lead against Tunis, rather than Syria (or Egypt), because of his interests in the area. Louis and a large part of his army died in Tunis of dysentery. In 1291 Acre and what remained of the crusading states fell to the Turks, although Cyprus remained in Western hands until the latter half of the sixteenth century. . . .

The Crusades extended over the greater part of the twelfth and thirteenth centuries. In the judgment of many scholars, these were the most progressive of the Middle Ages, the centuries when western Europe made its greatest advances in economic, political, and cultural growth. In view of the hundreds of thousands of men and women who participated directly and indirectly in these military operations, of the many popes and churchmen, of the kings and scores of powerful lords who took part, of the Italian cities which capitalized on the expeditions, it is not too much to affirm that the Crusades exerted a profound influence upon the economic, political, and cultural developments which took place during those centuries.

A BYZANTINE PRINCESS COMMENTS ON THE CRUSADES

ANNA COMNENA

Pope Urban II, who called the First Crusade in 1095, was responding to a plea for military assistance from the Byzantine emperor, Alexius. Alexius was facing a new Islamic threat, the Seljuk Turks, who had conquered Jerusalem and were threatening Byzantine territory.

Urban saw great opportunity in Alexius' plea. He hoped, first, to unite Europe's warring nobles in a Christian army under papal authority. Secondly, Urban wanted to establish jurisdiction over all Christians, including the Byzantine Christians of the east. The Turkish presence in Jerusalem gave Urban a useful pretext for assembling his army and sending it eastward. Little did Urban know, however, that his call to crusade would send everyday people as well as knights to the Holy Land. Indeed, the pope's call seemed to inspire a kind of crusading fever.

In the following selection Anna Comnena, Alexius's daughter, comments on what she sees as the rash and violent behavior of the "Franks," or Europeans, as they passed through the Byzantine capital, Constantinople, and entered Turkish territory. Her focus is on the Peasants' Crusade, a huge migration of some thirty-five thousand common people led by Peter the Hermit, which actually reached Constantinople before the official soldiers of the First Crusade.

From *Alexiad*, by Anna Comnena, translated by E.A.S. Dawes (London: Kegan Paul, Trench, Trubner, 1928). Reprinted by permission of Routledge.

L et me, however, give an account of this subject more clearly and in due order. According to universal rumour, Godfrey [a French nobleman who was one of the leaders of the First Crusade], who had sold his country, was the first to start on the appointed road; this man was very rich and very proud of his bravery, courage and conspicuous lineage; for every Frank is anxious to outdo the others. And such an upheaval of both men and women took place then as had never occurred within human memory, the simpler-minded were urged on by the real desire of worshipping at our Lord's Sepulchre, and visiting the sacred places; but the more astute, especially men like Bohemund [another Crusade leader, of Norman or Viking descent] and those of like mind, had another secret reason, namely, the hope that while on their travels they might by some means be able to seize the capital itself, looking upon this as a kind of corollary. And Bohemund disturbed the minds of many nobler men by thus cherishing his old grudge against the Emperor. Meanwhile Peter, after he had delivered his message, crossed the straits of Lombardy before anybody else with eighty thousand men on foot, and one hundred thousand on horseback, and reached the capital by way of Hungary. For the Frankish race, as one may conjecture, is always very hot-headed and eager, but when once it has espoused a cause, it is uncontrollable.

The Emperor, knowing what Peter had suffered before from the Turks, advised him to wait for the arrival of the other Counts, but Peter would not listen for he trusted to the multitude of his followers. So he crossed and pitched his camp near a small town called Helenopolis. After him followed the Normans numbering ten thousand, who separated themselves from the rest of the army and devastated the country round Nicaea, and behaved most cruelly to all. For they dismembered some of the children and fixed others on wooden spits and roasted them at the fire, and on persons advanced in age they inflicted every kind of torture. But when the inhabitants of Nicaea became aware of these doings, they threw open their gates and marched out upon them, and after a violent conflict had taken place they had to dash back inside their citadel as the Normans fought so bravely. And thus the latter recovered all the booty and returned to Helenopolis. Then a dispute arose between them and the others who had not gone out with them, as is usual in such cases, for the minds of those who had stayed behind were aflame with envy, and thus caused a skirmish after which the headstrong Normans drew apart again, marched to Xerigordus and took it by assault. When the Sultan heard what had happened, he dispatched Elchanes against them with a substantial force. He came, and recaptured

Xerigordus and sacrificed some of the Normans to the sword, and took others captive, at the same time laid plans to catch those who had remained behind with Cucupeter. He placed ambushes in suitable spots so that any coming from the camp in the direction of Nicaea would fall into them unexpectedly and be killed. Besides this, as he knew the Franks' love of money, he sent for two active-minded men and ordered them to go to Cucupeter's camp and proclaim there that the Normans had gained possession of Nicaea, and were now dividing everything in it. When this report was circulated among Peter's followers, it upset them terribly. Directly they heard the words "partition" and "money" they started in a disorderly crowd along the road to Nicaea, all but unmindful of their military experience and the discipline which is essential for those starting out to battle. For, as I remarked above, the Latin race is always very fond of money, but more especially when it is bent on raiding a country; it then loses its reason and gets beyond control. As they journeyed neither in ranks nor in squadrons, they fell foul of the Turkish ambuscades near the river Dracon and perished miserably. And such a large number of Franks and Normans were the victim of the Ishmaelite sword, that when they piled up the corpses of the slaughtered men which were lying on either side they formed, I say, not a very large hill or mound or a peak, but a high mountain as it were, of very considerable depth and breadth—so great was the pyramid of bones. And later men of the same tribe as the slaughtered barbarians built a wall and used the bones of the dead to fill the interstices as if they were pebbles, and thus made the city their tomb in a way. This fortified city is still standing to-day with its walls built of a mixture of stones and bones.

PETER THE HERMIT ESCAPES THE MASSACRE

When they had all in this way fallen a prey to the sword, Peter alone with a few others escaped and re-entered Helenopolis; and the Turks who wanted to capture him, set fresh ambushes for him. But when the Emperor received reliable information of all this, and the terrible massacre, he was very worried lest Peter should have been captured. He therefore summoned Constantine Catacalon Euphorbenus (who has already been mentioned many times in this history), and gave him a large force which was embarked on ships of war and sent him across the straits to Peter's succour. Directly the Turks saw him land they fled. Constantine, without the slightest delay, picked up Peter and his followers, who were but few, and brought them safe and sound to the Emperor. On the Emperor's reminding him of his original thoughtlessness and saying that it was due to his not having obeyed his, the Emperor's, advice that he had incurred such disasters, Peter, being a haughty Latin, would not admit that he himself was the cause of the trouble, but said it was the others who did not listen to him, but followed their own wills, and he denounced them as robbers and plunderers who, for that reason, were not allowed by the Saviour to worship at His Holy Sepulchre. Others of the Latins, such as Bohemund and men of like mind, who had long cherished a desire for the Roman Empire, and wished to win it for themselves, found a pretext in Peter's preaching, as I have said, deceived the more single-minded, caused this great upheaval and were selling their own estates under the pretence that they were marching against the Turks to redeem the Holy Sepulchre.

THE CRUSADERS ADAPTED TO LIFE IN THE MIDDLE EAST

ANTONY BRIDGE

Both the Byzantine Empire and the Islamic world of the Arabs, Persians, and Turks enjoyed far higher standards of civilization than western Europe, the homeland of the crusaders. While Europe was still heavily forested and rural, and dominated by illiterate warrior nobles, Asia Minor, Syria, and Palestine had been centers of civilization for thousands of years. Their cities had stood for centuries as military and trade outposts and their wealthy, educated classes were literate and refined. An Arab nobleman, for instance, was expected to be a poet and thinker as well as a warrior.

In the following selection Antony Bridge explores some of the ways in which crusaders, or "Franks," adapted to life in the Middle East after settling there following the successful Crusade of 1099. Their adjustments ranged from changes in dress, professions, and leisure pursuits to, occasionally, intermarriage with local people. While, as Bridge notes, barriers to full assimilation remained, the Franks of the crusader kingdoms enjoyed a higher standard of living than they had imagined in Europe.

A professional painter and ordained minister, Antony Bridge is also the author of *Richard the Lionheart*.

Many of the original Crusaders went home, but others settled down to spend the rest of their lives in Outremer. Many of the minor knights and most of the rank

From *The Crusades*, by Antony Bridge (New York: Franklin Watts, 1982). Reprinted by permission of HarperCollins Publishers Ltd.

and file had little or no incentive to make the return journey. But perhaps the words 'settled down' are misleading, for life in the Crusader kingdoms throughout their history was turbulent and unsettled. Internally it was beset by dynastic quarrels between the great ruling families, who were violently jealous of one another and chronically incapable of living in peace together, while externally it was lived against a background of almost perpetual war with the Moslems. . . .

BECOMING MIDDLE EASTERNERS

The first Crusaders were nearly all either Norman or French, and the states they founded were unmistakably created by Frenchmen; everyone spoke French, and the feudal structure of contemporary French society was faithfully reproduced in Outremer, while the Orthodox Church and its Greek liturgy was ousted by the Catholic Church and its Latin rite. During the two centuries of their existence, the Crusader kingdoms did not change in these respects. In all sorts of other ways, however, the way of life there was profoundly changed by the climate, the physical conditions and the natural resources of the land, and as the years went by the Franks of Outremer succumbed to a slow process of orientalisation, the results of which regularly shocked newcomers from the West. Perhaps if they had been more numerous, more of their western ways and customs might have remained unchanged over the years, but during the whole course of their history they were a tiny minority both racially and socially in the lands which they ruled. It has been estimated that there were never as many as a thousand knights resident in the Kingdom of Jerusalem, although their numbers were swollen by visitors from time to time; and much the same was true of the entire knightly population of the Principality of Antioch and the Counties of Edessa and Tripoli taken together. The rank and file were more numerous, but even they were vastly outnumbered by the local people. These consisted of Greek-speaking Christians alongside Armenians, Jews, Egyptians and Arabs, some of whom were Christians and some Moslem, but there was not much social contact between the Franks and those whom they ruled. Intermarriage was exceedingly rare; in aristocratic circles members of the ruling families tended to marry only members of similar families, although a few of them married well-bred Armenians or Byzantines, all of them Christian. Any kind of sexual intercourse with a Moslem, in marriage or in concubinage, was strictly outlawed; indeed, the Council of Nablus in 1120 decreed that a man found guilty of going to bed with a Moslem woman should both be castrated and have his nose cut off. But members of less exalted Frankish families felt free to marry the daughters of local Christians, whatever their ethnic origins might have been; and the result was that, as time went by, their descendants, who were known as *poulains,* were often difficult to distinguish from other members of the native population. In contrast, the Venetians, the Pisans and the Genoese, who as time went by were to be found acting as merchants and *entrepreneurs* in almost every city, kept their identity better than most of the Franks, partly because they lived together in streets allocated to them by the various princes with whom they had made treaties, and partly because they travelled to and from Italy on their mercantile occasions, and so never lost touch with their native cities.

EVERYDAY LIFE

Life in the villages was much the same as it had been in Old Testament times, so little had it changed, but very few Franks settled in them. Wherever it was possible, they were built on the tops of hills, both because such sites were more easily defended than more accessible settings, and also because they were windier and thus both cooler in summer and better suited for winnowing at harvest time. Those Franks who did live in the villages had to endure the primitive conditions endured by the native villagers, and this was one reason why they were unpopular. Those who lived in the towns enjoyed much better amenities. Some lived in simple, single-storeyed houses, but most had homes with two floors, and the rich lived in much grander abodes, which they called 'palaces'; these were built in a style inherited from Graeco-Roman days, as much else had been by Arab civilisation in that part of the world. Usually they consisted of a square of rooms on two floors surrounding a central *patio;* apart from the main entrance, all the doors and windows opened onto the central court, as did a row of verandas in the more luxurious houses, and their roofs were flat. People slept upstairs, while the living-rooms, dining-rooms and kitchens were on the ground floor. Unlike their oriental subjects, who reclined to eat their meals as the Romans had before them, the Franks sat around a table when they ate together; the table was covered with a cloth, lit by candles or oil lamps at night and, as the years went by and old prejudices slowly died, it was furnished with just such luxuries as knives, spoons and forks, glass decanters and goblets, elegant dishes and plates, as had aroused the angry derision of the first Crusaders to pass through Constantinople and observe the 'effeminate' table manners of Emperor Alexius' court.

The Franks' personal habits changed in many ways too, although not in all. The men continued to wear their hair long to their shoulders and to shave their chins, although a few grew beards like those of the Greeks and Syrians. In Jerusalem there was a barbers' quarter near the Church of the Holy Sepulchre, to which many people went to be shaved once or twice a week, while others were shaved by attendants at the public baths; and presumably other cities had similar amenities. The women wore their hair in two long plaits, painted their faces and dressed superbly. A Spanish traveller who was in the Kingdom of Jerusalem in 1181, a man named Ibn Jubayr, was dazzled by a Frankish bride whom he saw on her wedding day in Tyre. 'She was most elegantly arrayed in a beautiful dress,' he wrote, 'from which there floated, according to their traditional style, a long train of silk. On her head she wore a golden diadem covered by a net of woven gold, and on her breast there was a similar ornament.' The men were scarcely less splendid; for some time they continued to wear European clothes, which consisted of long stockings, a shirt with long tight sleeves, and over it a short jacket with short sleeves, but whether these garments were made of fine wool, cotton, linen or silk, invariably they were brilliantly coloured and embroidered with gold or silver thread. But as the years passed most of the knights abandoned Western fashions altogether and, returning from whatever battlefield happened to have been claiming their professional attention at the time, removed their armour and put on a silk burnous in summer and furs in winter.

But perhaps the single biggest change in their habits took place in their attitude to personal hygiene. In Europe, washing had been despised, but in the climate of Outremer they began to patronise the public baths, to be found in every city. They were similar to the Turkish baths of today or the Roman baths of antiquity; the bather first undressed, and then donned a towel and sandals, although apparently some of the Franks sometimes dispensed with the towel; the Prince Usamah, a member of an independent dynasty of Munqidhite Arabs with a castle at Shaizar near Hama, who travelled widely through Outremer, made many Frankish friends, and wrote his *Memoirs*, complained that some people did not bother with a towel but bathed naked. But whether clothed or not, the bather entered a heated room, where he began to sweat; then, when he had sweated enough, he called an attendant, who soaped him all over, rubbed him down, and dried him with another towel. Before leaving he rested in an ante-room where couches were provided on which he could lie in comfort. Bathing became so much a part of everyone's way of life that it was even required on certain occasions; for instance, young men seeking admission as novices to one or other of the Military Orders were obliged to bathe in a communal bath-house before they were formally admitted. Women bathed as frequently as men, going to the baths two or three times a week, although needless to say they bathed separately from the men.

If the Franks were cleaner in Outremer than they had been at home in Europe, they were much better fed too; for not only was their food rich and varied, but it was cooked by local people who were artists in the kitchen. Chicken, crane, quail, pigeon and partridge were plentiful; mutton, beef, wild boar, ibex, roebuck and hare were cooked with garlic and herbs and seasoned with mustard and pepper, or served with delicious sauces; there was an abundance of freshwater fish, and eels were much prized as delicacies; cooked vegetables included such things as beans, peas, artichokes, asparagus and rice, while lettuces and cucumbers were eaten raw. When they first arrived, the Franks were astonished by the novelty and variety of the various kinds of fruit which they found growing everywhere, many of which they had never even heard of let alone seen or eaten; there were bananas, oranges, lemons, dates, carobs, the fruit of the sycamore tree which they named 'Pharaoh's figs', grapes, peaches, plums, quinces and ordinary figs, and with them various nuts including almonds. Since wine was forbidden to Moslems, there were no vineyards, but that was a deficiency soon remedied, and after the first few years wine was plentiful and much of it was good. In the heat of summer it was chilled with snow from the mountains of Lebanon, which was brought south protected from the heat of the sun by straw, and it was drunk both in private houses and in taverns. Beer brewed from barley was also popular, and fruit juices were cheap and easily available.

TRADES AND PASTIMES

In the intervals between wars, some of the Franks practised trades of various kinds. They were great builders, as both their churches and their castles still testify, and although much of the work of building them must have been done by local Arabs and other native people, the masons' marks to be found on some of their stones proves that Frankish craftsmen were also active. The area around Tyre was famous for its pottery and glass, and a Frankish glass-smelting furnace has been found at Samariya near Acre, so some of the Crusaders must have learned how to blow glass from their Arab neighbours, who had been manufacturing it since Roman days and before; the Venetians, who held large parts of Tyre and the country round it, seem to have learned to be glass-makers there. There was a thriving textile industry in Outremer too, and probably some Franks were employed in the manufacture of silk and cotton fabrics. But then as now the most thriving industry was the manufacture of religious souvenirs for the pilgrims who came in large numbers to visit the holy places of the Christian faith, and the resident Franks must have been involved in this highly lucrative trade.

But if involvement in trade was not beneath the dignity of some of the less aristocratic Frankish citizens of Outremer, the knights scorned it as unworthy of their nobility; war was their profession, and when they were not fighting one another or their Moslem neighbours, they spent most of their time hunting. Mounted and armed with spears, they pursued such beasts of prey as lions, leopards, bears and wolves for the sheer enjoyment of the chase, while they also hunted wild boar, deer, ibex and hares for the pot. Needless to say, there were accidents from time to time and men were hurt or even killed; but this deterred no one. . . .

LUXURIOUS HOMES

When they were not enjoying themselves out of doors, the Franks spent their time at home or visiting their friends, and as the years passed some of their houses became astonishingly luxurious: so luxurious indeed that they shocked newcomers from the West. Like the houses of wealthy Byzantines, the palaces of some of the richer Franks were adorned with Persian carpets, damask hangings, mosaic floors, inlaid marble walls, carved furniture of ivory or rare wood and dinner services of silver or Chinese porcelain brought by caravan from the East. Their owners slept in comfortable beds between fine linen sheets, and in some of the northern cities, where water was abundant the biggest houses had their own private bathrooms with running water. People played dice a great deal, and such games as chess were also played; they drank a lot, both at home and in taverns, and drunkenness was common. Musicians, strolling players and mimes performed in the squares of the cities and in other open spaces; their performances were popular and well attended, but the performers themselves were regarded as the lowest of the low, little better than prostitutes. These, too, were to be found on the streets of every city.

Most of these pursuits were, however, masculine preserves; it is difficult to discover what the Frankish women did in their spare time. No doubt the greater part of their lives was spent either preparing to be married or, after their marriages, bearing children, even if desperately few of their babies survived to the age of five. But everyone was used to the fact that in the midst of life they were in death, and they took the deaths of many of their children as much for granted as they took the way in which their

marriages were arranged for them. It was not at all unusual for
the children of the upper classes to be married when they were
five or six years old in the hope that one day they might grow up
to consummate their union and produce some dynastically desirable children, while on other occasions a child might be married to a much older adult in order to join two dynasties in a desirable political union; for instance, Baldwin III of Jerusalem
married a little Byzantine princess named Theodora when she
was thirteen years old and he was twenty-seven. . . .

Just as the standard of living of the Franks in Outremer was
much higher than anything they had ever known at home in Europe, so they enjoyed a much higher standard of medical care
too. The skill of their physicians was borrowed over the years
from the Arabs, who were far in advance of doctors in the West.
Indeed during the early years of the Crusader kingdoms everyone consulted local physicians in preference to men of their own
race; the chronicler, William of Tyre, noticed how his contemporaries 'scorned the medicines and practice of our Latin physicians
and believed only in the Jews, Samaritans, Syrians, and Saracens'.
At the height of their prosperity and power, the Crusader kingdoms probably had more hospitals than any other countries of
comparable size; in Jerusalem alone there were four, and Acre,
Nablus, Ascalon, Jaffa and Tyre each had its own. . . .

A HIGHER STANDARD OF LIVING

Throughout their whole history the Franks in Outremer remained a conquering race. Rather like the British in India, . . .
they found themselves far better off in their new home than they
had ever been in Europe, and so there was a fairly constant
stream of new arrivals from the West. Fulcher of Chartres described the situation. 'Every day our dependents and our relatives follow us, leaving behind, unwillingly perhaps, all their be-
longings. For he who was poor there now finds that God has
made him rich here. He who had little money now possesses
countless gold coins. He who did not hold even a village over
there now enjoys a town which God has given him. Why should
anyone return to the West, who has found an Orient like this?'
Why indeed! Moreover, as time went by, in many little ways the
Franks learned to live on friendly terms with their Moslem
neighbours, and as the process of orientalisation continued to
change their habits, the superficial differences between them diminished, and an ever firmer *modus vivendi* [way of life] was established by the two sides. 'We who had been occidentals have
become orientals,' wrote Fulcher of Chartres; 'the man who had
been a Roman or a Frank has here become a Galilean or a Pales-

tinian; and the man who used to live in Rheims or Chartres now finds himself a citizen of Tyre or Acre. We have already forgotten the places where we were born; already many of us know them not, or at any rate no longer hear them spoken of. Some among us already possess in this country houses and servants which belong to them as of hereditary right. Another has married a wife who is not his compatriot: a Syrian or an Armenian woman perhaps, or even a Saracen, who has received the grace of baptism. He who was once a stranger here now a native.'

HINDRANCES TO FULL ASSIMILATION

But two things prevented this process of slow assimilation from resulting in a full acceptance of the Franks by their non-Christian neighbours: the Moslems never forgot the massacres of their compatriots by the Christians in Antioch and Jerusalem; and during the whole history of the Crusader kingdoms there was a steady influx of newcomers from the West, whose first question on arrival was, 'Where are some Moslems that I may kill them?' Again and again, enthusiastic knights would arrive bursting with determination to do God service by slaughtering some of the enemies of Christ, with whom the citizens of Outremer might just have made a treaty or concluded a truce, which was not only necessary to their own welfare but sometimes essential to their survival. But such political arrangements seemed almost blasphemous to the less sophisticated Christians from the West, and usually nothing deterred them from charging out of Christian-held territory in a fine flurry and fury of faith, hell-bent on a little godly bloodshed. The fact that they often got themselves killed in the process was little consolation to the long-suffering Franks, who had to live with the consequences of their aggression, which often included renewed warfare with their neighbours when they least wished it. Yet they could not afford to discourage immigrants from the West, for they were perennially short of manpower, and only reinforcements from overseas made up for the twin evils of a chronically low birth rate and a chronically high rate of infant mortality, which between them crippled Outremer. It was a dilemma which was destined never to be solved except by the eventual extinction of the kingdoms founded by the first Crusaders; for while recruits from the West could still be found who were willing to fight for the triumph of the Cross, as they understood it, Moslem hostility was inevitably replenished; and when their enthusiasm eventually faded, and no more recruits were forthcoming, the fate of the Crusader kingdoms was sealed.

THE CRUSADES ENRICHED EUROPE ECONOMICALLY AND CULTURALLY

MARTIN ERBSTÖSSER

The Crusades resulted in much greater contact between Europe and the richer and more cultured Byzantine and Islamic worlds. Not only did European nobles establish kingdoms in the Middle East, ships traveled back and forth from Europe to the eastern Mediterranean with pilgrims and trade goods, and scholars and scientists exchanged ideas with their counterparts from Spain to Baghdad.

In the following selection, Martin Erbstösser describes some of the ways by which the Crusades made Europeans more worldly. He describes the vast array of produce that arrived from the "Orient," or "East." In particular, crusading opened Europe up to the vast spice trade of Asia. Europeans also were exposed to Asian knowledge in papermaking, navigation, and medicine. Erbstösser also points out that the Arab gentleman, a model of both fighting ability and refined behavior, may have had a direct influence on the age of chivalry, which took hold in Europe in the twelfth century.

Martin Erbstösser is professor of history at the University of Leipzig in Germany.

From *The Crusades*, by Martin Erbstösser, translated by C.S.V. Salt (Leipzig: Edition Leipzig, 1978). Reprinted by permission of Dornier Medienholding, Berlin.

As a result of European expansion in the Orient, Europeans were introduced to a large number of crops and fruits hitherto unknown to them: lemons, oranges, apricots, peaches, plums, cucumbers, melons, maize, rice, saffron, artichokes, sesame, carob, dates, sugar cane and others. Many descriptions of the milieu in the Crusader states are full of praise for the extensive gardens and their tasty fruits. Europe heard about this and many Crusaders and pilgrims brought seeds back with them on their return. However, this had little effect on the spread of these plants since the feudal lords knew little about their cultivation or propagation. From contemporary accounts, it seems that their attempts were regarded more as curious experiments than as serious efforts to bring about changes in European agriculture. The route by which these plants actually came to Europe was via Spain, Sicily and Southern Italy. The Muslim peasants had the necessary knowledge and skills for the cultivation of these crops and it is known that a rapid change took place in the character of agriculture in these areas after the Islamic conquest. In Sicily, for instance, date palms were planted immediately afterwards in a totally systematic manner. They then gradually spread from here to Italy and Southern France in particular. This was a matter of major importance for the producers and not for the feudal lords— which was likewise the case in Spain and Italy, too. However, it was during the time of the Crusades that this change was initiated and it continued during the centuries that followed. A second route, which was especially significant for Eastern Europe, was from Byzantium via the Balkans so that it seems likely that many of these crops, such as melons, maize and cucumbers, became known in Central Europe by way of the Balkans.

AN INCREASE OF ASIAN MERCHANDISE IN EUROPE

From the 12th century onwards, the trade with the Orient and Byzantium led to a substantial increase in the consumption of spices, dyes and perfumes and a wide variety of artisan products. Pepper, cloves, nutmeg, amber, incense, saffron, alum, indigo, red sandalwood, lacquer, damask, muslin, silk, velvet, atlas and other products were constantly offered for sale at the great markets of Europe, in addition to splendid apparel and blankets. Oriental carpets were in great demand and high prices were paid for jewellery of pearls and precious stones, enamel work, fine glassware and ceramic articles, ivory carvings and other objets d'art. The same applied to gold and silver work and ornamental weapons of Damascus steel.

To some extent, these and other products were imports obtained through commercial channels. But in the 12th and 13th centuries many of the artisan products in particular had originally been secured as booty or represented gifts from Crusaders. The events of the 4th Crusade provide especially clear evidence of this. Unfortunately, no detailed accounts have survived but many of the collections which still exist in churches and monasteries were originally donated by persons who took part in the Crusades.

Every castle must have possessed at least a few luxury objects from the Orient and churches and monasteries were furnished with them. Altar cloths, chasubles and liturgical vessels frequently bore Arabic inscriptions or Islamic motifs. This did not seem to bother the people of the time to any great extent, perhaps because they thought that these were Hebraic symbols. The main thing was that they contributed to the solemn atmosphere.

The "reliquary trade" did unexpectedly well. Every large church and monastery of this period fought for a share of the relics and precious reliquaries stolen from the churches of the Orient and Byzantium since the reputation of the Church depended to a not insignificant extent on the value of its relics. In Halberstadt (GDR), for example, the day on which the treasures from the fourth Crusade became the property of the Church was long celebrated by a solemn procession. The fact that it originated from the plundering of a Christian city probably never occurred to anyone anymore.

Although Oriental products were so popular, local artisans were relatively slow in making the change to similar products. Silk production spread to other regions in the course of the 13th century. In the middle of the 12th century, it seems that it was still restricted to Sicily. It was from here that it spread to Central and Northern Italy, Provence and finally to Northern Germany as well. Lucca became the great centre of the silk trade but Bologna, Venice, Augsburg, Ulm and other cities also raised silkworms or produced silk fabrics.

IMPORTED TECHNOLOGY WAS ADAPTED TO EUROPE

Up to the 13th century, paper was imported from Spain and the Orient but after this date there is evidence that it was manufactured in Europe, too. From this time onwards, merchants made increasing use of paper as a writing material. At the end of the 13th century, it was being made in Genoa and Ravensburg and shortly afterwards in Bologna, Padua, Venice and other cities as well.

The Crusaders and pilgrims had observed the windmills in use in the Orient, and, in this case, it was not long before the first examples appeared in Europe. There is evidence that windmills were in use in various regions of Europe as early as the middle of the 12th century.

There was much indirect influence on the production of high-quality handmade articles, this resulting from attempts to imitate Byzantine and Oriental imports. However, this influence was often nothing more than a stimulus. After the 13th century, the cities of Northern Italy became noted for the production of high-quality woollen fabrics. The raw materials—alum, dyes and wool—were mainly imported from the Orient and Byzantium. Enamel work had been produced in Europe before the expeditions to the Orient but it was only from the 13th century that it achieved real artistic excellence, not least because of the quality of Byzantine enamel work which Europeans had learnt to appreciate. Glass production, especially in Venice, had survived the decline of Antiquity but the art of glass painting by the appropriate fusion process, the making of ground crystal dishes and other techniques date only from after the 12th century. The products of the Orient had a similar influence on the emergence of ivory carving, faience ware and the work of the gold and silversmiths.

The material production of Europe in general and of Italy in particular was stimulated in numerous ways through the contacts with Islamic Arabic and Byzantine culture. Accumulation from intermediate trade and high productivity in the crafts were two of the essential conditions for the development of that stage of history known as the Renaissance. . . .

THE INFLUENCE OF EASTERN SCHOLARS

Under the influence of the Church and with few exceptions, theology and its philosophical consequences was the principal subject studied at the universities. Nevertheless, the natural sciences such as mathematics, physics, biology, medicine, chemistry and others were gaining in importance.

The foundations of this new interest in knowledge were provided by the teachings of Islamic Arabic and Antique authors. Translations from Arabic into Latin of the scientific and philosophical works of Greek Antiquity and the Islamic world had started to appear from the early 12th century. The translation schools were centred in Spain, Sicily and the Crusader states, Spain being the most important. The most favourable conditions existed here on account of the relatively large group of Jews and native Christians who were familiar with Hebraic, Arabic, Greek and Latin and able to make translations. One of the most outstanding of these was John of Seville, also known as John of Spain and Ibn Daud. He was a Jew who had grown up in the cultural tradition of the Omayyad empire in Spain and was a convert to Christianity. He was responsible for a large number of mathematical, astronomical, medical and astrological translations during the first half of the 12th century. A few years later, Gerard of Cremona came to the fore. He was active in Toledo in the years after 1165, probably in association with other native translators. It is said that he was responsible for seventy-one translations. It was mainly Greek authors, such as Aristotle, Euclid and Archimedes, in whom he was interested but he also translated the works of Arab Islamic scholars such as Al-Razi, Ibn Sina, Al-Kindi and others. . . .

By way of Spain and the Norman empire in Southern Italy, this mass of learning and scientific knowledge flowed to the universities of Europe. The Crusader states, concentrating only on conquest and later after the rise of Saladin, caught up in a complicated and hopeless military situation and afflicted by major losses of territory, were unable to offer the right atmosphere for scholarly work. In addition, the native population led a separate life, quite different from the situation in Spain and Southern Italy. Nevertheless, the indirect influence of the existence of the Crusader states on the acceptance of Oriental sciences in Europe appears to have been greater than is apparent from the direct evidence.

The great universities of Southern France and Italy were not only in the vicinity of Spain and Southern Italy but were also the traditional centres of the Crusades and the trade with the Orient. There is evidence that many scholars did not keep to the "contact zone" with the Orient but went further afield. Practitioners took part as personal physicians to kings and princes in the Crusades of the 13th century and used the opportunity to extend their knowledge. . . .

It is obvious that only few of the men of learning of the 13th century had first-hand experience of the Islamic world. From the 13th century onwards, the principal achievements of Arab Islamic science and of Antique authors who had influenced the Arab scholars were known in Europe. Manuscripts of these works were kept in universities and monasteries. For the following period, there also survives a series of examples of independent interpretations and modifications by scholars from various European countries. Nevertheless, it cannot be assumed from this that there was a widespread knowledge of these works or that they had a broad influence. Feudal society with its narrow economic basis was not in a position to apply this knowledge on a broad scale. This is why the process of "digestion" of these achievements continued until 1500 and later.

The extent and forms of the influence of the Crusades and the

Orient on the feudal nobility itself and especially the knights is the subject of controversy. The age of the Crusades was simultaneously the finest hour of chivalry. These were the centuries in which chivalry acquired its intellectual profile. Castle architecture experienced a climax and the observance of the code of chivalry, which laid down the moral qualities and principles of honour of the knights, was considered particularly important. Troubadours and minstrels sung not only about the forms of courtly wooing but also proclaimed the standards of chivalrous behaviour in general. Some of the characteristic features of knightly ethics, such as valour, Christian piety and so on, have already been indicated in connection with the development of the Crusade idea. The influence of the Orient on knightly culture is evident from the parallels between the internal developments within the class of the feudal lords and the Crusade movement.

Despite this, the social conditions influencing the development of the knights in Europe were so different from those of the Orient even as late as the 13th century that a closer rapprochement was out of the question.

The intellectual level of the European feudal lords did not approach that of their Islamic Arab counterparts nor did they strive to attain it in their concept of the ideal knight. Only in Spain and the Norman empire of Southern Italy did the rulers concern themselves with scientific problems and developments. Otherwise, the knights were practically illiterate and even many of the minstrels and entertainers had to dictate their songs and epics.

A series of moral concepts are related to this, such as valour in battle, religious piety, chivalrous behaviour towards women, generosity towards the vanquished and others. The Crusaders had first seen tournaments in the Orient and were not slow in emulating them. The same applies to courtly celebrations. Both Muslim and Christian lords cultivated the art of chivalrous poetry and both sides presented their works at the court of the Norman kings. Nevertheless, the points of contact should not be overemphasized since there was much which evidently followed an independent course and in which knowledge of the Orient was no more than a stimulus.

Challenges and Transitions in the Fourteenth and Fifteenth Centuries

CHAPTER 8

THE BLACK DEATH STRIKES THE OLD WORLD

ROBERT S. GOTTFRIED

Between 1320 and 1360, vast areas from China to Europe were devastated by the plague, a bacterial disease carried by rat-borne fleas. Humans were exposed to the disease through the bite of an infected flea. Both in its bubonic and pneumonic forms, the death rate from plague was high.

In Europe, which was hit by the plague between 1347 and 1352, the epidemic was known as the Black Death. It killed nearly one-third of the population, perhaps 25 million people. Those most at risk had been weakened by malnutrition or lived in Europe's crowded, unsanitary, and rat-infested towns. Although less is known about the effects of the plague elsewhere, estimates claim that the epidemic killed at least a third of the people in China, India, the Middle East, and North Africa.

In the following selection, Robert S. Gottfried suggests reasons for the devastating spread of plague over such a wide area, including the travels of Mongol warriors across Asia, changes in weather patterns, and the increase of international trade.

Robert S. Gottfried is professor of history at Rutgers University.

Sometime in the late thirteenth or early fourteenth century the ecological balance of Eurasia was violently disrupted. A result was the spread of *Y. pestis* [yersinin pestis, the plague bacillus] and plague from a permanent locus, the Gobi Desert, east into China, south into India, and west across central Asia to the Middle East and the Mediterranean Basin. This marked the onset of the Black Death and the coming of the second plague pandemic.

THE MONGOL EMPIRE HELPED THE PLAGUE SPREAD

There are several theories that try to explain the Black Death. One, developed in part by [historian] William McNeill, assigns a crucial role to the nomadic rulers of the Mongol Empire. Begun in the late twelfth century by Genghis Khan and still powerful in the fourteenth century, the Mongol Empire was important because it served as the link between less mobile Eurasian societies in China, India, the Middle East, and Europe. The Empire was bound together by highly mobile Mongol horsemen, who formed a network of military and governmental communications spanning Asia from Russia to Persia and from the Punjab to Manchuria. By the late thirteenth century, the Empire had reached the Yunan region in southern China. The Yunan is today an inveterate focus of plague, and many scholars believe that it has been such since the sixth century A.D., when *Y. pestis* came from east Africa during the first pandemic. McNeill and others argue that, by the early fourteenth century, Mongol horsemen and supply trains had picked up the infected insect or rodent hosts of *Y. pestis* and carried them back to Mongol headquarters at Karakorum, in the Gobi Desert. Local Gobi rodents were then infected and they and Mongol horsemen carried it throughout the far-flung Empire in the same fashion that they had brought plague into the desert. There are variations on this theory; many scholars believe that the Gobi region was itself an inveterate focus of *Y. pestis*. In either circumstance, the domination of much of Eurasia by the Mongols was crucial to the spread of plague.

A second interpretation recognizes the importance of the Mongols, but claims that environmental, rather than human, factors were most important in plague's origins and spread. . . . As the prevailing Eurasian wind patterns changed, western Europe, dominated by Atlantic breezes, became much wetter; by contrast, sirocco winds from the Sahara blew hot, dry air into the already hot and dry central parts of Asia. The environmentalists believe that this gradual dessication, which began in the mid-thirteenth century and continued into the early fourteenth century, caused Mongol and Turkic nomads to move their flocks—the most important part of their pastural economies—east and west in search of greener pastures. At the same time, central Asian wild rodents—marmots, susliks, tarbagons, ground squirrels, and the like—also moved in search of food and water, infecting local rodent populations with *Y. pestis* and thus extending the second plague pandemic.

Both theories are compelling, and the truth no doubt lies in some combination of the two. The importance of Mongolia, however, is paramount. The rodents and men of the steppes and desert were clearly the initial carriers of plague. The nomadic tribesmen seemed even to have a sense of the connection between plague and rodent intermediaries, and developed a series of customs to prevent the spread of *Y. pestis*. The trapping of marmots, usually the principal host to the flea *X. cheopis* [xenoptin cheopis, a rat flea], was generally forbidden; they could be shot, but only at a safe distance. Animals that moved slowly were untouchable, and there were widespread taboos about using furs from certain types of rodents. Whatever the precise cause or chronology, an epizoötic, and then an epidemic, of plague erupted in the Gobi Desert sometime in the late 1320s.

Wiping out nearly one-third of Europe's population, the Black Death thrived among people living in overcrowded, unsanitary conditions.

THE PLAGUE REACHES CHINA AND MOVES WEST

News of natural disasters in Asia began to filter back to the West from travelers early in the 1330s. A series of droughts and earthquakes from 1330 to 1333 and subsequent flooding in 1334 caused widespread famines, which were worsened by swarms of locusts that destroyed what remained of the crops. These adverse ecological blows continued into the 1340s and, at some point—perhaps as early as 1331—were joined by plague. The Chinese records are vague. An unspecified epidemic broke out in the province of Hopei in 1331 and allegedly killed 90% of the population, but both the mortality and the description of the disease cast doubt on whether it was the Black Death. The first unimpeachable references appear in 1353, when chroniclers claim that two-thirds of China's population had died since 1331. Whatever the precise dates and circumstances, by the mid–fourteenth century, the Black Death had struck China and, by 1393, after successive cycles of plague epidemics, the Chinese population had dropped to about 90 million from a thirteenth-century high of over 125 million.

The westward spread of the Black Death is better documented. Between 1330 and 1346, plague probably infected the Western world in two ways. The first was strictly ecological. Dislodged central Asian rodents infected local animal, and then human, populations—a gradual, but very comprehensive, process. The second was the work of man—the elaborate East-West trading system established in the twelfth and thirteenth centuries. There were three principal arteries of this East-West trade. The first was an overland path through northern China and across central Asia to the trading entrepôts along the northern shore of the Black Sea. This route was traversed primarily by caravans, which were protected by the Mongol Peace, a guarantee enforced by the Mongol khans. The second path was primarily by sea and involved the lucrative spice trade from south Asia. Ships sailed west across the Indian Ocean into the Persian Gulf, whence goods were transported by caravan across the northern Arabian Peninsula to the Levantine Coast. The third route also was primarily by sea and emanated from south Asia. Goods were carried across the Indian Ocean, around the southern Arabian Peninsula, past Yemen, and into the Red Sea. There, they were taken overland to Gaza or the ports of the Nile Delta.

At the end of each route were Italian merchants, primarily Genoese in the Black Sea and Venetians and Pisans in the Mediterranean, who carried the goods by ship to Italy, southern France, and Catalonia, where they were taken overland into northern Europe. In 1291, the intra-European routes of this system were facilitated when Genoese ships sailed for the first time through the Straits of Gibraltar, north into the Atlantic, through the English Channel and into the North Sea ports of the Netherlands. By the fourteenth century, the entire system was relatively quick and efficient. *Y. pestis* could be carried either by the fleas and rats aboard the trading ships or, in the case of pneumonic plague, by the merchants themselves. By the 1340s, the Eurasian commercial network was sufficiently fluid for an epidemic to pass through it before the disease's carriers fell victim themselves.

THE BLACK DEATH TRAVELED BY BOTH LAND AND SEA

Historians debate which of the three trading routes was most important in the spread of the Black Death. It is likely that the overland route through central Asia was most crucial, but the other two also played an important role in plague's spread, if not in its origins. For ships on these sea-based routes brought infected Asian black rats, plague's most prolific carriers, to the West.

The first records of the Black Death's westward movement are from 1339. Archaeological evidence shows that substantial portions of a Nestorian Christian community near Lake Issyk Kul, in the Tien Shan region of central Asia, died from bubonic plague. Narrative records show that later in the year plague reached Belasagun, Talas, and perhaps Samarkand, along the rivers Jaxartes and Oxus in Transoxiana. By 1345, it was at Sarai, a major trading center astride the Lower Volga. By 1346, it reached Astrakhan, the Caucasus, and Azerbaijan, and rumors of its devastation began to reach the ports of the Mediterranean. One chronicler claimed: "India was depopulated; Tartary, Mesopotamia, Syria, Armenia were covered with dead bodies; the Kurds fled in vain to the mountains. In Caramania and Caesaria [in Asia Minor] none were left alive."

THE PLAGUE IN ITALY

GIOVANNI BOCCACCIO

The Black Death reached Italy in 1347, probably via rats that had stowed away on Italian trade ships returning from the Middle East. As in the rest of Europe, the plague not only caused large numbers of deaths but also affected basic social behavior, as Giovanni Boccaccio reports in the following selection from his *Decameron.*

Boccaccio was a writer from Florence, which in the 1300s was becoming a major Italian economic and cultural center. He was one of the first to produce literary works in the vernacular, the common Italian spoken by everyday people, as opposed to the Latin of scholarship and the church. Moreover, his work focused on earthly activities and pleasures.

The *Decameron* is a collection of fictional stories of flirtation and adventure, told by a group of young, upper-class Florentines. But the context in which Boccaccio places the telling of these stories is the Black Death, which he estimates killed perhaps one hundred thousand people in Florence. His storytellers seek to escape the plague in the cleaner air of the countryside, but as Boccaccio points out in this introduction, escape from the disease and its social effects was difficult.

To the cure of these maladies neither counsel of physician nor virtue of any medicine appeared to avail or profit aught; on the contrary—whether it was that the nature of the infection resisted it or that the ignorance of the prescribers (of whom over and above professional men, the number, both men and women, who had never had any teaching of medicine, was become exceeding great) did not succeed in knowing whence it arose and consequently did not take due measures against it—

not only did few recover thereof, but well-nigh all died within the third day from the appearance of the aforesaid signs, this one sooner and that one later, and for the most part without fever or other complication. And this pestilence was the more virulent in that, by communication with those who were sick thereof, it got hold upon the sound, not otherwise than fire upon things dry or greasy, whenever they are brought very near to it. Nay, the mischief was even greater; for not only did converse and consortion with the sick give to the sound infection or cause of common death, but the mere touching of the clothes or of whatsoever other thing had been touched or used by the sick appeared of itself to communicate the malady to the toucher. A marvelous thing to hear is that which I have to tell and one which, had it not been seen by many men's eyes and by my own, I should scarcely have dared credit, much less set down in writing, even though I had heard it from one worthy of belief. I say, then, that of such virulence was the pestilence in question in communicating itself from one to another, that, not only did it pass from man to man, but this, which is much more, it many times visibly did—to wit, a thing which had pertained to a man sick or dead of the aforesaid sickness, being touched by an animal foreign to the human species, not only infected this latter with the malady, but in a very brief space of time killed it. Of this my own eyes (as has a little before been said) had one day, among others, experience in this way; to wit, that the rags of a poor man who had died of the plague, being cast out into the public way, two hogs came upon them and having first, after their wont, rooted amain among them with their snouts, took them in their mouths and tossed them about their jaws; then, in a little while, after turning round and round, they both, as if they had taken poison, fell down dead upon the rags with which they had in an ill hour intermeddled.

People React to the Plague

From these things and many others like them, or yet stranger, various fears and notions were begotten in those who remained alive, which well-nigh all tended to a very barbarous conclusion, namely, to shun and flee from the sick and all that pertained to them, and thus doing, each thought to secure immunity for himself. Some there were who conceived that to live moderately and keep oneself from all excess was the best defense against such a danger; wherefore, making up their company, they lived removed from every other, taking refuge and shutting themselves up in those houses where none were sick and where living was best; and there, partaking very temperately of the most delicate viands and the finest wines and eschewing all incontinence, they abode with music and such other diversions as they might have, never allowing themselves to speak with any, nor choosing to hear any news from without of death or the sick. Others, inclining to the contrary opinion, maintained that to carouse and make merry and go about singing and frolicking and satisfy the appetite in everything possible and laugh and scoff at whatsoever befell was a very certain remedy for such an ill. That which they said they put in practice as best they might, going about day and night, now to this tavern, now to that, drinking without stint or measure; and doing this yet more freely in the houses of others, if only they scented anything there that pleased or tempted them; and this they might easily do, because everyone—as though he were to live no longer—had abandoned all care of his possessions, as of himself, wherefore the most part of the houses were become common property and strangers used them whenever they happened upon them, even as the owner himself might have done; and with all this bestial preoccupation, they ever shunned the sick to the best of their power.

In this sore affliction and misery of our city, the reverend authority of the laws, both divine and human, was all in a manner dissolved and fallen into decay, for [lack of] the ministers and executors thereof, who, like other men, were all either dead or sick or else left so destitute of followers that they were unable to exercise any office, wherefore everyone had license to do whatsoever pleased him. Many others held a middle course between the two aforesaid, not limiting themselves so exactly in the matter of diet as the first, nor allowing themselves such license in drinking and other debauchery as the second, but using things in sufficiency, according to their appetites; nor did they seclude themselves, but went about, carrying in their hands, some flowers, some odoriferous herbs, and others various kinds of aromatic drugs which they often held to their noses, accounting it an excellent thing to fortify the brain with such odors, since the air seemed all heavy and tainted with the stench of the dead bodies and that of the sick and of the remedies used.

ABANDONING FAMILY, FRIENDS, AND NEIGHBORS

Some were of a more barbarous, though, perhaps, a surer way of thinking, affirming that there was no remedy against pestilences better than—no, nor any so good as—to flee before them; wherefore, moved by this reasoning and taking thought of nought but themselves, very many, both men and women, abandoned their own city, their own houses and homes, their kinsfolk and possessions, and sought the country seats of others, or, at the least, their own, as if the wrath of God, being moved to punish the iniquity of mankind, would not proceed to send this pestilence wheresoever they might be, but would content itself with afflicting those only who were found within the walls of their city, or as if they were persuaded that no person was to remain therein and that its last hour was come. And although these, who opined thus variously, did not all die, yet neither did they all escape; nay, many of each way of thinking and in every place fell sick of the plague and, well-nigh abandoned, languished away, having themselves, while they were well, set the example to those who remained in good health.

Indeed, leaving be that townsman avoided townsman and that well-nigh no neighbor took thought of other, and that kinsfolk seldom or never visited one another and held no converse together save from afar, this tribulation had stricken such terror to the hearts of all, men and women alike, that brother forsook brother, uncle nephew and sister brother and oftentimes wife husband; nay (what is yet more extraordinary and well-nigh incredible) fathers and mothers refused to visit or tend their very children, as if they had not been theirs. By reason of this there remained to those (and the number of them, both males and females, was incalculable) who fell sick, no other succor than that which they owed either to the charity of friends (and of these there were few) or the greed of servants, who tended them, allured by high and extravagant wages; although, for all this, these latter had not become many, and these were men and women of little understanding and for the most part unused to such offices, who served for well-nigh nought save to reach things called for by the sick or to note when they died; and in the doing of these services many of them perished with their gain. . . .

Moreover—not to go longer searching out and recalling every particular of our past miseries, as they befell throughout the city—I say that while so sinister a time prevailed in the latter, on no wise therefore was the surrounding country spared, wherein (letting be the fortified towns which in their littleness were like the city) throughout the scattered villages and in the fields, the poor miserable peasants and their families, without succor of physician or aid of servant, died not like men, but well-nigh like beasts, along the roads or in their tillages or about the houses, indifferently by day and night. By reason whereof, growing lax like the townsfolk in their manners and customs, they took no thought of any thing or business of theirs; nay, all, as if they looked for death that very day, studied with all their wit, not to help to maturity the future produce of their cattle and their fields and the fruits of their own past toils, but to consume those which were ready to hand. Thus it came to pass that the oxen, the asses, the sheep, the goats, the swine, the fowls, nay, the very dogs, so faithful to mankind, being driven forth from their own houses, went straying at their pleasure about the fields, where the very grain was abandoned, without being cut, much less gathered in; and many, almost like rational creatures, after grazing all day, returned at night, glutted, to their houses, without the constraint of any herdsman.

To leave the country and return to the city, what more can be said save that such and so great was the cruelty of heaven (and in part, perhaps, that of men) that, between March and the following July, what with the virulence of that pestiferous sickness and the number of sick folk ill tended or forsaken in their need, through the fearfulness of those who remained in good health, it is believed for certain that upward of a hundred thousand human beings perished within the walls of the city of Florence, which perhaps before the advent of that death-dealing calamity, would not have been accounted to hold so many? Alas, how many great palaces, how many goodly houses, how many noble mansions, once full of families, of lords and of ladies, remained empty even to the meanest servant! How many memorable families, how many ample heritages, how many famous fortunes were seen to remain without lawful heir! How many valiant men, how many fair ladies, how many sprightly youths, whom, not only others, but [ancient Greek physicians] Galen, Hippocrates or Aesculapius themselves would have judged most hale, breakfasted in the morning with their kinsfolk, comrades and friends and that same night supped with their ancestors in the other world!

FAMINE AND CHURCH CORRUPTION IN EUROPE

BARBARA TUCHMAN

For most of the Middle Ages, Europe was dominated by the Roman Catholic Church. The power of the church reached its peak during the Crusades, when the popes were able to command the support of both Europe's common people and the feudal nobles who controlled land and politics. During the fourteenth century, however, the church began to lose influence. A series of weak popes were dominated by nobles, particularly the king of France. For much of the century, in fact, the papacy was a pawn of the French king, and the popes lived not in Rome but in Avignon in southern France. Moreover, churchmen grew corrupt and worldly, concerned more with wealth and politics than religion.

According to historian Barbara Tuchman, author of the following selection, the decline in religious authority was only one crisis suffered by Europeans in the fourteenth century. Another was famine, which made Europeans more susceptible to the Black Death when it arrived in the 1340s. Combined with war and revolt, famine and religious corruption undermined the balance of society in medieval Europe.

Barbara Tuchman is the author of many popular works of history, including *The Guns of August* and *The Proud Tower*.

A physical chill settled on the 14th century at its very start, initiating the miseries to come. The Baltic Sea froze over twice, in 1303 and 1306–07; years followed of unseason-

From *A Distant Mirror*, by Barbara Tuchman. Copyright © 1978 by Barbara W. Tuchman. Used by permission of Alfred A. Knopf, a division of Random House, Inc.

able cold, storms and rains, and a rise in the level of the Caspian Sea. Contemporaries could not know it was the onset of what has since been recognized as the Little Ice Age, caused by an advance of polar and alpine glaciers and lasting until about 1700. Nor were they yet aware that, owing to the climatic change, communication with Greenland was gradually being lost, that the Norse settlements there were being extinguished, that cultivation of grain was disappearing from Iceland and being severely reduced in Scandinavia. But they could feel the colder weather, and mark with fear its result: a shorter growing season.

This meant disaster, for population increase in the last century had already reached a delicate balance with agricultural techniques. Given the tools and methods of the time, the clearing of productive land had already been pushed to its limits. Without adequate irrigation and fertilizers, crop yield could not be raised nor poor soils be made productive. Commerce was not equipped to transport grain in bulk from surplus-producing areas except by water. Inland towns and cities lived on local resources, and when these dwindled, the inhabitants starved.

In 1315, after rains so incessant that they were compared to the Biblical flood, crops failed all over Europe, and famine, the dark horseman of the Apocalypse, became familiar to all. The previous rise in population had already exceeded agricultural production, leaving people undernourished and more vulnerable to hunger and disease. Reports spread of people eating their own children, of the poor in Poland feeding on hanged bodies taken down from the gibbet. A contagion of dysentery prevailed in the same years. Local famines recurred intermittently after the great sweep of 1315–16.

Acts of man no less than change in the climate marked the 14th century as born to woe. . . . The most fateful was an assault on Boniface VIII by agents of Philip IV, King of France, surnamed the Fair. The issue was temporal versus papal authority arising from Philip's levy of taxes on clerical income without consent of the Pope. Boniface in response issued the defiant Bull *Clericos Laicos* in 1296 forbidding the clergy to pay any form of tax whatsoever to any lay ruler. He recognized in the growing tendency of prelates to hesitate between allegiance to their king and obedience to the Pope a threat to the papal claim to universal rule as Vicar of Christ. Despite formidable hostilities brought to bear on him by Philip the Fair, Boniface asserted in a second Bull, *Unam Sanctam*, in 1302, the most absolute statement of papal supremacy ever made: "It is necessary to salvation that every human creature be subject to the Roman pontiff."

Philip thereupon called for a council to judge the Pope on

charges of heresy, blasphemy, murder, sodomy, simony and sorcery (including consorting with a familiar spirit or pet demon), and failure to fast on fast days. At the same time Boniface drew up a Bull to excommunicate the King, prompting Philip to resort to physical force. On September 7, 1303, agents of the King, aided by anti-papist Italian armed forces, seized the 86-year-old Pope in his summer retreat at Anagni near Rome with the intention of forestalling the excommunication and bringing him by force before a council. After three days' turmoil, Boniface was freed by the citizens of Anagni, but the shock of the outrage was mortal and within a month he was dead.

THE PAPACY MOVES TO AVIGNON

The assault on the Pope did not rally support for the cause of the victim and the fact that it did not was a measure of change. The tide was receding from the universality of the Church that had been the medieval dream. The all-embracing claim of Boniface VIII was obsolete before he made it. The indirect consequence of the "Crime of Anagni" was the removal of the papacy to Avignon, and in that "Babylonian Exile" demoralization began.

The move occurred when, under the influence of Philip the Fair, a French Pope was elected as Clement V. He did not go to Rome to take up his See, mainly because he feared Italian reprisals for the French treatment of Boniface, although the Italians said it was because he kept a French mistress, the beautiful Countess of Périgord, daughter of the Count of Foix. In 1309 he settled in Avignon in Provence near the mouth of the Rhône. This was within the French sphere, though technically not in France since Provence was a fief of the Kingdom of Naples and Sicily.

Thereafter under six French popes in succession, Avignon became a virtual temporal state of sumptuous pomp, of great cultural attraction, and of unlimited simony—that is, the selling of offices. Diminished by its removal from the Holy See of Rome and by being generally regarded as a tool of France, the papacy sought to make up prestige and power in temporal terms. It concentrated on finance and the organization and centralization of every process of papal government that could bring in revenue. Besides its regular revenue from tithes and annates on ecclesiastical income and from dues from papal fiefs, every office, every nomination, every appointment or preferment, every dispensation of the rules, every judgment of the Rota or adjudication of a claim, every pardon, indulgence, and absolution, everything the Church had or was, from cardinal's hat to pilgrim's relic, was for sale. In addition, the papacy took a cut of all voluntary gifts and bequests and offerings on the altar. It received Peter's Pence from

England and other kingdoms. It sold extra indulgences in jubilee years and took a special tax for crusades which continued to be proclaimed but rarely left home. The once great impulse had faded, and fervor for holy war had become largely verbal.

Benefices, of which there were 700 bishops' sees and hundreds of thousands of lower offices, were the most lucrative source of papal income. Increasingly, the popes reserved more and more benefices to their power of appointment, destroying the elective principle. Since the appointees were often strangers to the diocese, or some cardinal's favorite, the practice aroused resentment within the clergy. If an episcopal election was still held, the papacy charged a fee for confirming it. To obtain a conferred benefice, a bishop or abbot greased the palms of the Curia for his nomination, paid anywhere from a third to the whole of his first year's revenue as the fee for his appointment, and knew that when he died his personal property would revert to the Pope and any outstanding dues would have to be paid by his successor.

FINANCIAL CORRUPTION AND ILLITERATE PRIESTS

Excommunication and anathema, the most extreme measures the Church could command, supposedly reserved for heresy and horrible crimes—"for by these penalties a man is separated from the faithful and turned over to Satan"—were now used to wring money from recalcitrant payers. In one case a bishop was denied Christian burial until his heirs agreed to be responsible for his debts, to the scandal of the diocese, which saw its bishop lying unshriven and cut off from hope of salvation. Abuse of the spiritual power for such purposes brought excommunication into contempt and lowered respect for clerical leaders.

Money could buy any kind of dispensation: to legitimize children, of which the majority were those of priests and prelates; to divide a corpse for the favorite custom of burial in two or more places; to permit nuns to keep two maids; to permit a converted Jew to visit his unconverted parents; to marry within the prohibited degree of consanguinity (with a sliding scale of fees for the second, third, and fourth degrees); to trade with the infidel Moslem (with a fee required for each ship on a scale according to cargo); to receive stolen goods up to a specific value. The collection and accounting of all these sums, largely handled through Italian bankers, made the physical counting of cash a common sight in the papal palace. Whenever he entered there, reported Alvar Pelayo, a Spanish official of the Curia, "I found brokers and clergy engaged in reckoning the money which lay in heaps before them."

The dispensation with most serious results was the one permitting appointment to a benefice of a candidate below the canonical age of 25 or one who had never been consecrated or never taken the required examination for literacy. Appointment of unfit or absentee clergy became an abuse in itself. In Bohemia on one occasion in the early 14th century, a boy of seven was appointed to a parish worth an annual income of 25 gulden; another was raised through three offices of the hierarchy, paying at each stage for a dispensation for non-residence and postponed consecration. Younger sons of noble families were repeatedly appointed to archbishoprics at 18, 20, or 22. Tenures were short because each preferment brought in another payment.

Priests who could not read or who, from ignorance, stumbled stupidly through the ritual of the Eucharist were another scandal. A Bishop of Durham in 1318 could not understand or pronounce Latin and after struggling helplessly with the word *Metropolitanus* at his own consecration, muttered in the vernacular, "Let us take that word as read." Later when ordaining candidates for holy orders, he met the word *aenigmate* (through a glass darkly) and this time swore in honest outrage, "By St. Louis, that was no courteous man who wrote this word!" The unfit clergy spread dismay, for these were the men supposed to have the souls of the laity in their charge and be the intermediaries between man and God. Writing of "incapable and ignorant men" who could buy any office they wanted from the Curia, the chronicler Henry of Hereford went to the heart of the dismay when he wrote, "Look . . . at the dangerous situation of those in their charge, and tremble!"

When Church practices were calculated at a money value, their religious content seeped away. Theoretically, pardon for sin could only be won through penitence, but the penance of a pilgrimage to Rome or Jerusalem had little meaning when the culprit could estimate the cost of the journey and buy an indulgence for an equivalent sum.

POPES LIVED LIKE EMPERORS

The popes—successors, as Petrarch pointed out, of "the poor fisherman of Galilee"—were now "loaded with gold and clad in purple." John XXII, a Pope with the touch of Midas who ruled from 1316 to 1334, bought for his own use forty pieces of gold cloth from Damascus for 1,276 gold florins and spent even more on furs, including an ermine-trimmed pillow. The clothing of his retinue cost 7,000 to 8,000 florins a year.

His successors Benedict XII and Clement VI built in stages the great papal palace at Avignon on a rock overlooking the Rhône, a

huge and inharmonious mass of roofs and towers without co-
herent design. Constructed in castle style around interior courts,
with battlements and twelve-foot-thick walls for defense, it had
odd pyramidal chimneys rising from the kitchens, banqueting
halls and gardens, money chambers and offices, rose-windowed
chapels, a steam room for the Pope heated by a boiler, and a gate
opening on the public square where the faithful gathered to watch
the Holy Father ride out on his white mule. Here moved the ma-
jestic cardinals in their wide red hats, "rich, insolent and rapa-
cious" in Petrarch's words, vying with each other in the magnif-
icence of their suites. One required ten stables for his horses, and
another rented parts of 51 houses to lodge all his retainers.

Corridors of the palace bustled with notaries and officers of
the Curia and legates departing on or returning from their missions. Petitioners and their lawyers waited anxiously in ante-
rooms, pilgrims crowded in the courtyards to receive the pontifical blessing, while through the halls passed the parade of the
Pope's relatives of both sexes in brocades and furs with their attending knights and squires and retainers. The household of
sergeants-at-arms, ushers, chamberlains, chaplains, stewards,
and servants numbered about 400, all supplied with board, lodg-
ing, clothing, and wages.

Tiled floors were ornamented in designs of flowers, fantastic
beasts, and elaborate heraldry. Clement VI, a lover of luxury and
beauty who used 1,080 ermine skins in his personal wardrobe,
imported Matteo Giovanetti and artists from the school of Si-
mone Martini to paint the walls with scenes from the Bible. The
four walls of Clement's own study, however, were entirely covered by scenes of a noble's secular pleasures: a stag hunt, fal-
conry, orchards, gardens, fishponds, and a group of ambiguous
nude bathers who could be either women or children depending
on the eye of the beholder. No religious themes intruded.

At banquets the Pope's guests dined off gold and silver plate,
seated beneath Flemish tapestries and hangings of silk. Recep-
tions for visiting princes and envoys rivaled the splendors of any
secular court. Papal entertainments, fetes, even tournaments and
balls, reproduced the secular.

"I am living in the Babylon of the West," wrote Petrarch in the
1340s, where prelates feast at "licentious banquets" and ride on
snow-white horses "decked in gold, fed on gold, soon to be shod
in gold if the Lord does not check this slavish luxury." Though
himself something of a lapsed cleric, Petrarch shared the clerical
habit of denouncing at double strength whatever was disap-
proved. Avignon became for him "that disgusting city," though
whether because of worldly corruption or the physical filth and

smells of its narrow, overcrowded streets is uncertain. The town, crammed with merchants, artisans, ambassadors, adventurers, astrologers, thieves, prostitutes, and no less than 43 branches of Italian banking houses (in 1327), was not so well equipped as the papal palace for the disposal of sewage. The palace had a tower whose two lower stories contained exclusively latrines. Fitted with stone seats, these were emptied into a pit below ground level that was flushed by water from the kitchen drains and by an underground stream diverted for the purpose. In the town, however, the stench caused the ambassador from Aragon to swoon, and Petrarch to move out to nearby Vaucluse "to prolong my life."

ENGLAND'S HENRY V TRIUMPHS DURING THE HUNDRED YEARS' WAR

CHRISTOPHER HIBBERT

The Hundred Years' War (actually fought from 1337 to 1453) was a long-lasting drain on the human, financial, and territorial resources of both its main participants, England and France. The war's origins lay in the claim of King Edward III of England (reigned 1327–1337) to the throne of France, a claim the French resisted. Both kingdoms settled into a conflict that, it seemed, would never end.

England's great moment of triumph in the war came during the reign of the young king Henry V, whose unexpected victory over a much larger French force at Agincourt in 1415 was celebrated by, among others, Shakespeare. Henry's victory gave him the French throne, and he took the opportunity to marry the French princess. A complete English victory seemed imminent until Henry died in 1422 at the age of just thirty-four.

In the following selection, Christopher Hibbert describes Henry's return to England following his successes in France. He notes that while Henry could be cruel and reckless, the people of England loved him. Henry V and Agincourt, Hibbert concludes, reflect one of the most significant legacies of the Hundred Years' War: the emergence of patriotism and nationalism.

From *Agincourt*, by Christopher Hibbert (London: Batsford, 1964). Copyright © Christopher Hibbert, 1964. Reprinted by permission of Chrysalis Books.

Popular historian Christopher Hibbert is the author of many books, including *The Rise and Fall of the House of Medici*, *The Days of the French Revolution*, and *The Great Mutiny*.

A s on landing in France, so now on returning home King [Henry V] knelt in prayer. He prayed on the beach at Dover and at Canterbury he prayed at the shrine of St Thomas and kissed the Cathedral's holy relics. God had brought him his victory. With God's help he would strive to be worthy of it.

Travelling by way of Eltham, he set out for London on the morning of 23 November. At Blackheath he was met by the new Lord Mayor, Nicholas Wolton (known as 'Witless Nick' in the city), twenty-foot aldermen and thousand upon thousand of citizens and craftsmen, all dressed in scarlet and wearing the devices of their companies. The Mayor formally congratulated the King on the great victory that he had won, and then the long cavalcade rode off towards Southwark and London.

For days the city had been preparing a welcome worthy of so magnificent a victor; and as he entered it by way of the gatehouse at the Stoops by London Bridge Henry could see how triumphal his greeting was to be.

On either side of the gatehouse, at the top of its two towers, a gigantic statue had been erected. One of these figures 'of amazing magnitude' was of a sentinel who held a battle-axe in his right hand and offered the King the keys of the city in his left. By his side stood a female figure, almost as immense, clothed in a scarlet cloak and decorated with jewels and sparkling ornaments. All around both figures, banners and standards flew in the wind from the turrets of the towers, while 'trumpets, clarions and horns sounded in various melody'.

London Welcomes Its Triumphant King

The King and his retinue stood still for a moment, wondering at the sight and sound of their welcome. Then the King said in a loud voice, 'Hail to the royal city!' and they went on towards the bridge.

They passed between two tall wooden columns covered with linen painted to represent blocks of whim marble and green jasper. Looking up towards the top of the column on their right, they saw the figure of an antelope with the royal arms hanging on a shield from his neck and with the royal sceptre grasped between the paws of his right forefoot; and turning to the left they saw a lion holding a staff from which hung the royal standard.

Beyond the bridge they came towards an immense arch raised

across the street, and on top of the arch, inside a pavilion of crimson tapestry, there was a statue of St George in armour, his helmet covered with a laurel wreath studded with pearls and precious stones. And as they passed beneath the arch, 'innumerable boys, representing the angelic host, arrayed in white with their faces painted gold and with glittering wings and virgin locks set with precious sprigs of laurel, sang in melodious voices'. . . .

The procession wound up Fish Hill through the Cornmarket in Grass Church towards the rough and narrow streets that stretched from Leadenhall to St Paul's. At the Tun in Cornhill, there was another tower draped in crimson cloth, the hem of the cloth held out on long red poles in representation of an open tent. As the King passed by the tent and looked inside,

> a company of prophets, of venerable hoariness, dressed in golden coats and mantles, with their heads covered and wrapped in gold and crimson, sent forth a great quantity of sparrows and little birds, as a sacrifice agreeable to God in return for victory. Some birds alighted on the King's breast, some rested on his shoulders, and some fluttered round about him. And the prophets sang with sweet harmony, bowing to the ground, this psalm of thanksgiving: 'Cantate Domino canticum novum, Alleluia! Quia mirabilia fecit, Alleluia!'

On through Cheapside, past vast tapestries on which were worked scenes representing the deeds of English heroes, past great banners and standards, escutcheons and shields, flags fluttering on velvet-covered poles, by miniature forts and linen-covered castles that 'seemed to grow out of the buildings' on either side, beneath damask awnings and arches of halberds that stretched from roof to roof above their heads, the King and his friends and his awestruck prisoners went towards St Paul's.

Here, on one side of the Cathedral, were more old men 'having the names of the twelve apostles written on their foreheads, together with the twelve Kings, Martyrs and Confessors of the succession of England, their loins girded with golden sceptres, sceptres also in their hands and crowns on their heads, chanting with one accord at the King's approach'. And there, on the other side, were raised pavilions filled with 'most beautiful virgin girls, standing motionless like statues, decorated with very elegant ornaments of modesty and crowned with laurel and girt with golden girdles, having in their hands cups of gold from which they blew, with gentle breath scarcely perceptible, round leaves of gold upon the King's head as he passed beneath them'. And in front by the steps of the Cathedral itself, more beautiful girls, clothed all in white, came out towards him, 'singing with timbrel and dance, this song of congratulation: *'Welcome, Henry the Fifte, Kynge of Englond and of Fraunce'*; while little boys, also dressed in white, their hair covered in jewels, threw down from the towers of a 'very fair castle made of wood with no less ingenuity than elegance', gilt wavers and laurel leaves.

And everywhere,

> besides the pressure in the standing places, and of people crowding through the streets, and the multitudes of men and women looking through openings and apertures, the lattices and windows on both sides were filled with the most noble ladies and women of the realm and with honourable and honoured men who flocked together to the wonderful sight and were so very gracefully and elegantly dressed in fine garments of gold and crimson and various other apparel, that a greater assembly or a more splendid spectacle was not recollected to have been seen in London ever before.

The King himself, amidst all the excitement and the adulation, passed quietly along in a purple robe, modest and thoughtful. He had been pressed to wear the helmet that had been battered by the axe at Agincourt, but he insisted on walking through the crowds bareheaded and on foot. He had few attendants with him, and often he was obliged to wait patiently while they cleared a path for him through the crowds. When men raised their voices to praise him extravagantly, he asked them not to praise him but God.

At the door of St Paul's he was greeted by eighteen bishops in their pontificals, and he followed them to the High Altar where he sank humbly to his knees.

THE CONTROVERSIAL "STAR OF ENGLAND"

The character of this remarkable man has long puzzled historians. To his English contemporaries he was *'sans peur et sans reproche'* [without fear and without reproach], a 'noble prince and victoriouse Kynge, floure in his tyme of Cristen chivalrie', a 'Julius in intellect, a Hector in valour, an Achilles in strength, an Augustus in morals, a Paris in eloquence, a Solomon in dialectic, and a Troilus in love', 'al nobleness, manhode and vertue', 'felicitous in all things'.

Even French contemporaries, who had little good to say of English people, could not but admire their King. He was 'above all the prince of justice, both in relation to himself for the sake of example, and in relation to others, according to equity and right; he gave support to none out of favour, nor did he suffer wrong to go unpunished out of regard for kinship.'

It was an opinion which Shakespeare's contemporaries endorsed. They recognised in *King Henry V* a noble soldier, selfless, brave, patriotic, honourable, human and just, the 'true monarch of Elizabethan idealism', as Professor E.F. Jacob [an authority on Henry V] has put it, 'a figure dominant over State and Church alike, an instrument of the divine will'.

To a people who looked back on his time as a golden age, Henry was, indeed, 'this star of England'. Fortune made his sword. He possessed all the virtues of the good mediaeval king. His piety, his courage, his sense of justice and his brilliant generalship were all unquestioned. His supposedly wild youth added a pleasing touch of humanity to his stern nobility.

In more recent years this unqualified approval of the paragon of paladins has not been found acceptable. Was there not much that was unfeeling and bigoted in the strict morality of his adult life, much that was priggish and sanctimonious in his piety, deceitful in his diplomacy, selfish in his patriotism, secretive in his reserve? He may have been a great soldier but he was a hard, domineering and, on occasions, cruel man. It was remembered that as a young prince of twenty-three, five years before the battle of Agincourt, he had supervised the burning of a blacksmith who had maintained that the Sacrament was not the body and blood of Christ; that during the battle itself he had ordered the slaughter of unknown numbers of defenceless prisoners in the face of a threat which turned out to be a false alarm; and that three years after the battle, while besieging Rouen, he had refused to let 12,000 old men, women and children—*bouches inutiles* [useless mouths]—pass through his lines during the cruel severities of an appalling winter in which most of them died. Rouen was his own city, it was withheld from him against all justice and God's will. He would not bargain with them.

The tremor of distaste is inevitable. But the King was a man of his age, and it is the age, which by the modern liberal conscience, must be condemned as distasteful. Henry V may have been more concerned with the future of the House of Lancaster than with that of the Kingdom of England; he may have been less concerned with the conquest of France as a step to the conquest of the Infidel than he pretended; he may have been more of an adventurer than a statesman; he may have had many, if not all, of the faults of character that have reliably been attributed to him. But he was still the greatest Englishman of his time. He was also England's greatest soldier. . . .

HENRY WAS A CHARISMATIC AND LUCKY GENERAL

He brought to the direction of his army a special quality of leadership that was as rare as it was effective. His men admired his dash and spirit, the energy and stamina, the force and determination, the verve and panache of the ideal mediaeval knight. It was in these qualities that his greatness lay. He was not a powerful-looking man, but he was lithe and athletic and he wore his armour 'as though it were a light cloak'. His features, an apparently accurate refection of his musical and liturgical tastes, were more those of a monk or an intellectual than those of the fighting soldier; but he *was* a fighting soldier. And his troops recognised him as one. He shared their hardships; he spoke to them in words they could understand. He was a king but he showed that he understood the feelings and aspirations of common men. He was not excitable, neither wildly elated in victory nor obviously dismayed by defeat, and he never gave way to hysteria or panic. His calm and contemplative eyes became terrifying when he was angry, but his anger did not rise without good cause. He was stern, relentless, even implacable but his soldiers found him just and he was a man of his word; he succeeded in imparting to them much of his own dedicated enthusiasm and moral fervour. They grumbled when he refused to allow them to plunder, but they respected him and most of them obeyed him. He was masterful, decisive and competent with a sense of authority that was at once impressive and reassuring. He was, in short, a natural leader of men.

So much is undoubted. Whether or not he was a great general is, however, a question which requires investigation. He owed much to luck, of course—but then all successful generals have done; he made mistakes—they all do that; he profited as much from his enemies' blunders as from his own unerring decisions—few do not. Beyond these considerations, there is, though, an element of doubt about his capacity as a general which an examination of his strategy and tactics during the Agincourt campaign—and his later campaigns were almost entirely limited to sieges—does nothing to dispel. . . .

Even so, leaving aside his faith in God's guidance and help, Henry's *chevauchée* [cavalry march] across the Somme through Picardy might, perhaps, more accurately be termed, in [military historian] Colonel Alfred Burne's phrase, 'a justifiable and commendable risk', than a 'foolhardy and reckless adventure'. To set out, however, for the Blanche-Taque ford on the Somme without ensuring that it would still be open when he arrived there was a mistake which involved a long, painful and dangerous march that could have been disastrous. He did instruct the Captain of Calais to send a force down towards the Somme, but he did not himself send forward an advance-guard or even a reconnaissance party, to discover whether or not the troops from Calais had succeeded in their task, although he had eight days—while awaiting the Dauphin's answer to his challenge—in which to do so. And it was consequently not until he had crossed the Bresle and was coming down towards the Somme estuary that he learned that the small force of 300 men that had been sent down from Calais by Sir William Bardolf had been driven back long before it reached the Blanche-Taque ford, which was by then guarded by a strong French force.

The march eastwards towards the boggy headwaters of the Somme was now inevitable; and it was only after the army had reached Fouilly that Henry learned—not from his own scouts, apparently, but first from prisoners of war and then from intimidated peasants anxious to get rid of so many hungry men—of a suitable crossing place. The immediate change of direction across the downland from Fouilly to Voyennes and Béthencourt, since it enabled him to cross the river without interference by the French army which until then had been shadowing him, has been described as a 'brilliant step on the part of the English King', though it seems, in fact, if not actually forced on him by necessity, more adventitious than adroit.

The subsequent seventy-mile march from Athies to Agincourt was undoubtedly a tribute to the endurance and discipline of Henry's army, but the French troops—most of whom had already come heavily equipped with both guns and wagons a hundred miles from Rouen, and some of whom had come much further, and were not all mounted—went by a longer route and got there before him to close the road to Calais. It cannot, I think, be doubted that up to this stage of the campaign Henry was out-generalled.

THE FRUITS OF VICTORY AT AGINCOURT

Nothing, however, succeeds like a victory. And whether or not Henry's triumph owed more to the obsolete tactics of the French army and the reckless and insubordinate behaviour of the French men-at-arms than to his own prowess, it *was* a great triumph. The results of the campaign—limited as they were to the possession of Harfleur—a doubtful asset—and the acquisition of ransom money, cannot be said to be impressive. Nor can it be denied that Normandy could have been conquered later, had Agincourt never been fought. But the whole Christian world was impressed and the prestige that Henry had acquired made it possible for him to return to France as a feared and respected conqueror.

Henry went back in the summer of 1417 with hopes of recovering Normandy and extending his possessions in south-western

France. He lay siege to Caen and it fell without a struggle; the Duke of Gloucester entered Bayeux unresisted; Falaise surrendered at the beginning of January 1418. Rouen offered stronger resistance, but that too fell to the English a year later; and with its fall came the conquest of Normandy. In the following year the Treaty of Troyes was signed and Henry was made heir and regent of France and married Catherine, the King's daughter. The leadership of all Christendom was now within his grasp and his thoughts turned once more to a new crusade against the Infidel. But his health broke down in the summer of 1422 and on 31 August at the age of thirty-four he died at Vincennes.

When he lay dying, as though answering unspoken charges, he justified his attack on France:

> It was not ambitious lust for dominion, nor for empty glory, nor any other cause, that drew me to these wars, but only that by suing of my right, I might at once gain peace and my own rights. . . . And before the wars were begun I was fully instructed by men of the holiest life and the wisest counsel that I ought and could with this intention begin the wars, prosecute them, and justly finish them without danger to my soul.

Later he interrupted his confessor and chaplains, who were saying with him the psalms of penance, and added:

> O Good Lord, thou knowest that, if thy pleasure had been to have suffered me to live my natural age, my firm purpose and intent was, after I had established this realm of France in sure peace, to have gone and visited Jerusalem and to have re-edified the walls thereof, and to have repulsed from it the miscreants, thine adversaries.

It was for this ultimate purpose he now felt sure, and, perhaps, always had felt sure, that the battle of Agincourt had been fought. But it was not God's will that he should fulfil that purpose.

He died to leave his country in the care of a regent and a baby-king who eventually, not having his powers of leadership or his degree of parliamentary support, and having to contend with the rising force of French national pride and its inspired epitome, Joan of Arc, was to lose all that his father had fought for.

Henry V's life, though, had not been in vain. He had bequeathed England something far more valuable than foreign territory. For all his faults, for all the contradictions of his character and the selfishness of his motives, he had re-awakened a new national consciousness and pride that the advances and victories of the previous century had first engendered. Patriotism can be a dangerous emotion, and the sort of patriotism brought about by the Hundred Years War often amounted to no more than complacency and insularity, but at its most pure and unselfish it is an inspiration. Henry's life and achievement awakened Englishmen to this truth, and to the awareness that their country was not only their home but that it could represent an ideal worth dying for.

JOAN OF ARC TURNS THE TIDE OF WAR

ROBIN NEILLANDS

After Henry V's victory at Agincourt during the Hundred Years' War gave the throne of France to the English, the French forces were in disarray. The dauphin Charles VII (the French claimant to the kingdom of France) finally turned to a young peasant woman, Joan of Arc (Jeanne d'Arc), who claimed to have heard angelic voices since girlhood. The voices had convinced her that she must stand at the head of France's armies and, after lifting a siege the English mounted at the important city of Orléans, lead the dauphin to the city of Rheims to be crowned king.

As Robin Neillands, the author of the following selection, asserts, Joan's uncommon charisma and strong faith impressed those around her. After some skepticism, Charles VII and his nobles allowed Joan to fight with them. She enjoyed victories at Orléans and elsewhere and gave France the same sense of national identity that Henry V had given England. Neillands notes that when Joan, the so-called Maid of Orléans, was betrayed and burned at the stake for witchcraft, France gained a martyr to its cause.

Popular historian Robin Neillands is the author of many books, including *The Great War Generals on the Western Front, The Bomber War,* and *Walking Through France.*

I t is more than curious that the Plantagenet [the English royal line] dominion in France had its beginnings with the Devil's Brood [rumors that the Plantagenet line had the devil's blood] and came to an end through the actions of a saint, but that is what happened. A girl came riding out of the east and within one

From *The Hundred Years War,* by Robin Neillands (London: Routledge). Copyright © 1990 Robin Neillands. Reprinted with permission from John Pawsey Literary Agency.

short summer, sent the English on a retreat which continued until they were expelled from the kingdom, years after her death.

Perhaps the most remarkable thing about the entire saga is not
that a young girl heard voices and believed she had a divine mission, but that the King of France believed her and entrusted her
with an army. There is now a popular belief, fuelled by [modern
playwright George Bernard] Shaw among others, that when Joan
arrived at Chinon the Dauphin was living in penury, his soldiers
disillusioned and unwilling to fight, his courtiers nothing but ef-
fete fops. None of this is true. The Dauphin already had plenty of
money and would experience no great difficulty in raising more.
His soldiers, if as yet none too successful in battle, were still in the
field, swiftly regaining any territory the Anglo-Burgundians captured and stoutly defending the walls of Orléans, while a stream
of defector knights arrived daily from Plantagenet holdings in the
north. The Dauphin still ruled in much of France, and among his
supporters were such warlike captains as La Hire, Ponton de Xaintrailles, Arthur de Richemont, and Dunois, Bastard of Orléans, a
host of knights and burghers and a mass of common people.

Joan's Importance to France

He still needed the Maid but the reason for this need must therefore be a cause of speculation. She never actually commanded
the army; her role was more that of a living standard, charging
recklessly at the head of the troops. Indeed, her only tactic was
the charge, her only policy a relentless determination to attack
the English wherever they could be found. Perhaps it was this
that made Charles support her; he was well aware that he lacked
what we now call charisma, while this girl dazzled his court, his
captains, and all who met her. Maybe, with her at their head, his
troops could defeat an English army in the field and put the
'Goddams' on the road back to their foggy island of Albion. Any-
way, it was worth the risk.

Jeanne d'Arc, St Joan, *La Pucelle* [the Maid], the Maid of Orléans
was, however, much more than a romantic creation, or a useful
tool of kings. She was and remains the embodiment of patriotic
France. Her chief appeal lay not with the King and his court, who
first used her, then ignored her, and finally abandoned her, but
the common people and the common soldier. In Jeanne, people
saw the hand of God, fulfilling all their hopes; hopes of an end to
this interminable war, the final expulsion of the English and the
Free Companies, and the creation of a France in which they, too,
might have some share in the future peace and prosperity.

According to some of those who knew her and testified at the
rehabilitation trial at Rouen in 1450, twenty years after her death,

Jeanne was born in Domrémy, a hamlet of Lorraine, on 6 January 1412, of fairly well-to-do peasant stock, and was christened in the village Church of St Rémy. The land around Domrémy was held for the Armagnacs by an experienced captain of the Dauphin, Robert de Baudricourt, who commanded the castle at nearby Vaucouleurs and led the garrison out from time to time on punitive raids against Burgundian incursions and the roving bands of English or French *routiers* [bandits], the *'Ecorcheurs'* or flayers, successors to the Tard-Venus of Edward III's time who were then ravaging the surrounding countryside.

JOAN CLAIMS DIVINE GUIDANCE

Sometime in the autumn of 1428, when she was aged about 17, Jeanne presented herself at the castle of Vaucouleurs and told her tale to the sceptical captain. Since her childhood, she said, she had heard heavenly voices. They spoke to her in the wind and in the bells of the village church, and they told her of the Dauphin Charles, of the plight of his kingdom, of how she must go to see him at Chinon. There the Dauphin would give her an army with which she would raise the siege of Orléans and then she would lead the Dauphin to his coronation at Rheims, and all of France would rise up singing and drive the 'Goddams' from the land they had usurped. It took several visits before Robert agreed to help her, and it was the first of her miracles that she finally convinced this grizzled old soldier of the French wars to risk his command and reputation by giving her his support. He found horses, helped her to disguise herself as a boy, sent a messenger to Chinon to give the Dauphin warning of her coming, and provided a small escort. If she could make her way to the court across hundreds of miles of hostile, harried territory, that in itself would be another miracle, and if not, there was little lost. Like his sovereign a little later, Robert de Baudricourt thought it was worth the risk. . . .

ENGLISH FORCES BESIEGE ORLÉANS

In July 1428, the English, led by Thomas Montague, Earl of Salisbury, had occupied Paris. With the capital secured from the slippery grasp of Burgundy, it was now possible to consider a major advance south across the Beauce towards the city of Orléans, which was the key to the Loire valley and roughly halfway between Paris and the French Dauphin's capital at Bourges. During this advance to the Loire, the English army, now some 4,000 strong, first took the city of Chartres. Salisbury began his investment of Orléans by sending Sir William de la Pole to capture three Loire towns: Jargeau which lies to the east of Orléans, and

Beaugency and Meung which lie to the west. This effectively prevented any supplies or men entering Orléans via the river, and this done, Salisbury's army appeared before the walls of the city on 12 October 1428 and began to dig in for a siege.

Salisbury's slow advance had given the garrison plenty of time to get in supplies and improve the defences. The garrison of some 3,000 men had hastily rebuilt the five-gate towers and added a large number of 'bombards' of cannon to the city's already formidable fire power. The walls of Orléans now mounted over seventy cannons of various size, some capable of firing cannon balls weighing up to 190 lb. A number of these cannons were built into two towers, 'Les Tourelles', which commanded the river bridge leading into the city.

The English pitched camp in the suburb of Olivet, where they were soon joined by a force of 1,500 Burgundian men-at-arms, and the siege commenced with a heavy bombardment of the Tourelles and the town's curtain walls. After three days this bombardment forced the French to abandon the Tourelles and the garrison withdrew into the city on 23 October, after making a breach in the bridge to prevent pursuit. The jubilant English promptly occupied the Tourelles, then moved their cannon forward to recommence the bombardment. On the following day they received a setback, when the Earl of Salisbury, studying the fortifications from a window high in one of the Tourelles, was hit by a shot from a cannon accidentally discharged by a young French boy playing in the defending battery. The cannonball hit the window lintel and one of the iron bars struck the Earl in the face. Grievously injured, Salisbury died of shock and gangrene at Meung, eight days later. The command of the siege fell for a while on to a more cautious general, the Earl of Suffolk, who was supported by several experienced captains: Lord Scales, Lord Ros and the Earl's brother, Sir William de la Pole.

ENGLISH FORCES WERE FORMIDABLE

It was now November and the weather was atrocious, so Suffolk moved his men into winter quarters in the suburbs, leaving only a token force before the city. This lapse enabled Dunois to enter the city with fresh troops and take command of the garrison, which with the addition of his men now actually exceeded the numbers of the besieging army. In December, however, the English returned to their flooded trenches, spurred on by their new commander, Lord Talbot, 'great marshal to our Lord King Henry VI, for all his wars within the realm of the French', who soon put pressure on the defence. This general, John Talbot, Earl of Shrewsbury, was to become the leading English commander in

France during the final phase of the Hundred Years War. He had been born about 1387, and was an experienced captain long before he came to France, having served with Henry IV and the Prince of Wales in their Welsh campaigns. He had fought at Shrewsbury in 1403, and at the sieges of Aberystwyth and Harlech in 1407–9. He was to soldier on for over fifty years, building a formidable reputation as a warrior, and is the only English knight that Jeanne d'Arc knew of by name. . . .

The first major effort to lift the siege came at the start of Lent in 1429, when on 12 February a force containing many Scottish soldiers, led by the Count of Clermont, attempted to enter the city from Blois. Near Janville this force ran into a large convoy of over 300 English waggons from Paris, commanded by Sir John Fastolf, which had a considerable escort of 1,000 archers and some light cavalry, or *hobelars*. The waggons contained salted fish, 'herrings and Lenten stuff,' the besiegers' supplies for the coming Lent, which gave to their encounter the name of 'The Battle of the Herrings'.

Fastolf was an experienced captain and had risen in the world since he had leapt into the surf before Harfleur. He was now a Knight of the Garter, and a well regarded soldier. Seeing the enemy about to charge, Fastolf circled his waggons into a laager, and had his archers screen them with their stakes. Although the French and Scots first bombarded the waggon circle with light field artillery and then sent in foot and cavalry attacks, they were beaten off by the English archers with great loss, until the ground around the waggons was carpeted with men and horses. Then, seeing his enemy hesitate, Fastolf and his men mounted and charged out from the waggon circle and turned the battle into a rout. The Count of Clermont was wounded and Sir John Stewart, the Constable of Scotland, was killed. This victory at the Battle of the Herrings greatly encouraged the besieging army, and plunged the Dauphin and the garrisons of Chinon and Orléans into the deepest gloom. This depression lifted somewhat on 6 March, when Jeanne the Maid arrived at Chinon. Dramatists like George Bernard Shaw have shown the Dauphin as hiding among his courtiers while they mocked the peasant girl, but it is more likely that he simply kept his distance until he had time to examine her more closely and make up his own mind, for he was well aware what his enemies would make of it if he was taken in by some charlatan.

Jeanne was not alarming. She was a small, rather plain girl, with a sturdy peasant frame, her short, cropped hair a dark frame to an open face. Only her enthusiasm for the war and her fervent faith marked her out from a hundred others who followed in the train of the armies. Charles admitted her to his presence on 8 March, and though he found her fascinating, he sensibly sent her first to Poitiers, where she was carefully examined by the *Parlement* [Parliament of Paris, advisers to the king] and by a number of clerics, who finally attested to her chastity, sincerity and orthodoxy. Jeanne returned to Chinon in early April, where the King supplied her with armour and horses and sent her on to the army outside Orléans, where matters were not going well.

JOAN ARRIVES AT ORLÉANS

The English investment had continued throughout March and by early April the English were ready to advance on the battered walls of the city and take it by storm. It was only then, when the English were massing to assault the city, that they heard some incredible news. A new French army was marching upon them from Blois and at its head rode a *girl*.

This Maid—doubtless a witch of Satan—announced her intentions in letters to Lord Talbot and the Regent of France, John, Duke of Bedford:

> You, the English captains, must withdraw from the Kingdom of France and restore it to the King of Heaven and his deputy, the King of France, while the Duke of Burgundy should return at once to his true allegiance. Take yourself off to your own land, for I have been sent by God and his Angels, and I shall drive you from our land of France. If you will not believe the message from God, know that wherever you happen to be, we shall make such a great Hahaye as has not been made in France these thousand years.

It is fair to say that the English captains and their Burgundian allies were quite unimpressed by this missive. English heralds promptly put it about that the Dauphin's new army was led by a witch, but to the French soldiers besieged inside the city, the coming of the Maid was a miracle.

The army sent to Orléans was actually commanded by the Duke of Alençon, recently released after his capture by Bedford at Verneuil. Most of the force, including Jeanne, entered the city on 30 April. The rest followed, and Alençon's whole army was inside the city by 4 May. The English had now been battering the walls of Orléans for six solid months and were greatly discouraged by the arrival of fresh supplies and more troops for the garrison. Exactly why Talbot was unable to prevent the French entering Orléans is still unclear, but apparently the eastern gate, the Burgundian Gate, was unguarded, and some slipped in there while others crossed the river by night in barges.

On the very day that Alençon entered the city, Jeanne rode out again with diversionary forces which overran the Bastille Saint-Loup before Talbot could send men from his base at Bastille Saint-Laurent. The English and Burgundians in Saint-Loup were massacred and a large convoy of food entered the city. Two days later, on 6 May, Jeanne was in action again when, at the head of 4,000 troops, she crossed the river to storm the English forts along the south bank. This battle on the south bank took two days and on the first day Jeanne was struck in the shoulder by an arrow and carried weeping from the field, the English archers dancing about and shouting out delightedly 'The witch is dead!'

In fact, she had only received a flesh wound, for the arrow had barely penetrated her armour, and next day, to the dismay of the English, Jeanne was back in the fray. The last English troops on the south bank were soon penned up in the shattered ruins of the Tourelles, which fell on 7 May to a combined assault from Jeanne's forces on the southern side, and the city militia advancing from the city. On the following day, Talbot lifted the siege and Jeanne rode back in across the repaired Tourelles bridge to receive a rapturous welcome from Alençon, the soldiers of the garrison and the citizens of Orléans, an event which has been repeated at Orléans on 8 May every year from that day to this.

The command of the large French army, numbering 8,000 men, and now assembled at Orléans, passed to Dunois, but even with Dunois' intelligent command and Jeanne, a living *Oriflamme* [the Sacred Banner of the French kings], the French were still wary of engaging English archers in open battle and held back when, having burned what they could not carry away, the English army left its camp and halted just north of the city, inviting combat. When the French declined to attack, the English army fell into column and began to withdraw sullenly across the Forêt d'Orléans, with the French army now dogging their footsteps. This withdrawal was a risky undertaking, for not only was the entire English army already smaller than the Dunois command, but men had been bled off to reinforce the garrisons of Jargeau, Meung and Beaugency.

THE ENGLISH RETREAT

Hearing of the debacle at Orléans, Bedford had ordered Sir John Fastolf, whose stock stood high after the Battle of the Herrings, to lead a fresh army of 5,000 men, 'many of them knights and squires of England', south to Janville to cover Talbot's retreat. Fastolf reached Janville without difficulty. Here he heard that the French had relieved Orléans and had also driven the English from the Loire towns of Beaugency and Jargeau, and were now investing Meung, news which, according to the chronicler Wavrin du Forestal, 'gave him great distress'. An hour later, however, Talbot rode into Janville with an escort, 'of two hundred men-at-arms and as many mounted archers. His arrival was very joyful for the English, for Lord Talbot was the wisest and most valiant knight of the Kingdom of England'. . . .

The English withdrawal in the usual three divisions was closely followed by the French, and the English were 'about a league' from the town of Patay, 20 miles north of Meung, when the French cavalry fell like a thunderclap upon the rearguard, which was commanded by John Fastolf. The English attempted to deploy for battle but on that open plain the French cavalry, led by La Hire and Xaintrailles, with Jeanne, to her disgust, forced to

Joan of Arc's actions revived morale and helped the French prevail over the English in the Hundred Years' War.

watch their attack from a position in the rear, were among the archers of the rearguard before they could plant their stakes in thick, defensive hedgerows, driving them back into the main body. Fastolf then galloped after the vanguard to recall it to the battle, but the captains of the vanguard took his headlong arrival as the signal for *'sauve qui peut'* [a little savagery] and the English army collapsed. The vanguard fled; the rearguard and centre were cut down. Lord Talbot was captured, along with Lord Scales and several other knights, while the French rode about the plain, cutting down every archer they could reach. Rounding up what men he could, Fastolf and the remainder of the army stood off the French until nightfall, and then fell back on Paris, while Jeanne led the victorious French and their prisoners back to Orléans. Back in Paris, the blame for this defeat was heaped upon Sir John Fastolf, who was briefly deprived of his Garter, but good soldiers were now in short supply and he was soon restored to favour.

JOAN BRINGS THE NEW KING TO HIS THRONE

At Chinon, Jeanne's star was now high and the Dauphin and his advisers quickly fell in with her major plan. According to her voices, her next task was not to pursue the demoralized English to Paris and Normandy, but to lead the Dauphin to Rheims. This she duly did, and the Dauphin was duly crowned Charles VII on 18 July 1429, seven years after the death of his father. After that there were no more taunts about 'The King of the Bourges'. This coronation, on top of the successes of the recent months and the inspiring presence of the Maid, seemed to melt all English and Burgundian resistance and French armies triumphed everywhere. French contingents swept north across the Beauce into the Brie and up to the Marne, taking the surrender of town after town and castle after castle, until the time was judged right for an attack on Paris. . . .

The coronation at Rheims gave a great boost to Charles's standing in France, for the young Henry VI of England and France was still uncrowned. This was a situation that the Duke of Bedford decided to remedy, and if Rheims could not be reached, then Bedford would settle for a coronation in Paris, though in September 1429, Paris too was under attack by the jubilant French forces. Although the young Henry was crowned King of England on 6 November 1429, he was not brought to Paris for his French coronation until December 1431, where the old Cardinal Beaufort crowned him Henry II of France. This coronation lacked both the setting of Rheims and the holy oil of St Rémy, and was ignored by the French and Burgundians. The young Henry returned to England in January 1432 and never set foot in France again.

Rumors of Witchcraft

Jeanne took the field again in the early months of 1430, attacking the English garrisons north of Paris, at Senlis and Melun, but her successes were limited. Her forces were composed of mercenary companies, commanded by Ponton de Xaintrailles and La Hire, quite unsupported by the main royal army. John of Bedford found himself in little better position, for his health and power were both waning. He was forced by circumstance to hand over more and more English towns to Burgundian troops under John of Luxembourg, who had already occupied Paris to free English troops for the field, and the Burgundians were using the gradual crumbling of the English position to extend their rule across the towns and castles of the Ile-de-France. Bedford was quite unable to maintain all the territory he had previously conquered, for he lacked both the men and the money and blamed much of his misfortune on the Maid. 'These blows', he told the young King Henry later, 'were caused in great part by that limb of the fiend called *Pucelle*, or the Maid, who used false enchantments and sorcery.'

It is strange that so level-headed a prince as the Duke of Bedford should place any belief in witchcraft, but witchcraft was not unknown, even in circles close to the throne. His stepmother, Henry IV's Queen Joan, had been accused of sorcery, and his sister-in-law, Eleanor, Duchess of Gloucester, was to be found guilty of witchcraft and forced to do public penance. Besides, Jeanne claimed to be guided by God, so it was simple and sensible propaganda to claim that she was, in fact, an agent of the Devil.

Bedford's problems in France were not eased by the strife at home between Cardinal Beaufort and Humphrey of Gloucester, and by the continuing reluctance of the English Parliament to vote more money for the French War. The war effort in France was starved for lack of funds, and was left more and more in the grasping hands of the Duke of Burgundy, who gave little help to his allies and was now seriously contemplating a return to his French allegiance.

In the meantime, he charged Bedford a steep price for his troops' services and, if not for his aid, at least for his neutrality. He extracted 13,000 crowns from Bedford in return for Jean of Luxembourg's service at Compiègne, and a further 250,000 crowns for his help in the campaigns against Jeanne d'Arc in 1429, while from 1431–5 he received a monthly pension from the English of 3,000 crowns, a great drain on English funds.

Joan Is Betrayed

In April 1430, Philippe the Good ordered his vassal, Jean of Luxembourg, to seize Compiègne. In an effort to prevent the town falling again into Burgundian hands, Jeanne entered the town on 13 May with a small body of reinforcements. On 23 May she led a sortie to attack a small group of Burgundians blockading the gate and on returning, with the Burgundians in hot pursuit, she found the gates closed against her. Fighting wildly, she was hauled from the saddle by a Burgundian soldier and handed over to Jean of Luxembourg. He sold her to the English for 10,000 *livres tournois*, and her fate was sealed.

The capture of the Maid dismayed the Valois and delighted the English, not least because with her capture their string of reversals suddenly stopped. This was taken, for so it must seem, as further evidence that she was indeed a witch. John of Bedford now had time to think of ways to reverse his misfortunes of the past year, and he began by bringing the young King Henry, now 9 years old, from England to Rouen, and then leading him across Normandy for his coronation as King of France, which took place in Paris on 12 December 1431.

Loaded with chains, Jeanne d'Arc was conveyed across France and imprisoned in Rouen to await her trial on charges of witchcraft and heresy, and Bedford held hopes that her trial would both restore English morale and blast the prospects of Charles VII.

The English declared Jeanne to be a witch, or at best a whore and a heretic, who had scandalized religion by dressing in men's clothes and wearing amour. Her trial for heresy and blasphemy, before a clerical court, was conducted by French clerics led by Pierre Cauchon, the Bishop of Beauvais, but it was seen by the English and Burgundians as the chance to demonstrate that her victories at Orléans and Patay and elsewhere were the work of the Devil. Jeanne's trial began on 21 February 1431, and on 21 May, worn down by weeks of interrogation, Jeanne submitted to the court and was sentenced to life imprisonment. When the full horror of what was meant by a lifetime's incarceration dawned upon her, she quickly recovered her nerve and recanted. On 28 May 1431, she was declared a relapsed heretic, handed over to the secular power—the English—and burned to death in the market place in Rouen two days later. The English declared they had destroyed a witch; the French believed the English had martyred a saint and would suffer for it. History was to prove them right.

A New Chinese Dynasty Demonstrates Its Power

Louise Levathes

The Mongols conquered China under Genghis Khan and Kublai Khan, but their hold on China was very brief. In 1368, after less than a century of Mongol rule, China was reconquered by a native Chinese rebel known as Hongwu. He adopted the phrase "Ming" or "brilliant," to refer to his new dynasty. The Ming dynasty governed China until 1644.

For much of its history the Ming dynasty was inward-looking and conservative, preferring limited contact with the outside world. During the early fifteenth century, however, the third Ming emperor, Yongle, mounted a series of expeditions that demonstrated to peoples of the Indian Ocean region that China was again powerful and wealthy. Yongle launched seven voyages, all led by his close adviser Zheng He. The treasure fleets, as they were called, were the largest oceangoing fleets assembled to that date, and included the largest ships ever built.

In the following selection, Louise Levathes describes the arrival of the Treasure Fleet at the East African trade center of Malindi, noting that after such a spectacle, the locals were unimpressed by the arrival of European explorers at the end of the century. She also notes that, despite the successes of the treasure fleets, Ming leaders chose to destroy them instead of sending the ships to West Africa and beyond.

Louise Levathes is a journalist who has worked for *National Geographic*, the *New York Times*, and the *Washington Post*.

A larm spread quickly through the East African town of Malindi. Across the sea, beyond the coral reef, strange storm clouds appeared on the horizon. Fishermen hastily dragged their outriggers to safety on dry land. As the clouds gathered, it suddenly became clear that they were not clouds at all but sails—sails piled upon sails, too numerous to count, on giant ships with large serpent's eyes painted on the bows. Each ship was the size of many houses, and there were dozens of these serpent ships, a city of ships, all moving rapidly across the blue expanse of ocean toward Malindi. When they came near, the colored flags on the masts blocked the sun, and the loud pounding and beating of drums on board shook heaven and earth. A crowd gathered at the harbor, and the king was summoned. Work ceased altogether. What was this menacing power, and what did it want?

The fleet moored just outside Malindi's coral reefs. From the belly of the big ships came small rowboats and men in lavish silk robes. And among the faces were some the king recognized. These men he knew. They were his own ambassadors, whom he had dispatched months ago on a tribute-bearing mission. Now emissaries of the dragon throne were returning them home, and they brought wondrous things to trade. But had so many men and so many ships come in peace, or had they come to make the citizens of Malindi subjects of the Son of Heaven?

The year was 1418.

TREASURES AND VISITORS FROM MING CHINA

The largest of the ships moored off Malindi were four-hundred-foot-long, nine-masted giant junks the Chinese called *bao chuan* (treasure ships). They carried a costly cargo of porcelains, silks, lacquerware, and fine-art objects to be traded for those treasures the Middle Kingdom desired: ivory, rhinoceros horn, tortoiseshell, rare woods and incense, medicines, pearls, and precious stones. Accompanying the large junks on their mission were nearly a hundred supply ships, water tankers, transports for cavalry horses, warships, and multi-oared patrol boats with crews numbering up to 28,000 sailors and soldiers. It was a unique armada in the history of China—and the world—not to be surpassed until the invasion fleets of World War I sailed the seas.

In the brief period from 1405 to 1433, the treasure fleet, under the command of the eunuch admiral Zheng He, made seven epic voyages throughout the China Seas and Indian Ocean, from

Taiwan to the Persian Gulf and distant Africa, China's El Dorado. The Chinese knew about Europe from Arab traders but had no desire to go there. The lands in the "far west" offered only wool and wine, which had little appeal for them. During these thirty years, foreign goods, medicines, and geographic knowledge flowed into China at an unprecedented rate, and China extended its sphere of political power and influence throughout the Indian Ocean. Half the world was in China's grasp, and with such a formidable navy the other half was easily within reach, had China wanted it. China could have become the great colonial power, a hundred years before the great age of European exploration and expansion.

But China did not.

Shortly after the last voyage of the treasure fleet, the Chinese emperor forbade overseas travel and stopped all building and repair of oceangoing junks. Disobedient merchants and seamen were killed. Within a hundred years the greatest navy the world had ever known willed itself into extinction and Japanese pirates ravaged the China coast. The period of China's greatest outward expansion was followed by the period of its greatest isolation. And the world leader in science and technology in the early fifteenth century was soon left at the doorstep of history, as burgeoning international trade and the beginning of the Industrial Revolution propelled the Western world into the modern age.

AFRICANS RECALL THE CHINESE VISIT

In 1498, when Vasco da Gama and his fleet of three battered caravels rounded the Cape of Good Hope and landed in East Africa on their way to India, they met natives who sported embroidered green silk caps with fine fringe. The Africans scoffed at the trinkets the Portuguese offered—beads, bells, strings of coral, washbasins—and seemed unimpressed with their small ships. Village elders told tales of white "ghosts" who wore silk and had visited their shores long ago in large ships. But no one knew anymore who these people had been or where they had come from. Or even if they had really come at all. The treasure fleet had vanished from the world's consciousness.

Zheng He and Vasco da Gama missed each other in Africa by eighty years. One wonders what would have happened if they had met. Realizing the extraordinary power of the Ming navy, would da Gama in his eighty-five to a hundred-foot vessels have dared continue across the Indian Ocean? Seeing the battered Portuguese boats, would the Chinese admiral have been tempted to crush these snails in his path, preventing the Europeans from opening an east-west trade route?

THE OTTOMAN EMPIRE THREATENS BYZANTIUM

ANDREW WHEATCROFT

Beginning in the eleventh century, Turkish-speaking nomads invaded and settled the Middle East, where they converted to Islam. Territorial as well as religious differences brought them into conflict with the Christian Byzantine Empire. In the early fourteenth century, one group of Turks, the Osmanli or Ottomans, began to establish an empire that quickly isolated the Byzantine capital of Constantinople.

The Greek-speaking Byzantine Empire was the remnant of the old Roman Empire. It had withstood numerous threats, ranging from Persians to Arabs to the marauding Christians of the Fourth Crusade, for over one thousand years. Constantinople was one of the great cities of the Middle Ages, rich with treasure and trade goods. The city stood on a peninsula commanding the straits between the Black Sea and the Mediterranean Sea. It was also surrounded by a system of walls and fortifications and notoriously difficult to attack.

In the following selection, Andrew Wheatcroft describes the expansion of the Ottoman Empire and its intention to conquer Constantinople and bring the Byzantine Empire to an end. The Turkish leader who took up the task was the sultan Mehmed II, who took the Ottoman throne in 1451.

Andrew Wheatcroft, the author of three popular histories, teaches at the University of Stirling in the United Kingdom.

From *The Ottomans*, by Andrew Wheatcroft (Penguin Books, 1993). Copyright © Andrew Wheatcroft, 1993. Used by permission of Penguin Books Ltd.

The cross of Christ had been the emblem of Constantinople for seventeen generations. The first Christian emperor of Rome, Constantine, had settled his capital in the old Greek city of Byzantium on the shores of the Bosporus, and on 11 May 330 had dedicated 'The New Rome which is Constantinople' to the Holy Trinity and to the Mother of God. The new city owed little to the old Rome and much to Greece, for the empire was Roman only by its political genealogy, which traced a lineage back to the Caesars. It was a Greek empire, gathering in all the residues of Hellenism in Asia Minor. For almost 700 years, this Greek empire had ruled as far south as Lebanon and the headwaters of the great rivers, Tigris and Euphrates. The Greek (Byzantine) armies had withstood the advance of Arabs from the south and the first Turkic nomads from the east. The power of the Byzantines had been checked at the battle of Manzikert in 1071, when the nomad Turkish warriors overcame the heavily armoured horsemen of Constantinople and took the emperor Romanus IV prisoner. But the most devastating blow had come from fellow Christians. In 1204, the Christian armies of the Fourth Crusade had turned on their Byzantine hosts and looted the city. The provinces which had formed the bulk of the old empire broke away from the Latin kingdom of Constantinople established by the crusaders, leaving only a rump state to be ruled from the great city. In 1261, the Greek kingdom had been restored by the Paleologues, one of the leading families of Constantinople, but the old empire could not be reclaimed.

The Ottoman Turks Establish Their Empire

The empire had been eaten away piecemeal. Turkish warriors whose ancestors had defeated Romanus IV at Manzikert filled the space left by the Byzantines. Who were these wild borderers whose name increasingly dominated the pages of the chroniclers? The name 'Turk' comes from the language spoken by many nomadic peoples of Central Asia, an idiom which could be understood from China to the frontiers of Europe. These Turks provided mercenary troops for many Eastern rulers: even the Byzantines used them. They were fearsome soldiers, with the mobility and speed that made the nomad tribes so deadly in war, but they also possessed an innate discipline and order. The Turks had come from the empty arid plains of central Asia to conquer the richer lands of Anatolia. In their turn they were overwhelmed by fresh surges of nomads—first the Mongols in the thirteenth century, and then the Tartars in the fifteenth. But these hordes came and went, while the Turkish tribes rooted themselves in Asia Minor. They displaced the earlier inhabitants, and abandoned their earlier nomadic way of life. The Turks built towns and cities, and hacked fields and orchards out of the harsh landscape of Anatolia. While sultanates and emirates fell to the waves of invaders, the Turks remained in control of the towns and villages. They banded together into groups of border warriors, and lived by raiding each other or the remaining Byzantine lands to the north. One of the most successful of these border tribes was the Osmanli or Ottoman clan, named after its founder Osman. From the time that Osman captured the ancient city of Bursa in north-western Anatolia in 1326 (after a ten-year siege), these Turks were a powerful and immovable force on the edge of Christendom. Twenty years later, under Osman's son Orhan, the Ottomans crossed the narrow sea into Europe. In 1361, the Ottomans captured Adrianapole (Edirne), the second city of the Byzantine empire after Constantinople, and made it their new capital.

The steady progress of the Ottomans was halted—temporarily —by an invasion from the east. The Tartars led by the terrible Tamerlane (Timur)—half Turk, half Mongol—trounced the Ottoman Turks in battle at Ankara in 1402. Ottoman invincibility proved mythical when Timur captured their sultan Beyazid I and carried this proud Turk around in a cage (some sources say a litter) for all to see his humiliation. But the all-conquering horde soon returned to the east, leaderless after the death of Timur in 1405, and the Ottomans revived.

The Tartar conquest provided only the briefest respite for the beleaguered Byzantines: the Ottoman advance continued remorselessly. By 1453, all that was left of the once huge Byzantine domain was the city of Constantinople itself, a Christian enclave in a terrain ruled by Muslim Turks. If the young emperor Constantine XI Dragases, the ninety-fifth ruler to sit on the throne of Constantine, had looked out from the walls of his city in May 1453, he would have seen only enemies, encroaching on every side.

CHRISTIAN CONSTANTINOPLE STANDS ISOLATED

Yet the Turks had already tried and failed to capture the city. In 1422 a Turkish army had besieged Constantinople, but all its assaults had broken on the city's massive defences. In 1453, optimists in the city found encouragement in this 'victory', and argued that Constantinople, the Queen of Cities, could hold out indefinitely, especially since the encircling walls had been strengthened. Moreover, there were promises that Christian Europe would rally to the defence of their co-religionists. These optimists ignored the most pronounced quality of the Turks: their doggedness. It had taken Osman ten years to take Bursa, but he had won in the end. The Turks never conceded defeat: they had failed once against Constantinople, but they would return again. If they lacked siege-engines to batter down the walls, then they would make them. If they required ships to control the narrow Sea of Marmara, the city's lifeline to the west, then they would build them. The city would fall once the Turks were determined to take it.

In 1453, the city was besieged by a man more determined than any of his ancestors to accomplish the long-awaited conquest. Mehmed II was in his twenty-second year, 'of middle height but strongly built. His face was dominated by a pair of piercing eyes, under arched eyebrows, and a thin aquiline nose that curved over a mouth with full lips. In later life his features reminded men of a parrot about to eat ripe cherries.' Mehmed was the third son of the sultan Murad II, and had never been expected to come to the throne. But his two elder brothers, Ahmed and Ali, had died unexpectedly, and Mehmed became the heir. In 1444 his father had abdicated, and the boy succeeded him briefly, only to be deposed in 1446 at the insistence of the great magnates of Anatolia. It was said that they objected to his plan for an assault on Constantinople. Murad was recalled to the throne, and his heir began a fearful life at Manisa, far from the capital, daily expecting a visit from the palace executioner. Mehmed's position became even more precarious when in 1450 one of his father's concubines gave birth to a baby boy. But in February 1451, after Murad had died of apoplexy at Adrianople, Mehmed occupied the throne without opposition from those who had deposed him before. But he took the precaution of having his infant half-brother smothered, so that there should be no future focus for rebellion.

MEHMED THE CONQUEROR PREPARES HIS ATTACK

Mehmed possessed two dominant traits. The first was patience. The second was cruelty. He never forgot an insult or a slight, but would wait for years to exact his vengeance. His childhood had taught him the value of wariness. These traits conditioned the manner in which he moved against Constantinople. After months of exchanging pleasantries with the Byzantine court, in the autumn of 1451 he found a pretext for breaking off relations. During the winter he assembled thousands of masons and labourers, and set them to work building a fortress on the European shore of the Bosporus directly opposite an old Turkish fort at Anadolu Hisari. His intention was clear: once the new strongpoint (named Rumeli Hisari) was complete and guns were mounted in both fortresses, the Turks would control all traffic up and down the straits. The emperor Constantine wrote in protest, and as a contemptuous response Sultan Mehmed cut off the heads of the Byzantine envoys. All the signs were of war.

By August 1452, three huge cannon were mounted on the ramparts of Rumeli Hisari and the Turks closed the straits to all ships which had not sought permission to pass. Most of the ships passing through the straits were from Genoa and Venice. Genoa had a colony at Galata, on the far shore of the Golden Horn, while Venice was still a great power in the Aegean and on the Greek mainland. A few intrepid commanders ran the blockade, but finally a Venetian ship was sunk by cannon fire and her crew were captured. The seamen suffered the same harsh fate as the Byzantine envoys, but worse was reserved for their captain: he was impaled. This terrible death was intended as a message to the city of Constantinople, and to the doge and council of Venice far away to the west. Mehmed had signalled that it would be a war without mercy.

THE CONQUEST OF CONSTANTINOPLE

KRITOVOULOS

In 1453 the Ottoman Empire, under the sultan Mehmed II, conquered the Byzantine capital of Constantinople. The Eastern Roman Empire was brought to an end, and Greek-speaking Byzantine Christians were no longer a power in the Middle East. The entire region, from southeastern Europe to Egypt to India, was now controlled by Muslims.

The conquest of Constantinople, however, was not easy. The Ottoman Turks had to mount a series of attacks and overcome numerous defenses, including three massive cannon, a weapon that was relatively unknown in the Middle East and Europe. Nevertheless, as the Greek chronicler Kritovoulos describes in the following passage, the Turks were finally able to enter the city. The final Byzantine emperor, Constantine, was killed in the fighting, and the Turks proceeded to devastate and plunder the city.

---

230. Instead, the hapless Romans were destined finally to be brought under the yoke of servitude and to suffer its horrors. For although they battled bravely, and though they lacked nothing of willingness and daring in the contest, Giustinianni [a Byzantine mercenary commander] received a mortal wound in the breast from an arrow fired by a crossbow. It passed clear through his breast plate, and he fell where he was and was carried to his tent in a hopeless condition. All who were with him were scattered, being upset by their loss. They abandoned the palisade and wall where they had been fighting, and thought of only one thing—how they could carry him on

From *History of Mehmed the Conqueror*, by Kritovoulos, translated by Charles T. Riggs. Copyright © 1954, renewed 1984 by Princeton University Press. Reprinted by permission of Princeton University Press.

to the galleons and get away safe themselves.

231. But the Emperor Constantine besought them earnestly, and made promises to them if they would wait a little while, till the fighting should subside. They would not consent, however, but taking up their leader and all their armor, they boarded the galleons in haste and with all speed, giving no consideration to the other defenders.

232. The Emperor Constantine forbade the others to follow. Then, though he had no idea what to do next—for he had no other reserves to fill the places thus left vacant, the ranks of those who had so suddenly deserted, and meantime the battle raged fiercely and all had to see to their own ranks and places and fight there—still, with his remaining Romans and his bodyguard, which was so few as to be easily counted, he took his stand in front of the palisade and fought bravely.

233. Sultan Mehmed, who happened to be fighting quite nearby, saw that the palisade and the other part of the wall that had been destroyed were now empty of men and deserted by the defenders. He noted that men were slipping away secretly and that those who remained were fighting feebly because they were so few. Realizing from this that the defenders had fled and that the wall was deserted, he shouted out: "Friends, we have the City! We have it! They are already fleeing from us! They can't stand it any longer! The wall is bare of defenders! It needs just a little more effort and the City is taken! Don't weaken, but on with the work with all your might, and be men and I am with you!"

CAPTURE OF THE CITY

234. So saying, he led them himself. And they, with a shout on the run and with a fearsome yell, went on ahead of the Sultan, pressing on up to the palisade. After a long and bitter struggle they hurled back the Romans from there and climbed by force up the palisade. They dashed some of their foe down into the ditch between the great wall and the palisade, which was deep and hard to get out of, and they killed them there. The rest they drove back to the gate.

DEATH OF EMPEROR CONSTANTINE

235. He had opened this gate in the great wall, so as to go easily over to the palisade. Now there was a great struggle there and great slaughter among those stationed there, for they were attacked by the heavy infantry and not a few others in irregular formation, who had been attracted from many points by the shouting. There the Emperor Constantine, with all who were with him, fell in gallant combat.

236. The heavy infantry were already streaming through the little gate into the City, and others had rushed in through the breach in the great wall. Then all the rest of the army, with a rush and a roar, poured in brilliantly and scattered all over the City. And the Sultan stood before the great wall, where the standard also was and the ensigns, and watched the proceedings. The day was already breaking.

Great Rush and Many Killed

237. Then a great slaughter occurred of those who happened to be there: some of them were on the streets, for they had already left the houses and were running toward the tumult when they fell unexpectedly on the swords of the soldiers; others were in their own homes and fell victims to the violence of the Janissaries and other soldiers, without any rhyme or reason; others were resisting, relying on their own courage; still others were fleeing to the churches and making supplication—men, women, and children, everyone, for there was no quarter given.

238. The soldiers fell on them with anger and great wrath. For one thing, they were actuated by the hardships of the siege. For another, some foolish people had hurled taunts and curses at them from the battlements all through the siege. Now, in general they killed so as to frighten all the City, and to terrorize and enslave all by the slaughter.

Plunder of the City

239. When they had had enough of murder, and the City was reduced to slavery, some of the troops turned to the mansions of the mighty, by bands and companies and divisions, for plunder and spoil. Others went to the robbing of churches, and others dispersed to the simple homes of the common people, stealing, robbing, plundering, killing, insulting, taking and enslaving men, women, and children, old and young, priests, monks—in short, every age and class.

Here, too, a Sad Tragedy

240. There was a further sight, terrible and pitiful beyond all tragedies: young and chaste women of noble birth and well-to-do, accustomed to remain at home and who had hardly ever left their own premises, and handsome and lovely maidens of splendid and renowned families, till then unsullied by male eyes— some of these were dragged by force from their chambers and hauled off pitilessly and dishonorably.

241. Other women, sleeping in their beds, had to endure nightmares. Men with swords, their hands bloodstained with murder,

breathing out rage, speaking out murder indiscriminate, flushed with all the worst things—this crowd, made up of men from every race and nation, brought together by chance, like wild and ferocious beasts, leaped into the houses, driving them out mercilessly, dragging, rending, forcing, hauling them disgracefully into the public highways, insulting them and doing every evil thing.

242. They say that many of the maidens, even at the mere unaccustomed sight and sound of these men, were terror-stricken and came near losing their very lives. And there were also honorable old men who were dragged by their white hair, and some of them beaten unmercifully. And well-born and beautiful young boys were carried off.

243. There were priests who were driven along, and consecrated virgins who were honorable and wholly unsullied, devoted to God alone and living for Him to whom they had consecrated themselves. Some of these were forced out of their cells and driven off, and others dragged out of the churches where they had taken refuge and driven off with insult and dishonor, their cheeks scratched, amid wailing and lamentation and bitter tears. Tender children were snatched pitilessly from their mothers, young brides separated ruthlessly from their newly-married husbands. And ten thousand other terrible deeds were done.

PLUNDERING AND ROBBING OF THE CHURCHES

244. And the desecrating and plundering and robbing of the churches—how can one describe it in words? Some things they threw in dishonor on the ground—ikons and reliquaries and other objects from the churches. The crowd snatched some of these, and some were given over to the fire while others were torn to shreds and scattered at the crossroads. The last resting-places of the blessed men of old were opened, and their remains were taken out and disgracefully torn to pieces, even to shreds, and made the sport of the wind while others were thrown on the streets.

245. Chalices and goblets and vessels to hold the holy sacrifice, some of them were used for drinking and carousing, and others were broken up or melted down and sold. Holy vessels and costly robes richly embroidered with much gold or brilliant with precious stones and pearls were some of them given to the most wicked men for no good use, while others were consigned to the fire and melted down for the gold.

246. And holy and divine books, and others mainly of profane literature and philosophy, were either given to the flames or dishonorably trampled under foot. Many of them were sold for two or three pieces of money, and sometimes for pennies only, not for gain so much as in contempt. Holy altars were torn from their

foundations and overthrown. The walls of sanctuaries and clois-ters were explored, and the holy places of the shrines were dug into and overthrown in the search for gold. Many other such things they dared to do.

247. Those unfortunate Romans who had been assigned to other parts of the wall and were fighting there, on land and by the sea, supposed that the City was still safe and had not suffered reverses, and that their women and children were free—for they had no knowledge at all of what had happened. They kept on fighting lustily, powerfully resisting the attackers and brilliantly driving off those who were trying to scale the walls. But when they saw the enemy in their rear, attacking them from inside the City, and saw women and children being led away captives and shamefully treated, some were overwhelmed with hopelessness and threw themselves with their weapons over the wall and were killed, while others in utter despair dropped their weapons from hands already paralyzed, and surrendered to the enemy without a struggle, to be treated as the enemy chose.

CHRONOLOGY

220

The Han dynasty falls in China, giving way to the era of the Six Dynasties.

325

The Roman emperor Constantine transfers his capital to Byzantium, or Constantinople; he later becomes the first Christian emperor.

451

Huns from Central Asia invade India, ultimately toppling the Gupta dynasty; India is largely disunified for over one thousand years.

476

The German warlord Odoacer conquers the Western Roman Empire; his leadership of the West is recognized by the Eastern, or Byzantine, emperor.

507

Clovis, king of the Germanic Franks, converts to Roman Catholic Christianity; most other Germanic tribes cling to Eastern Orthodox Christianity.

527–565

The reign of the Byzantine emperor Justinian; among his many accomplishments are the construction of the Church of Hagia Sophia and the compilation of the Roman Body of Civil Law.

570–634

The life of the Islamic prophet Muhammad, originally a merchant from the city of Mecca in Arabia.

589–618

The Sui dynasty reunites China.

600–800

Maya civilization thrives at Tikal in Guatemala and elsewhere.

618–970

The Tang dynasty rules China from its magnificent capital of Chang'an; the Silk Road, a long overland trade route connecting China with India, the Middle East, and Europe, begins in Chang'an; the Tang dynasty is an era of territorial growth and cultural greatness in China.

622

Muhammad and his followers make the hejira, or exile, to Medina; from there they return to Mecca and conquer it for Islam.

650s

The Koran, the Islamic holy book, is compiled.

661

The beginning of the Ummayad Caliphate, which rules an Arabian and Islamic Empire stretching from Spain to Persia.

732

At the Battle of Poiters in France, a European force led by the Germanic Franks defeats an invading Muslim army.

750

The Abbasid Caliphate replaces the Ummayads; the Arabian capital is shifted to Baghdad, which becomes an important economic and cultural center.

768

Charlemagne becomes king of the Franks.

786–809

The reign of Harun al-Rashid at Baghdad.

800

Charlemagne is crowned Holy Roman Emperor by Pope Leo III; both men attempt to revive a Catholic version of the Roman Empire in western Europe.

960–1279

The Song dynasty in China; until 1127, Song emperors govern from the northern capital of Kaifeng; after Central Asian nomads conquer the north, the Song are forced to relocate to Hangshou in southern China.

1024

Paper money first appears in China. By the same era the Chinese have also invented the magnetic compass, gunpowder, and printing using moveable type.

1055

Baghdad is sacked by invading Turks, converts to Islam who are originally nomads from Central Asia.

1071

At the Battle of Manzikert, Turks defeat a large Byzantine force and take control of Jerusalem.

1095

Responding to the Byzantine emperor Alexius's request for military help against the Turks, Pope Urban II issues his "call to crusade," setting off two centuries of Crusades from western Europe to the Holy Land.

1099

The First Crusade captures Jerusalem.

1192–1194

The Third Crusade, led by the German emperor Frederick Barbarossa and the English king Richard the Lion-Heart, fails to regain Jerusalem, now under the control of the Arab warlord Saladin.

1202–1204

The Fourth Crusade nearly destroys the Byzantine Empire as crusaders involve themselves in the politics of Constantinople.

1206

Turkish Islamic conquerors establish the Delhi Sultanate in northern India. Genghis Khan is proclaimed leader of the Mongols.

1211

The Mongols begin the conquest of China.

1221

The Mongols conquer Persia.

1230–1255

The reign in West Africa of Sundiata, who establishes the Empire of Mali. It is estimated that during the thirteenth and fourteenth centuries two-thirds of the gold circulated in the Old World was mined in Mali.

1258

The Mongols sack Baghdad and end the Abbasid Caliphate.

1271–1295

The Venetian merchant Marco Polo travels across Asia to Mongol China. His tales of the wealth of Kublai Khan's court and the splendors and riches of China enthrall European merchants and explorers.

1279

The Mongol conquest of China is completed; Kublai Khan, Genghis Khan's grandson, becomes the first ruler of the Yuan dynasty, the Mongol dynasty in China; the Mongol Empire stretches from Poland in Central Europe to Korea on the Pacific coast of Asia.

1307

The papacy is moved from Rome to Avignon in France, where it stays until 1379; many claim that the Roman Catholic Church has lost its authority as popes and bishops live luxuriously and kings and nobles dominate religious institutions.

1310–1350

The Ottoman Empire establishes itself in Turkey and threatens the Byzantine Empire.

1324–1325

Mansa Musa, emperor of Mali, makes the Islamic pilgrimage to Mecca; he gives away a great deal of gold to impress the Islamic world with the wealth of West Africa.

1320s

The Black Death, an epidemic of bubonic and pneumonic plague, breaks out in China; the epidemic kills between one-third and one-half of the population.

1330s

The Black Death reaches India, the Middle East, and North Africa, where it also kills one-third of the population.

1330–1360

Ibn Battuta travels throughout Asia and Africa, reporting on trade, customs, and adherence to Islamic beliefs.

1337–1453

The Hundred Years' War between England and France devastates western Europe.

1347–1352

The Black Death reaches Europe on Italian trade vessels coming from the Middle East; 25 million people, one-third of Europe's population, fall victim to the epidemic.

1368

The Mongol Yuan dynasty is overthrown by Hongwu, who inaugurates the Ming dynasty.

1404–1433

The Ming dynasty sponsors seven voyages of "Treasure Fleets" across the Indian Ocean; partly an attempt to find pretenders to the Ming throne, the voyages also serve diplomatic purposes; the fleets are the largest ever built, including ships as long as four hundred feet.

1414–1415

The Council of Constance reestablishes religious stability in western Europe.

1453

The Byzantine Empire comes to an end when the Ottoman sultan Mehmed II conquers Constantinople; the Ottoman Turks now completely dominate the Middle East and much of southeastern Europe.

FOR FURTHER RESEARCH

PRIMARY SOURCES

Ibn Battuta, *Travels in Asia and Africa: 1325–1354*. London: Routledge and Kegan Paul, 1929.

Benjamin of Tudela, *Itinerary*. Trans. Marcus Nathan Adler. London: Oxford University Press, 1907.

Giovanni Boccaccio, *Decameron*. Trans. John Payne. Rev. and ed. Charles S. Singleton. Berkeley and Los Angeles: University of California Press, 1982.

The Book of the Thousand Nights and One Night. Vol. 3. Trans. J.C. Mardrus. Ed. and rev. E. Powys Mathers. New York: Dingwall-Rock, 1929.

Anna Comnena, *Alexiad*. Trans. E.A.S. Dawes. London: Kegan Paul, Trench, Trubner, 1929.

The Jade Mountain: Three Hundred Poems of the Tang Dynasty. Trans. Witter Bynner from the texts of Kiang Kang-Hu. New York: Knopf, 1929.

The Koran. Trans. from the Arabic by J.M. Rodwell. London: Everyman's Library/J.M. Dent and Sons, 1909.

Kritovoulos, *History of Mehmed the Conqueror*. Trans. Charles T. Riggs. Princeton, NJ: Princeton University Press, 1954.

The Secret History of the Mongols. Trans. F.W. Cleaves. Cambridge, MA: Harvard University Press, 1984.

The Song of Roland. Trans. Robert Harrison. New York: Mentor Books, 1970.

The Travels of Marco Polo. Trans. W. Marsden. Ed. Manuel Komroff. New York: Boni and Liveright, 1926.

CHINA AND THE MONGOLS

Peter Brent, *The Mongol Empire*. London: Weidenfeld and Nicolson, 1976.

Arthur Cotterell, *China: A Concise Cultural History*. London: John Murray, 1988.

C.P. Fitzgerald, *The Empress Wu*. Melbourne: Australian National University, 1955.

Harold Lamb, *The March of the Barbarians*. New York: Literary Guild of America, 1940.

Louise Levathes, *When China Ruled the Seas*. New York: Oxford University Press, 1994.

Franz Michael, *China Through the Ages*. Boulder, CO: Westview, 1986.

Joseph Needham, *Science in Traditional China*. Cambridge, MA: Harvard University Press, 1981.

J.A.G. Roberts, *A History of China*. Vol. 1. New York: St. Martin's, 1996.

Morris Rossabi, *Kublai Khan: His Life and Times*. Berkeley and Los Angeles: University of California Press, 1988.

THE ISLAMIC WORLD AND INDIA

Philip K. Hitti, *Islam: A Way of Life*. Minneapolis: University of Minnesota Press, 1970.

Nehemiah Levitzion, *Ancient Ghana and Mali*. London: Methuen, 1973.

M. Lombard, *The Golden Age of Islam*. Trans. Jon Spencer. New York: American Elsevier, 1973.

Dominique Sourdel, *Islam*. Trans. from the French by Douglas Scott. New York: Walker, 1949.

Romila Thapar, *A History of India*. Baltimore: Penguin Books, 1966.

William Montgomery Watt, *A Short History of Islam*. Oxford, England: Oneworld, 1996.

Andrew Wheatcroft, *The Ottomans*. London: Viking Press, 1993.

EUROPE AND THE BYZANTINE EMPIRE

Antony Bridge, *The Crusades*. New York: Franklin Watts, 1982.

Fred A. Cazel, ed., *Feudalism and Liberty: Articles and Addresses of Sidney Painter*. Baltimore: Johns Hopkins University Press, 1961.

Joseph Dahmus, *The Middle Ages: A Popular History*. Garden City, NY: Doubleday, 1968.

Alfred Duggan, *The Story of the Crusades, 1097–1291*. New York: Pantheon, 1963.

Martin Erbstösser, *The Crusades*. Trans. C.S.V. Salt. Edition Leipzig, 1978.

Robert S. Gottfried, *The Black Death: Natural and Human Disaster in Medieval Europe*. New York: Free Press/Macmillan, 1983.

H.G. Koenigsberger, *Medieval Europe 400–1500*. Harlow, Essex, UK: Longman, 1987.

Cyril Mango, *Byzantium: The Empire of New Rome*. London: Weidenfeld and Nicolson, 1980.

Henri Pirenne, *A History of Europe*. Vol. 1. Trans. Bernard Miall. Garden City, NY: Doubleday Anchor Books, 1956.

Pierre Riché, *The Carolingians: A Family Who Forged Europe*. Trans. Michael Idomir Allen. Philadelphia: University of Pennsylvania Press, 1993.

Jonathan Riley-Smith, *The Crusades: A Short History*. London: Athlone, 1987.

Steven Runciman, *Byzantine Civilization*. London: E. Arnold, 1933.

Armando Sapori, *The Italian Merchant in the Middle Ages*. Trans. P.A. Kennen. New York: Norton, 1970.

Joseph R. Strayer, *Western Europe in the Middle Ages: A Short History*. New York: Appleton-Century-Crofts, 1955.

Barbara Tuchman, *A Distant Mirror*. New York: Knopf, 1978.

THE MAYAN EMPIRE

Michael D. Coe, *The Maya*. London: Praeger, 1987.

John S. Henderson, *The World of the Ancient Maya*. Ithaca, NY: Cornell University Press, 1981.

TRADE, TRAVEL, AND CULTURE

Jerry H. Bentley, *Old World Encounters*. New York: Oxford University Press, 1993.

Luce Boulnois, *The Silk Road*. Trans. D. Chamberlain. New York: Dutton, 1966.

K.N. Chaudhuri, *Trade and Civilization in the Indian Ocean*. Cambridge, England: Cambridge University Press, 1985.

A.C. Crombie, *Medieval and Early Modern Science*. Garden City, NY: Doubleday Anchor Books, 1959.

Ross Dunn, *The Adventures of Ibn Battuta*. Berkeley and Los Angeles: University of California Press, 1986.

Richard C. Foltz, *Religions of the Silk Road*. New York: St. Martin's, 1999.

Peter Hopkirk, *Foreign Devils on the Silk Road*. London: John Murray, 1980.

Stephen F. Mason, *A History of the Sciences*. New York: Collier Books/Macmillan, 1962.

John Middleton, *The World of the Swahili: An African Mercantile Civilization*. New Haven, CT: Yale University Press, 1992.

Auguste Toussaint, *History of the Indian Ocean*. Trans. from the French by June Guicharnaud. Chicago: University of Chicago Press, 1966.

INDEX

Jeff Hay received a Ph.D. in history from the University of California, San Diego, where he taught in the innovative Making of the Modern World program. He now teaches world history at San Diego State University. In addition to editing two volumes of Greenhaven Press's Turning Points in World History series, Hay is working on a three-volume encyclopedia on the history of the Third Reich.